inspirational
TEACHERS
inspirational
LEARNERS

inspirational TEACHERS inspirational LEARNERS

by Will Ryan

A book of hope for Creativity and the Curriculum in the Twenty First Century

Edited by Ian Gilbert

Crown House Publishing Ltd
www.crownhouse.co.uk
www.crownhousepublishing.com

First published by

Crown House Publishing Ltd
Crown Buildings, Bancyfelin, Carmarthen, Wales, SA33 5ND, UK
www.crownhouse.co.uk

and

Crown House Publishing Company LLC
6 Trowbridge Drive, Suite 5, Bethel, CT 06801-2858, USA
www.crownhousepublishing.com

First printed 2011. Reprinted 2011, 2012, 2013, 2014.

British Library Cataloguing-in-Publication Data
A catalogue entry for this book is availablefrom the British Library.

Print ISBN 978-184590443-2
Mobi ISBN 978-184590722-8
ePub ISBN 978-184590723-5
LCCN 2010937330

Printed and bound in the UK by
TJ International, Padstow, Cornwall

Thunks® is the registered trademark of Independent Thinking Ltd.

The characters in this book are purely fictional. Any similarities between them and real individuals are purely coincidental.

To Daniel and Christina

Contents

Foreword

It means to 'breath life into', inspiration. Not 'perspire' or 'expire' but 'inspire'. To take something inert and lifeless and make it live. Like God with clay when he made humans according to many religions. Only for teachers it is with eight-year-olds. With clay. And paints. And pens. And a sparkle in their eyes.

It's great to hear a charismatic speaker. One who can transfix and then transform an audience with some well-turned words, a few early jokes and a decent PowerPoint. Many of us can point to charismatic teachers who sought to transform our childhoods with their character, their wit, their humour, their energy, their passion for a particular subject, their love of learning (although you have to watch out for the old joke about how primary teachers love children, secondary teachers love subjects and university lecturers love themselves).

Will Ryan takes things one step further, though, with a distinction that I hadn't thought about until he put it to me in one of our first meetings.

When it comes to being an inspirational teacher, it's not about you.

If the children in your classroom are spellbound by your performance in the classroom then you are charismatic but not inspiring. And if you want to inspire children then you must learn to stop taking their breath away.

I remember visiting a very successful secondary school near the Lake District several years ago as part of my day job. They boasted a particularly charismatic head whose character permeated the entire school and whose name impregnated every sentence. There was not a conversation that I had with student or teacher that did not include this man. Like 'Blackpool' in a stick of rock, wherever you sliced this school his name was there. This man didn't inspire the school, he *was* the school. And if like Alan Bradley he went under a Blackpool tram the day after my visit, then that school wouldn't so much grind to a halt as come off the rails completely. Charismatic this man may have been but inspiring he was not.

The very much flavour of the month PISA reports constantly highlight the importance of good teachers when it comes to riding high on the international league tables. 'The quality of an education system cannot exceed the quality of its teachers' as the 2007 McKinsey Report on the PISA findings, *How the world's best-performing school systems come out on top*, trumpets. This is something that the current UK government has picked up on (I say 'current' in case things have changed by the time this book comes to print. I can dream can't I … ?). Teaching is back centre stage again in the UK and elsewhere. But putting teaching centre stage does not mean putting teachers centre stage as Will Ryan points out in this game-changing book.

On another school visit I remember observing a VIth Form sociology lesson, led by a forceful, erudite and obviously well-educated lady teacher of a certain age. Part of my role was to try and engage the class in a range of thinking skills activities but every time I put a question to the students, she would pipe up with her answer whilst the students looked on in a combination of embarrassment and frustration. Her classroom, and I have seen this in many other teachers at all levels of the education system, is the place where she showed the world how clever she was. A visit from someone like me was her time to shine and she was not going to let it go. The saddest thing was that I don't think she even noticed what she was doing.

Next time you find yourself in a classroom with a group of young people, take the time to step back from yourself and observe who is at the epicentre of things. Are you the one leading the lesson? Are you the one with all the great one-liners and funny quips? Are you the one to whom all the questions are asked and from whom all the answers emanate? Are you the one who is coming out looking great? Are you the one coming out looking clever? Are you the one coming out looking tired … ?

The time after that when you are sitting down to plan your next lesson, at the top of the planning sheet, write those words, 'It's not about you'. Then plan the sort of lessons that allows for children to be inspirational, to amaze and confound you with just what they are capable of thinking and doing.

And, if you have trouble doing this, then this is where the book in your hands will help. The following pages are a distillation of Will Ryan's many years of experience in the classroom, as a headteacher and as a highly-regarded advisor in planning opportunities that bring the best out of children, all children, by designing wonderfully creative learning that is relevant, useful, engaging and comes from the heart, not from the government-led scheme of work.

At a time when there is so much pressure on teachers to teach children things to pass exams to make other people look good, it is all the more important that we remember the power that teachers have to change lives. The child who leaves your lesson walking ten feet tall because of the chance they had to be wonderful has learned something much more valuable than if all they got to do was to memorise the kings and queens of England while the teachers showed how clever they were.

The difference between the two sorts of lesson is down to you.

Ian Gilbert
Santiago de Chile
January 2011

Overheard in the Classroom

Teacher: Right, come out here in front of the class. Now then, what is the staple diet of the Boro Indian of the Amazon Basin?

Mickey looks for help from the class but there is none.

Mickey: Fish Fingers.

Teacher: Just how do you hope to get a job when you never listen to anything?

Mickey: It's borin'.

Teacher: Yes, yes, you might think it's boring but you won't be saying that when you can't get a job.

Mickey: Yeh, yeh, and it'll really help me get a job knowing what some soddin' pygmies eat for their dinner.

Willy Russell, *Blood Brothers* (1983)[1]

Chapter 1

Inspirational Teachers, Inspirational Learners

The only time my education was interrupted was whilst I was at school.
Winston Churchill

The Prologue

It was 1993 and the early spring sunshine was streaming through high Victorian windows as I walked into the classroom. Skies were blue, trees were turning green and the birds sang. I was feeling positive because I thought I was turning the corner in my second headship. At last, I thought, the school was on the way up. I moved towards a table with a spare chair and sat with a group of children. I turned to Jenny, a rather sweet eight-year-old with flowing blonde hair, and asked, 'Tell me, Jenny, what are you learning about today?' In gruff, flat Yorkshire vowels she replied, 'Well, if you ask me it's all a load of rubbish.'

The thing about working in primary education is that the highs can be very high but the lows can be very low.

The children were cutting out parts of diagrams from a pre-published worksheet and sticking them onto another piece of paper to depict the water cycle under the heading of 'The Journey of a River'. The activity was relatively undemanding and there was little evidence of pride in what was going on.

I asked Jenny to explain why she wasn't enjoying the lesson. She told me to walk to the end of the lane and look at the river because there were dead fish floating on the surface. She then told me that her grandfather and a group of friends (who were local miners) had in the past 'clubbed together' to buy fishing rights. They told her how they had racked their brains to prevent kingfishers and herons from robbing them of their investments. She knew about the boats that used to travel between the local coal mine and the power station pulling huge floating skips full of coal that would be used to generate electricity. She spoke of paddling and damming the small brook that feeds into the river. Then she told me how the river would eventually flow under Europe's largest suspension bridge and into the Humber ports. She concluded: 'We shouldn't be doing the journey of a river – we should be doing the story of a river.'

Those thoughts stayed with me for many years. I learned so much from her comments and further researched the idea of using an emotional hook to engage pupils' learning. I started to explore the concept further and found out how the limbic system in the brain works in precisely that manner. I also spent much time considering the key elements that would be in Jenny's story of a river. I pictured the group of enterprising miners and their need to think in order to seek solutions. I thought about how literacy and the arts could be involved and how the 'story of a river' would create a sense of awe, wonder and spirituality. As I did this, a new model of pupil creativity started to emerge in my mind that would be fit for the century we live in.

Time moved on. Jenny continued to point out the school's failings to me. She was a 'school council' all on her own. Jenny moved to secondary school and I moved on to join the local authority's school improvement service.

More or less fourteen years after that fateful day in Jenny's classroom I was sent to a school with several newly qualified teachers to observe them teach as part of the borough's monitoring programme. The head took me to the first classroom and introduced me to one of the NQTs, saying, 'Will, may I introduce Jenny Cole.' We both looked at each other and said, 'Oh no,' followed by, 'We have met before.' Both phrases were uttered in perfect unison. I was looking straight into the eyes of the former pupil who had seemed to invent the concept of student voice.

I asked about the lesson that I was about to watch and I was told it related to the journey of river. I was handed the lesson plan which had been downloaded from the internet. The session involved a diagram and the children sequencing sections of text so that they could piece together the story of the water cycle. In Ofsted terminology the lesson would have been graded satisfactory.

The thing about working in primary education is that the highs can be very high but the lows can be very low.

When it came to providing feedback, I reminded her of our conversation all those years ago and told her how I had learned so much from her remarks.

Without further comment from me, she said, 'I didn't follow my own advice then, did I?'

With the trace of a tear in her eye, she went on to say that she found the job so frustrating because her mind was full of ideas. She had wanted to take the class to different locations along the local river. She had wanted to take them to an abandoned warehouse by the wharf and sketch the disused buildings and then set an adventure story there. She had wanted to take her class of disadvantaged children up into the Pennine mountains to find the source of the river and feel the icy cold water as they paddled in the youthful beck. She had wanted the children to go to the river estuary before it flows into the sea, to watch the fish being unloaded onto the dockside and then to meet the crew of the lifeboat. She concluded that sometimes her mind was so full of plans that her head hurt.

I asked her why none of her ideas were possible and got the response: 'I am not allowed. We have all been told that there can be no time for extras because we have to raise standards by 5% in English and mathematics. The literacy subject leader said the class couldn't do story settings until next term. I was not able to go to the coast because the Year 6 class always do contrasting environments. I was also told the health and safety issues are too great and there would be problems because the parents wouldn't pay the voluntary contributions. And besides, the leadership team told me that we all followed the Qualifications and Curriculum Development Agency (QCDA) schemes and there was no need to deviate because all I had to do was make sure the children covered the journey of a river.'

The constraints were too great. And while we are simply managing them we will not be inspiring young lives. This book is based on an analysis of what our most inspirational teachers do. So ask yourself these questions:

- When did you last inspire someone?
- Are you content with the answer?
- Do you feel the need to read on?

This is a book that tells you what inspirational teachers do.

The difference between a person achieving their expectations and exceeding them is inspiration

They say a good book should keep the readers guessing until the last sentence. Oh well, what the heck. I will give you the answer in the first paragraph. What is it that inspirational teachers do? In short, they plan for their pupils to be inspirational. This book will tell you about the wonderful things that creative teachers do to make such a difference to children. I often ask teachers why they came into their chosen profession in the first place. Many of them reply that they were taught by inadequate teachers who made them want to provide a far better and more exciting education for our youngsters. Others speak with a clarity of detail about stimulating and influential teachers who inspired their lives and how they wanted to do the same for others. I have listened to these people with envy – I have heard descriptions of inspiration that can put a lump in the throat and a tear in the eye.

So let us consider those unnerving questions that all teachers should ask of themselves: When did you last inspire someone? Are you happy with the answer? Because teachers should always be seeking to inspire young lives. If you want to know more then read on. This book will give you a model to develop inspirational teaching in your school or classroom that will make a genuine difference for the twenty-first century.

Me, fail English? That's unpossible

> How is education supposed to make me feel smarter? Besides, every time I learn something new, it pushes some old stuff out of my brain. Remember when I took that home winemaking course, and I forgot how to drive?

This question, along with the heading to this section are just two of the many famous lines from *The Simpsons*. You may love it or hate it, but you cannot doubt its success. Over the years it has had a string of famous guest stars queuing up to be part of the show including Tony Blair, three out of the four Beatles, Elton John, Dustin Hoffman, Pierce Brosnan, Sting, Buzz Aldrin and soccer star Ronaldo. The show has grossed over US$54,000,000. So why introduce the subject of *The Simpsons* at this stage? The creator Matt Groening was told by his teachers that his drawings and stories would never catch on and he should pursue a more solid profession. By contrast he was so inspired by his first grade teacher Elizabeth Hoover that she exists as a key character in the programme. She clearly spotted Matt's talents at an early age and said to him: 'I like those pictures and stories. Can I have them?' Those simple words of encouragement inspired him and gave him the self-belief that helped him on a journey to riches and success. Teachers should never doubt their capacity to make or break lives.

It has been said that every person born has six significant talents. Two come to the surface quickly. The next two are brought out by other inspirational individuals who are often teachers. The final two talents are taken to the grave. Teachers have sometimes been very poor at spotting talent. Jilly Cooper's school report stated: 'Jilly has set herself a very low standard which she has failed to maintain.' John Lennon's observed that he was 'certainly on the road to failure … hopeless … rather a clown in class and wastes other pupils' time'. Lord David Owen's teacher savagely wrote: 'If I had to select an expedition to go to the South Pole he would be the first person I would choose. But I would make sure he was not on the return journey'.

However other school reports have spotted significant hidden talents. Jeremy Paxman famously asked Conservative politician Michael Howard the same question twelve times on a *Newsnight* broadcast in 1997. The answer to the question was simply either yes or no. On each occasion Howard tried to wriggle out of providing a direct answer. Many political pundits argued that the interview did considerable damage to Howard's career. So what did Jeremy Paxman's school report say: 'Jeremy's stubbornness could be an asset if directed towards sound ends.'[2]

The school of failures

But first of all, let's pretend that you are a teacher marking your register. Is this the class from heaven or hell?

Imagine the following list of names being on your register: Simon Cowell, Richard Branson, Thomas Edison, Billy Joel, Christina Aguilera, Walt Disney, Sean Connery, Freddie Laker, Bill Gates, Rosa Parks, Snoop Dogg, Eric Hoffer, Michael J. Fox, Alan Sugar, Martin Luther King, the Wright Brothers, Jacqueline Wilson, J. K. Rowling and Judi Dench. Would you rub your hands with glee at having a class of such talent and capability or would you put your head into your hands in fear because of the awesome challenge you might face in extending these individuals?

The people listed above are all wonderfully successful and therefore potentially a source of inspiration to the rest of us. Some are great thinkers, some have a true sense of enterprise, some have great literary and artistic qualities, others have considerable spiritual and emotional intelligence. If we were to score them on the scales produced by England's now defunct QCDA relating to their (very much alive) personal learning and thinking skills (PLTS) this class would score very highly. To a greater or lesser extent these are people who are communicators and critical and creative thinkers who can solve problems. They are reflective learners who can demonstrate resilience. They are effective participators in society and also team workers. However if you were to ask if they learned these considerable qualities at school, or did they become inspirational because they were taught by a string of inspirational teachers, then the answer would be a resounding NO!

The truth is that these individuals never made it onto any school's register of gifted and talented pupils. But they do have something in common. They are all listed on various internet sites of famous 'high school dropouts'. The list also includes Albert Einstein, who once famously said, 'Don't worry about your problems with mathematics. I assure you mine are far greater,' and Frank Zappa, who on the notes for one of his album sleeves urged others to 'drop out of school before your mind rots from a mediocre educational system'.

A further analysis of those who seemingly 'failed' at school would reveal at least eighteen billionaires, hundreds of millionaires, ten Nobel Prize winners, eight US presidents and dozens of best-selling authors. Mensa, the high IQ group, includes many who failed at school amongst their ranks.

This list of people who fell short of reaching their true potential at school is daunting. As a result, each one of them will have had to demonstrate significant personal qualities in order to achieve their subsequent success. We live in a world that requires these strengths, but we operate a dated education system that focuses heavily on testing and imparting academic knowledge.

I write these comments on the twenty-first anniversary of the 1988 Education Reform Act which brought us the National Curriculum and primary school league tables. I recently had a bizarre dream in which teachers and school leaders up and down the country held street parties to celebrate the coming of the age of the National Curriculum. Most of the festivities were informal affairs where the revellers designed and made their own slippers and created pizza toppings. This seemed appropriate as there was a period in the midst of the era where nearly every school followed QCDA schemes of work and where such activities were commonplace in almost every primary classroom in the country. Heavy prescription through the National Curriculum, testing, targets and league tables has resulted in an impoverished curriculum in too many schools. These last twenty-one years represent dark days. Many schools just stopped thinking for themselves. This suited successive governments as they sought to create a compliant workforce of school leaders and classroom practitioners who followed the rhetoric to the letter because they were fearful of the real or perceived penalties of failure.

Over more recent years some brave and exhilarating head teachers alongside talented teachers have turned their back on central diktats and started to lead a revolution. The best of them have done it with true style and created an exciting, rich and vivid curriculum in their schools which meets the needs of the children in their care whilst achieving high standards and positive Ofsted inspection outcomes along the way. The purpose of this book is to provide passion, energy, belief and values, to add further fuel to the flames and to provide strategies to create inspirational teachers who create inspirational pupils.

Having identified those who did not achieve well at school, you might take the view that schools have served many others perfectly well. You could also argue that the individuals on the list 'came good' anyway. However many people with the same qualities as Richard Branson or Sean Connery left school simply believing they were deemed to be a failure. They will have under-achieved as individuals; their true talents will have been forever hidden leaving the rest of us poorer because we never benefited from their potential excellence.

The Bash Street Kids

Lovers of *The Beano* will remember with affection the strange collection of misfits who attended Bash Street School. In the twenty-first century the kid in blue trainers at Bash Street School should be able to rise to the fore despite the adversity that may exist around him. This is the era of the information superhighway – the internet. Access to sporting and cultural activities is available to all. Schools receive funding and training to spot those children who are academically able – or gifted – and those who are talented. However schools don't have a sufficiently successful track record of changing lives and too often a child's life chances are significantly determined by where and to whom they are born. The Sutton Trust reports that social mobility is currently no better now than it was in the 1970s.[3]

Why is this the case? In 2007 a Unicef report on the well-being of children ranked the UK as the worst of the twenty-one wealthy nations surveyed using a range of measures, including the degree to which pupils are happy at school.[4] Children get just one childhood: it should be a magical and happy time and their primary education should leave a host of positive and deep meaningful memories that last for the rest of their lives. However there is evidence that many children find school life stressful. On the opening day of the Key Stage 2 Standard Assessment Tests (SATs) in 2008 I was sitting with a colleague who told me that her son had gone through thirty-five mock SAT papers prior to the tests. In my role as school improvement partner I spoke to a child who told me that in Year 6 children didn't do science, they just worked through revision books. The government puts tremendous pressure on local authorities to get schools to improve their results. In turn, local authorities put pressure on schools which then put pressure on teachers, and this can affect the educational diet received by vulnerable children who are often at the bottom of the chain. Even the former head of the QCDA, Dr Ken Boston, has stated that 'the assessment load is huge and far greater than other countries and is not necessary for the purpose'.[5]

However there has never been a time in our history when the need to develop inspirational pupils has been so acute.

The future of the world as we know it

In 2009 a string of huge businesses crashed. High street names like Woolworths and MFI boarded up their shopfronts. Established banks were on the verge of collapse and a seven-year-old in an inner city school turned to me and said, 'Eh mister, this credit crunch is right frightening.'

I asked him to expand further and he explained how his mother who was a single parent was already holding down three different jobs in order to make ends meet and how the disappearance of household names was unnerving him. I listened to his concerns for a while and then told him to get on with colouring in his Roman soldier because it would take his mind off it. It was poor advice. Children growing up in the twenty-first century are deeply worried about their futures and they know that the current generation of primary school pupils will have to solve a series of significant problems, including:

- Global warming and other international issues including fighting starvation and disease in developing countries.
- Finding a replacement for oil and increasing competition for dwindling natural resources.
- Creating a sense of social cohesion at a time of a declining sense of local identity.
- The threats of terrorism and the proliferation of nuclear weapons.
- Providing care and finance for an increasingly elderly population.
- The effects on physical and mental health in a nation where too many people seem to work twenty-four hours a day and seven days per week, sometimes just to make ends meet financially.

I am fully aware that not all the students currently passing through our schools are going to solve the world's problems. However viewers of the YouTube favourite 'Shift Happens' will have digested the following stark information:[6]

- By 2012 the nation with the most English speaking citizens will be China.

- Those responsible for the US labour market predict that most school leavers will have had ten to fourteen jobs by the time they are thirty-eight.
- One in four people have been working for their current employer for less than a year and one in two for less than five years.
- The number of text messages sent every day exceeds the population of the earth.
- The amount of technical information doubles every two years.
- Three thousand new books are produced daily.
- There are five times as many words today as during Shakespeare's time.
- There are 2.7 million searches on Google every month.
- One in eight couples who married in the US and UK in 2008 met online.

In short, we are educating children to do jobs that don't yet exist, using technologies that don't yet exist to solve problems that don't yet exist. Now this makes the problem of inspiring young lives even more difficult.

Lord Sandy Leitch, in his report on employability skills in 2006, identified a new skill set that the nation would need.[7] These include:

- Critical thinking
- Problem solving
- Communication
- Collaboration
- Creativity
- Self-directed learning
- Information and media literacy
- Accountability and adaptability
- Social responsibility
- Literacy and numeracy
- Information technology.

Yet too many schools under the guidance of the government, the national frameworks and Ofsted simply trundle along teaching key facts about the Ancient Greeks, stressed vowels and the six wives of Henry VIII, and seem all but oblivious to the fact that today's youngsters will live and work in a knowledge making world and not a knowledge applying world. In order to equip our children well for the future they need to encounter inspirational teachers who absorb their students in learning. This new learning will include not only knowledge (because children do need *something* to study) but also an array of skills that are pertinent to the twenty-first century.

Through the best teachers our children will be inspired to develop life-changing attitudes. They will understand the importance of global awareness, human rights, empathy and ethics. They will embrace business and enterprise skills including risk taking and how to work collaboratively by influencing and negotiating with others. Learners will heighten their sensitivity and creativity through a love of literacy and the arts. Children will feel increasing positivity through understanding the fantastic power of their own brains as they imagine and develop new solutions. They will also develop willpower and resilience and recognise the importance of giving and receiving feedback.

So what kind of lessons are required?

For individuals to feel fulfilled in life they need to discover their own meeting point between natural aptitude and personal passion. This is what Ken Robinson calls 'the element'.[8] People in their element connect with something fundamental to their sense of identity, purpose and well-being. Being there provides a sense of self-revelation, of defining who they really are and what they are meant to be doing with their lives. To achieve it we have to help youngsters find aptitude and passion through instilling positive attitudes and creating opportunity. Some people are fortunate and can look back to particular teachers who had them bounding through the doors each school day and leaving them wanting more. These teachers inspired pupils and changed lives. They excelled on a daily basis, engaging hearts, minds and souls, often in spite of the basic culture and mindset of our education system which frequently seeks to push aside learning activities that require an emotional response, the senses or a good portion of our brains.

So what is it that inspirational teachers do? Well, the first thing they do is to recognise that achieving inspirational responses from children favours the well-prepared mind, and therefore some direct teaching is required. They then seek to get the balance right in several key areas, such as:

- The balance between teacher talk/modelling and pupil activity should be in the proportion of 1:4. The trouble with this ratio is that only teachers with the very highest expectations have the confidence to hand over the responsibility for learning to the children. Ian Gilbert, writing in my book *Leadership with a Moral Purpose*, talks of the need to replace, as the quote goes, the 'sage on the stage' with the 'guide from the side'.[9]

- The balance between the teaching of knowledge, skills, understanding and attitudes, recognising that the latter will be significant in developing the child as a good learner.

- The balance between dependency on the teacher, independence and interdependence on the other pupils around them. After fifteen minutes of sitting with their teacher on a carpet for the opening part of a lesson too often children shuffle off to groups to work alone.

- The balance of time, recognising that great and deep learning cannot necessarily be achieved within the middle part of a three-part lesson. Many children are frustrated by bells and timetables and wish to absorb themselves in their tasks and challenges and return to them again. Teachers often come to me with work produced by their pupils saying, 'Look at this, it's a piece of work with real quality.' When I ask them what constitutes 'quality work' the silence can be deafening as they strive for the right words. So here is my definition of high quality work:
  - It reflects pride and perseverance.
  - There is evidence of creativity, originality and/or uniqueness.
  - There have been high levels of independence and/or collaboration.
  - The work clearly builds on prior learning.
  - The challenge contributes towards the child achieving one or more of their learning targets.

The notion of schools and teachers having their own qualitative definition of high quality work that is separate to the national frameworks and level descriptors is important. Just take a look at the two samples below of children's' writing taken from the 2009 Key Stage 2 SATs for Writing. There is a world of difference between the two extracts. The second was produced by a pupil who had been in the country for less than one year and clearly contains many errors. However they do have something in common: they were awarded exactly the same score by the markers.

> The noise subsides as students settle down. What a cacophony louder than a rock festival is now a murmur quieter than a cricket. Stragglers rush past in dribs and drabs worrying about how angry their teachers will be.
>
> (Extract from a 140-word answer to the task)

> I was in the market and all people were rushing around. It smell like a pig! Everone was droping the food in the basket. The food was nice but the people wasn't. I was woking round the market to buy a chocolate.
>
> (Extract from a 70-word answer to the task)[10]

When a school has its own definition of high quality work which has been discussed with pupils, or comes from the pupils themselves, it will help the quality of the children's endeavours to spiral in an upwards direction. Learners will understand what they have to submit to their teacher, especially if they want the rewards of seeing their work displayed or being included in celebration assembly.

There are however a number of other key balances to get right. Guy Claxton in his brilliant book *What's the Point of School?* talks about the conflict between 'just in case learning' and 'just in time learning'.[11] The first of these is a traditional model that exists in many schools. A classic example would be teaching the children about the key events in Victorian Britain *just in case* they will need it in later life. And to be fair it might be helpful in the pub quiz at The Dog and Partridge. Using a *just in time* learning model the teacher may say to his or her class, 'Next term we are going to study the Victorians and at the end of the term you will be required to run a museum for the day with key exhibits which will inform others about Victorian life. You need to have interactive presentations and a digital film to show the visitors. Now children, what do we need to learn and when do we need to learn it?' This format will work because it is real-life learning based upon the notion of getting something interesting done. Usually we learn best when the process is a means to an end in itself. In real life significant learning often takes place when the timing is opportune because in real life people zoom in on a specific bit of information just when they need it. A practical example of this approach is included in Chapter 4.

Another balance that needs to be achieved relates to 'the dollops curriculum' (where children receive a dollop of literacy followed by a dollop of history followed by a dollop of PE and so on), and the need to secure steady improvement within a range of key learning skills. In redesigning the secondary curriculum in 2008 the then government identified six generic skills that pupils must develop if they are to become successful learners, responsible citizens and confident individuals. Much transformational work will need to take place if children are genuinely to become, as the personal learning and thinking skills framework suggests, independent enquirers, creative thinkers, reflective learners, team workers, self managers and effective participators. Inspirational teachers have intuitively recognised the importance of these skills and sought to develop them through rich activities in the lessons they teach. They have always recognised that real and deep learning does not come from merely delivering pre-packaged programmes of study. Chapter 2 is designed to help school leaders to develop their own personalised and outstanding curriculum that fulfils the needs of children growing up in the twenty-first century.

If children are genuinely to achieve the goal of being successful learners, responsible citizens and confident individuals they need to encounter inspirational teachers who will have sufficiently high expectations to encourage them to take far greater responsibility for their learning. Schools and teachers need to make learning deep through giving them real issues to explore and not presenting tired topics that have been covered time and time again. Children need the opportunity and challenge of 'getting stuck in' to significant problems and challenges and feel they can make progress with them. Finally pupils need to work in collaboration with each other so they can influence each other through negotiation and thus learn together.

So how does it all fit together? Here is my model of how inspirational teachers create inspirational pupils.

Inspirational teachers, inspirational pupils

You know when you are in the presence of an inspirational teacher. Yes, there will be an element of direct teaching involved because, in the famous words of R. F. Dearden in his landmark text on primary education, 'discovery favours the well prepared mind'.[12] In the best primary classroom there will be the direct teaching of phonics and calculation and guided reading and many other aspects of essential learning. However as you walk into the classroom you will realise that teachers are *guiding* the learning rather than being the font of knowledge.

Next you experience an electricity that seems real and you can sense the hairs tingle and feel goosebumps appear. The sensation is similar to static electricity. The classroom buzzes. There is an air of expectation. The children are learning from every word that is spoken, there are eyes transfixed and they are desperate to rise to the challenges that will be set for them.

But what will these challenges look like? I have had the privilege of being in very many classrooms and observed closely what our best teachers do. I have asked questions of school inspectors and local authority advisers and come up with the following conclusions.

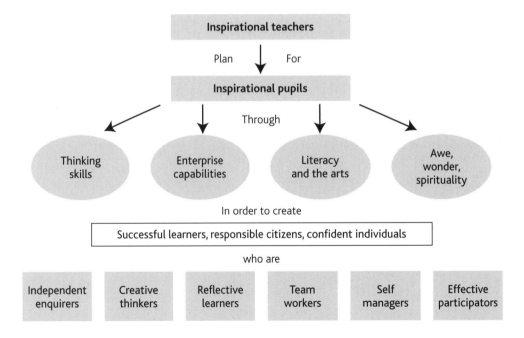

Make them think and make them think hard

The first thing that inspirational teachers do is to make pupils think – and think very hard. Their brains work so hard that there is the metaphoric smell of burning in the air. But they do this willingly in the knowledge that their thoughts and contributions will be valued and respected. In his book *And the Main Thing is … Learning*, Mike Hughes argues that in some lessons it can take as long as seventeen minutes for pupils to be required to think hard.[13] As a local authority adviser/inspector I have sat through many lessons where the children have not made significant strides in their learning because the steps they are required to follow are too small or on other occasions too many steps are included in the lesson. In contrast the inspirational teacher has a class-room that is akin to a gymnasium of the brain where it is stretched and made to work very hard. This gymnasium is not a self-inflicted torture chamber of unpleasant and tedious chores. (When I go to the fitness centre I refuse to enter if I can't get a parking space near the door!) This gymnasium of the brain is closer to a labour of love. A rich range of thinking opportunities is provided. This helps the children to conceptualise new information, create a sense of empathy, develop a moral purpose and enhance emotional and spir-itual intelligence as well as constantly maintaining concentration and focus.

In short, the inspirational teacher believes that classrooms should be places where thinking, questioning, predicting, contradicting and doubting are *actively* promoted. They develop children as active creators of their own knowledge. This is done through providing high quality opportunities for sequencing and sorting, classifying and comparing, making predictions, relating cause and effect, drawing conclusions, generating new ideas, problem solving, testing solutions and making decisions. Chapter 3 will provide further information about the importance of developing thinking classrooms – ideas for you to exploit and grids that will help you to examine the effectiveness of thinking skills in your school.

Creating enterprising individuals

Young children are naturally enterprising. It is one of their most striking fea-tures. Seven- and eight-year-olds during their school holidays, through play, will quickly turn their home into a restaurant or a television studio or a school.

Resources are made, roles allocated and a business plan devised. Older children (often boys) will create their own football tournaments, decide how long each game will last, organise league tables, cup draws and maybe even a transfer system. Inspirational teachers fully recognise the value of enhancing learning though developing activities that allow the children to be enterprising.

From my travels around schools over the last year I have seen many wonderful lessons in which teachers have allowed children to take an enterprising approach to learning. It works. The growth in knowledge and understanding is phenomenal as is the development of key life skills and positive attitudes. I have encountered seven-year-olds who have been required to run a restaurant for a day following a term's study around food and healthy eating. Another class were asked to stage their own version of *We Will Rock You* following a fabulous visit to London's West End. Rotherham schools regularly run a project called, 'Make £5 Blossom' whereby each child in a class is given £5 to set up their own business that will return a profit in six weeks time, but the school provides nothing for free and everything must be paid for. The products and services provided by the children are ingenious. Pupils carry out their own mergers and takeovers, and extra staff (in the form of classmates) are recruited. The children learn and develop significant key skills including team work, negotiating and influencing, creative and original thinking and the essential but often overlooked skills of financial literacy. Additionally many of the best enterprise topics can have a strong ethical dimension. Chapter 4 will provide further information about enterprise education including an array of ideas for you to exploit and self evaluation tools that will help you to examine the effectiveness of enterprise education in your school.

Literacy and the arts provide magic

Many inspirational teachers have recognised the power of the arts and literacy in providing children with the essential skills of communication, representation and expression. In 2000 Ofsted stressed their importance:

> Many of the schools we visited make particularly strong provision for expressive arts and have developed extensive programmes of special events and performances. Work in the arts is

seen as providing opportunities to demonstrate success, promote pupils' confidence and strengthen their communication skills. Many teachers argued that success in the arts has particular value for those who have little success out of school and that the improved confidence it brings transfers to other subjects.[14]

The arts and literacy have the wonderful capacity to engage the part of the brain that creates an emotional response. In the nineteenth century educationalists like Descartes would have argued that emotions in learning were a nuisance. Excitement and empathy would have been seen as disruptive to the learning process. Our knowledge of neuroscience now paints a totally different picture. The neurologist Antonio Damasio argues that learning without emotion or intuition simply produces intellectually clever people who behave stupidly.[15] Equally, a great deal of learning takes place through the senses. We think in sounds and pictures and movements. We can learn through stories and poetry, dance, music and art. The neurophysiologist J. Z. Young was right to argue that 'human life depends upon language, art and the complications of culture as much as on food and that it would ultimately collapse without them'.[16] For many experienced teachers this form of creativity dates back to the 1970s. It was sometimes associated with a laissez-faire form of learning through creativity that lacked any form of genuine rigour. Often that criticism was deserved. However in the hands of our best teachers it could lead to truly magical and life-changing learning, as shown in this account from the United States:

> I was supposed to be a welfare statistic ... it is because of a teacher that I sit at this table. I remember her telling us one cold, miserable day that she could not make our clothing better; that she could not provide us with food; she could not change the terrible segregated conditions under which we lived. She could introduce us to the world of reading, the world of books and that is what she did.

> What a world! I visited Asia and Africa. I saw magnificent sunsets. I tasted exotic foods. I fell in love and danced in wonderful halls. I ran away with escaped slaves and stood beside a teenage martyr. I visited lakes and streams and composed lines of verse.

I knew then that I wanted to help children do the same things,
I wanted to weave magic.[17]

Chapter 5 will provide further information about how schools can make best use of literacy and the arts and promote communication, representation and expression. It provides ideas for you to exploit and self-evaluation tools that will help you to examine the effectiveness of the provision with in this area in your school.

Awe, wonder, emotional and spiritual Intelligence

During a conference at which educational pioneer and devisor of the multiple intelligence approach to human genius, Howard Gardner, was launching his book *The Unschooled Mind* he was asked, 'Is there anything that a child must learn at school?' He answered that children should learn about what is good and what is evil, what is right and what is wrong, what is fair and what is unfair, what is beautiful and what is not, and the holocaust.[18] It is a statement worthy of deeper analysis and careful consideration.

Children get just one childhood and it should be memorable and life form-ing. School leaders and teachers need to ask themselves: If we don't create a sense of awe, wonder and spirituality in children *then who will*? It is certainly the case that not all children can rely on their parents to do so. Therefore the first element of this work is to create wonderful, rich and vivid life-changing experiences that might lead to either a sense of electricity coursing through the body or alternatively a sense of inner calm and peace. We seem to live in an era of safeguarding, risk assessments and sterile learning environments where children are protected from falling over and getting scabs on their knees. The importance of protecting children at all times is obvious. However primary education should still be about taking children to the coast to see stormy seas and to mountain tops via waterfalls and fast flowing streams. They should feel the frost with their fingertips and the wind and driving rain on their face. In winter they should build snowmen and in autumn kick up the leaves. Away from the natural world they should see mighty steam engines, elegant build-ings and sit in places of worship. These are all sensations that bring a true sense of awe and wonder. However they also bring a sense of spirituality which helps them understand and care for the world in which they live.

It is important that children develop a spiritual intelligence that allows them to make sense of their complex world. In a period of global warming, depleting mineral resources and a rapidly increasingly and mobile population, children need to learn how to care for the planet and its people. The diversity of Britain's population is changing fast. Recent statistics show that the number of babies with foreign-born mothers has almost doubled in the last decade. In some cities, including London, Slough and Luton, more than half the babies have mothers born overseas and in the London borough of Newham the figure is 75%.[19] Many people wrongly see this as a negative which brings with it a sense of friction. In contrast Robert Putnam, a political scientist and Professor of Public Policy from Harvard University, states that evidence suggests that creativity is enhanced by immigration and diversity. Immigration is associated with rapid economic growth rather than a loss of jobs.[20] When I was the head teacher of an inner city multicultural school I was amazed by the curiosity and respect the children had for each other and the richness and diversity of life. I greatly missed this when I moved to an all-white school.

When children develop an understanding of what is special about each other they are more likely to understand what is special about themselves. This in turn will raise self-esteem, self-belief and aspiration. This is important. Daniel Goleman would tell us that a person's life chances are more dependent on their emotional intelligence rather than their IQ.[21] Over recent years there has been a recognition of the importance of the social and emotional aspects of learning. Schools are now teaching children to have self-belief and also modelling a culture of respect and tolerance. But the reality is that they spend just 15% of their time in school and then they go home to watch Ann Robinson on *The Weakest Link* and a host of celebrity and talent shows in which they learn that disparagement is not only acceptable but amusing.

Chapter 6 will provide further information about how schools can develop a sense of awe and wonder and develop pupils' spiritual and emotional intelligence. It provides ideas for you to exploit and self-evaluation tools that will help you to examine the effectiveness of the provision for developing emotional and spiritual intelligence in your school.

Using the book

Having read the above synopses and studied the diagram at the start of this section you may be expecting that each chapter will be discrete and a separate entity. You would be wrong. Whilst each chapter can be used individually each one is deliberately influenced by the others. The chapter you are reading at any one time should have the spirit of the other seven. This is deliberate and is designed to give a holistic rather than a compartmentalised view of the work of inspirational teachers. I hope it gives school leaders and classroom teachers the courage and faith to create exceptional learning experiences for the youngsters in our care.

Have courage, have faith

As an inspector and local authority adviser I have observed many lessons. The exceptional quality of a few has blown my mind away, whilst others are like that famous quote about Wagner's music – they have wonderful moments but tortuous half-hours.

Prior to carrying out lesson observations I like to meet the staff, set the criteria for the visit and have an animated discussion about what their best might look like. Too often when teachers are being observed they pull back and play safe rather than grasping the opportunity to excite and excel. I remember once leading a staff meeting where we watched a video recording of a young teacher instructing his pupils about seed dispersal. For part of the lesson he took the children out onto the field to look at examples of how seeds are spread. One teacher watching the recording became very animated and announced: 'That's disgusting. You would never take the children out on the school field during a lesson observation.' I urge teachers to grasp *every* opportunity to engage and enthuse their learners and demonstrate their energy, commitment and passion for the learning process. I urge them to take risks and exploit the creativity and curiosity of pupils whilst recognising that such lessons will take the greatest amount of planning of all.

After this staff meeting I observed one of the best science lessons I have ever seen. It involved a very young and relatively quiet teacher exploring resistance by having balloons zipping along different types of wires and cables set at varying tensions. The children excitedly blew up balloons until they reached the predetermined size then released them along their self-constructed frames. The balloons whizzed along making loud raspberry noises. No child laughed, joked or used the freedom to entertain one another. Many teachers would have been fearful that this activity would lead to over-excited pupils who would lose sight of the purpose of the task. Only teachers with the highest expectations would have taken this gamble. This teacher did and it was a phenomenal success. The pupils excitedly constructed their fair tests and demonstrated their capacity to work purposefully in collaboration. When the teacher gently raised her arms above her head the whole room fell into a silent hush and children explained to her their well-constructed hypotheses and conclusions. Nobody in the room wanted the lesson to come to an end.

I share the view of Her Majesty's Chief Inspector of Schools that the overall quality of teaching and learning has never been higher. However I am deeply concerned that too much practice has become formulaic and that there is a deeply held view that a lesson can only be judged to be 'good' or 'better' if it follows a set format. Lesson objectives must be shared through WALT (We are Learning To) and the outcomes clarified through differentiated WILFs (What I'm Looking For). Lively starters incorporate talk partners. Teaching assistants support the different ability groups. Teachers assess the progress of benchmark pupils using Assessing Pupil Progress (APP) techniques. Pupils move into a plenary to draw their learning to a close and highlight the next steps. Children assess their own progress with thumbs up or thumbs down or using traffic lights. And Ofsted inspectors can tick all the boxes because they know all is well with the world.

Now all of these are good techniques. However let us assume that Jesus of Nazareth was one of the greatest teachers ever because it seems to me that his lessons have lasted for two thousand years. The question is, what would he have done that would have been different? Clearly this humble carpenter had the benefit of neuroscience because the first thing he always did was to engage the brain's limbic system which is situated in the mid brain. It governs learning, memory and the emotions. It is the part of the brain that is responsible for character building and creating a set of values and beliefs. The second thing this inspirational teacher did was to provide his followers with a sense of spiritual and emotional intelligence that would equip them to cope with life's challenges. He was clearly a historic forerunner to Daniel Goleman because he recognised that a person's life chances are more determined by emotional intelligence than academic achievement. The third thing he did was to equip his disciples with a set of life skills that would allow them to make a success of their lives in those demanding times. Too often these qualities are missing in twenty-first century classrooms.

Non vitae sed scholae discimus

For years I thought these famous words written by Seneca meant 'no school discos' but in reality it is a satirical statement which implies that too much of what we do in the name of 'education is for school and not for life', and that this should be reversed. There are many others who argue that real education starts when the child leaves formal schooling and enters the workplace. When academic learning becomes of no further use and a new set of generic skills is required. The reality is that we do not have an education system that equips children for life and work in the twenty-first century. In the late 2000s there was evidence that the cumbersome world of education was finally moving. The formal recognition of the six key personal learning and thinking skills alongside ability in English, mathematics and ICT will equip young people for life in a rapidly changing world. However if we are serious about a seam-less education system then the teaching of the personal learning and thinking skills is just as important for the youngsters in our primary schools as they are for secondary students. A useful assessment tool for this work is included as an appendix to this book, This book is built on the belief that they should become a key focus within the primary curriculum. Since then there has been a change of government and we wait to see if this forward thinking initiative will be maintained.

If the ideas outlined in this book are explored in more detail and put into prac-tice then our best teachers will create inspirational pupils. They will produce children who are *independent enquirers* who can process and evaluate informa-tion in their investigations, planning what to do and how to go about it. They will take informed and well-reasoned decisions, recognising that others have different beliefs and attitudes. The young people will be able to:

- Identify questions to answer and problems to resolve.
- Plan and carry out research, appreciating the consequences of decisions.
- Explore issues, events or problems from different perspectives.
- Analyse and evaluate information judging its relevance and value.
- Consider the influences of circumstances, beliefs and feelings on decisions and events.
- Support conclusions, using reasoned arguments and evidence.

Furthermore they will also develop young people who are *effective participants* and engage with issues that affect them and those around them. They will play a full part in the life of their school, college, workplace or wider community by taking responsible action to bring about improvements for others as well as themselves. The pupils will:

- Discuss issues of concern seeking resolution where needed.
- Present a persuasive case for action.
- Propose practical ways forward, breaking these down into manageable steps.
- Identify improvements that would benefit others as well as themselves.
- Try to influence others by negotiating and balancing diverse views to reach workable solutions.
- Act as an advocate for views and beliefs that may differ from their own.

The third key learning skill achieved by the pupils will relate to how they function as *reflective learners* who evaluate their strengths and limitations by setting themselves realistic goals with criteria for success. They will monitor their own performance and progress, inviting feedback from others and making changes to further their learning. The young people will:

- Assess themselves and others, identifying opportunities and achievements.
- Set goals with success criteria for their development and work.
- Review progress and act on the outcomes.
- Invite feedback and deal positively with praise, setbacks and criticism.
- Evaluate experiences and learning to inform future progress.
- Communicate their learning in relevant ways for different audiences.

The pupils will develop as *team workers* who work confidently with others, adapting to different contexts and taking responsibility for their own part. They will listen and take account of different views. They will form collaborative relationships and resolve issues to reach agreed outcomes. The young people will:

- Collaborate with others to work towards common goals.
- Reach agreements, managing discussions to achieve results.
- Adapt their behaviour to suit different roles and situations including leadership roles.
- Show fairness and consideration to others.
- Take responsibility, showing confidence in themselves and their contribution.
- Provide constructive support and feedback to others.

The pupils will also develop their skills as *self managers* who can organise themselves showing personal responsibility, initiative, creativity and enterprise with a commitment to learning and self-improvement. They will actively embrace change, responding positively to new priorities, coping with challenges and looking for opportunities. The young people will:

- Seek out challenges or new responsibilities and show flexibility when priorities change.
- Work towards goals showing initiative, commitment and perseverance.
- Organise time and resources, prioritising actions.
- Anticipate, take and manage risks.
- Deal with competing pressures, including personal and work-related demands.
- Respond positively to change, seeking advice and support when needed.
- Manage their emotions and build and maintain relationships.

Finally the pupils will develop as *creative thinkers* who generate and explore ideas and make original connections. They will try different ways to tackle a problem working with others to find imaginative solutions and outcomes that are of value. The young people will:

- Generate ideas and explore possibilities.
- Ask questions to extend their thinking.
- Connect their own and other's ideas and experiences in inventive ways.
- Question their own and other's assumptions.

- Try out alternatives or new solutions and follow ideas through.
- Adapt ideas as circumstances change.[22]

Learning from Clinton Cards

The entrance to Clinton Cards is the most important space in the store. It seeks to hook you in so that you feel compelled to make purchases. It follows key events in the calendar. The reds and greens of Christmas displays are cleared away for the over-sized heart-shaped Valentine's Day gifts. Next comes Mothering Sunday and Easter, then as it gets towards July and the end of the school year there are cards and gifts for the 'best teacher in the world'. This is because the astute business people behind Clinton Cards and similar retailers have stumbled across an important fact – the vast majority of pupils genuinely want their teacher to be the best teacher in the world. They want to succeed and do well for them. They want their teacher to be proud of them. They want their teacher to believe that they are the best pupil or student in the world. This book aims to fulfil that purpose.

Overheard in the Classroom

Pupil: Please, Sir, I have finished my essay for the competition entitled 'My Ideal School'.

Teacher: I bet it's brilliant, why don't you read it to me?

My ideal school could never exist. There is no reality in idealism. I dream of happiness and learning united. I dream of no interruptions. If I went to my ideal school I wouldn't wake up every morning and dread the next day, the next week, the next year and the rest of my life. In my perfect school we would only have teachers who knew and understood what they were talking about, they would all be passionate about their subjects and help us to unleash our passions. In my perfect school there would still be rules, but they would guide us, not confine us. Teachers and children would mesh harmoniously. There would be no grading, praise only for working hard not for your mental capability. I wouldn't have to compete with my friends and they wouldn't all want to be better than each other. We would not be concerned about whether we did the best in the class, but only whether everyone was happy with what he or she was doing and how he or she was progressing.

We wouldn't be confined within walls of stone, we would go outside and experience the weather. We would travel and experience other pleasures. We would gain an understanding of the way of the world. Exams would be abolished, people would work together and alone, they would use other people's knowledge to enrich themselves and others would do the same with them. In my perfect school there would be no bullies, there would be no insecurities. We would discuss our opinions in every lesson and everyone would listen and respect each other. Teachers and pupils would be equals, no privileges or disadvantages; everyone would be in the same boat. In my school the only things they would ban would be unhappiness and pain, no room for lying, revenge and deceit.

But to have my perfect school you need a perfect world, and if the world was perfect there would be no room for dreaming.[23]

Chapter 2

The Curriculum is Designed
Not to Cover but Uncover

How Inspirational Leaders and Teachers
Create a Powerful Curriculum

*The prior task of education is surely to inspire, to give a sense of values and the
power of distinguishing in life as in lesser things what is first-rate and what is not.*
Sir Richard Livingstone

Overheard in the Classroom

Pupil: Now we are in Year 5 will we be doing the Tudors? My brother and sister both did the Tudors in Year 5 and so did our next-door neighbour and he is seventeen now.

To be continued on page 65.

The Prologue

Are school car park gates more important than the curriculum?

This book takes the view that every child deserves to be taught by inspirational teachers who create an inspirational response from their learners through the creation of an inspirational curriculum. The core purpose of a school is to provide high quality memorable teaching and learning that leads to pupil progress and attainment. However it can be hard to be inspirational when the stakes are so high. Overall Ofsted reports on curricula in schools consist of a few bland statements. Inspection teams are weak at scrutinising the wider curriculum even though it is the lifeblood of the school. In recent years the government and Ofsted have discouraged any form of curricular innovation by making school leaders paranoid about limiting judgements relating to standards and safeguarding. During the autumn and spring of 2009–2010 Ofsted ran amok. The number of schools crashing into Ofsted categories of concern doubled whilst the proportion being judged outstanding halved. In March 2010 the *Times Educational Supplement* stated: 'For heads, teachers and those who represent them these figures represent more than just figures. They represent lost jobs, ruined careers, damaged morale and schools already struggling in difficult circumstances being pushed into steeper decline as alarmed parents take flight.'[24] The following week the same publication stated: 'Heads are being advised that it is no longer worth their while complaining or appealing to an independent adjudicator about Ofsted inspections.'[25] This was an extremely damaging time for many schools and fear levels rose to an all time high.

So let me tell you the following story to illustrate how the 'powers that be' bled the confidence out of one organisation. I hope it makes you smile first and angry second.

It was a Thursday afternoon. I was in a meeting with two government officers when I was told that I had to meet an inspection team who were about to place a school into a category of concern because they were failing to meet safeguarding regulations. As a senior member of the school effectiveness service I was told that I also had to bring with me the council's health and safety officer and the buildings manager. I arrived at the school in driving wind and rain. The institution had been told it would fail the inspection because there was a significant issue with the car park gates which had been left unlocked for a period of time on the first day of the inspection. We were told to meet in a small room at the end of a corridor that overlooked the car park and await the lead inspector's arrival so that she could discuss the problem with us all.

It was now around 2 p.m. and the head teacher, deputy head teacher, buildings manager, health and safety officer and I were squashed into the room awaiting the arrival of the lead inspector. There was a door into the room on the right hand side, another door on the left hand side and a very large pot plant stood in the corner. Please do not forget the pot plant as it has a significant and starring role to play in this story.

As we looked out towards the offending car park gates a little blue van arrived, a man in overalls climbed out and proceeded to unlock the gates. He then entered the car park leaving the gates wide open behind him. The head's heart sank, but she dived out of the room and accosted the driver of the van. She demanded who he was, how he had got the key and why he was there. He looked up and with a nervous tremble in his voice said, 'I've only come for my missus – she works in the kitchen. I'll only be ten minutes.'

The head demanded that he locked the car park gates straight away. As soon as this was done the now bedraggled head teacher dashed back into the room through the door on the left. A split second later the lead inspector entered through the door on the right. The doors opened and closed with the precision timing you might see in a Whitehall farce.

The lead inspector then went into a long lecture about the fact that the car park gates had been left open during the first day of the inspection and children could have wandered out, and that we all had to make a personal commitment that the gates would be locked in future. She also informed us that she would be writing our full names and job titles on her evidence form and sending it straight off to Ofsted as soon as the inspection was completed.

We duly provided the necessary information. We were all thinking of easing out of the cramped little room and escaping from the over-officious inspector when she added: 'Just a moment. There is one final question to complete. If the gates are going to be locked how will the fire engines get onto the site in an emergency?'

The day before I had been reading in *HELLO!* magazine (or was it *Cosmopolitan*? – I'm a big fan of such publications!) that 34% of adult females had experienced some kind of fantasy involving a fireman. All of a sudden I had visions of fire engines screeching to a halt with sirens sounding and lights flashing saying, 'We would like to put your fire out but we can't get through the gates.' It somewhat dampens their heroic image.

It was at this point that the so far silent buildings manager spoke up and said, 'I don't know if you are aware of this, love' (that made the lead inspector bristle) 'but fire engines are designed to rip gates open, but if you don't believe me we can take that pot plant out and bring the fire officer in and you can write his name on your piece of paper too!'

One and a half hours had been spent on this ridiculous situation. It takes less than thirty seconds to say, 'You need to keep the car park gates locked.' By comparison the time and energy put into inspecting the curriculum was minimal.

Schools should create a curriculum based around powerful, memorable and well-structured learning opportunities that hook children into learning for the rest of their lives. The curriculum is the lifeblood of the school and this inspection report contained a few bland comments about the curriculum in just 125 words, which focused mainly on extracurricular chess and sporting activities. If you compare this with the energy that went into the safeguarding issue then you could easily take the view that car park gates are more important than the school curriculum.

Here is one final thought. Finland, Singapore and Canada are three very high performing and yet contrasting countries in terms of education. However they do have one thing in common: they don't have any equivalent of Ofsted!

Emerging from the dark ages

The prime duty of any school leader is to take a dynamic and inspirational lead on the curriculum. It is the lifeblood of the school and therefore should course through every vein to create a passionate community where everyone wants to learn, believes they have a duty to learn and a duty to help others to learn.

However the period since the advent of the National Curriculum has represented the 'dark ages' for curriculum design in many of our schools. Some writers have called the era the 'ball and chain' years. Wave after wave of centrally prescribed initiatives have led to some school leaders abdicating their responsibility for curriculum design and adopting a national one-size-fits-all model regardless of the school's unique situation. Too often even when there has been a willingness for change the focus on testing, targets and league tables has resulted in a tired and impoverished curriculum. Over the last twenty-two years the policy makers responsible for educational reform have confused imposing structures with the fundamental purpose of education, measurement with accomplishment and the achievement of quick wins instead of longer term gains. In too many of our schools the definition of the curriculum relates to subjects and programmes of study that need to be covered – and 'covered' has been the optimum word. Too often very little attention is placed on deep learning or creating a set of knowledge, values and skills that will see a child through their life. Fortunately this is not always the case. In some schools inspirational leaders have set about creating their own outstanding curriculum that is personalised to the needs of the children growing up on the streets around the school. These leaders have become increasingly influential and the work of this minority is now starting to bring change. Even in those ball and chain years some of the peasants started to revolt!

Enter the inspirational mavericks

The word 'maverick' often has negative connotations. But I love the word! It is the people with maverick qualities who have the capacity to either bend or break the rules and bring about change for the better. Whilst the majority of schools were following a centrally prescribed methodology, the mavericks refused, with many setting about creating something unique and special. Sometimes they devised a curriculum from well-founded research into how children learn best; sometimes it was though a deep understanding of the community; sometimes it was far more intuitive and came from deep down within their heart and soul. When such curriculum models are devised, articulated and disseminated with clarity and pursued with rigour they regularly produce spectacular results.

Slowly, and it was very slowly at first, the influence of the mavericks started to spread. Sometimes there was intense criticism from outside forces when a school was failing to follow the QCDA schemes of work or was devising its own version of the literacy hour. However many mavericks modelled bravery and resilience and stood by their beliefs – and it led to them creating highly successful schools. As a consequence their influence began to spread. By the start of the twenty-first century more and more schools were looking at the curriculum afresh. However this was a very demanding process and time was needed if it was to be carried out in an appropriate manner and yield the right outcomes. Unfortunately the government continued with more and more centrally imposed changes thus restricting the time available for curriculum reform. But the voice of the growing band of mavericks was getting louder and louder. In 2007 it was announced that there was to be an independent review of primary education in England led by Professor Robin Alexander.

It was very clear from the early stages and interim reports that the Cambridge Review was likely to be scathing of the primary curriculum. The following extract captures the spirit of the report:

> As children pass through the primary phase their entitlement to a broad and balanced education is increasingly and need-lessly compromised by a 'standards agenda', which combines high stakes testing and the national strategies exclusive focus on literacy and numeracy. The most conspicuous casualties are

the arts, humanities and those kinds of learning which require time for talking, problem solving and the extended exploration of ideas. Memorisation and recall have come to be more valued than understanding and enquiry and transmission of information more than the pursuit of knowledge in its fuller sense.[26]

The review also considered the primary curriculum as a nettle that was 'ungrasped'. It was described as being detached from a clear set of aims. The report criticised an over-emphasis on prescription and micro-management. It used phrases such as 'the pernicious dichotomy which led to a muddled discourse between subjects and skills and a curriculum divided between the basics and the rest'. The review called for all schools to devise a new curriculum which:

- is firmly aligned with aims, values and principles;
- is grounded in the review's findings about childhood, society, the wider world and primary education;
- guarantees children's entitlement to breadth, depth and balance and to high standards in all the proposed domains and not just some of them;
- ensures that language, literacy and oracy are paramount;
- combines a national framework with protected local elements; and
- encourages professional flexibility with creativity.

It also called on the government to wind up the National Strategies and ensure that literacy and mathematics were incorporated into the rest of the curriculum.

Those people carrying the banner and shouting for curriculum reform now had significant backing behind them. They were getting more and more influential and persuasive. As a consequence, part way through the Cambridge Review the then government called on Sir Jim Rose to carry out their review of the primary curriculum in England. As a result of this report the influence of the inspirational mavericks won through. The Rose Review of 2009 promoted a new National Curriculum which:

- provided more flexibility and less prescription;
- focused on deep learning and not just coverage;

- secured the essentials in a range of ways;
- secured a wider range of skills and especially social and emotional skills;
- provided balance across all subjects and areas of the curriculum;
- created more scope for local interpretation and connecting learning to contemporary issues.

Whilst this represented progress, the challenge for all school leaders is to become an inspirational maverick, to reclaim education from the politicians and return it to the professionals – accepting that this comes with full accountability. There is no finer and more principled starting point for this work than creating an outstanding curriculum that fully meets the needs of the learners. The following guidance is based on observations of how our best and most inspirational school leaders have proceeded in the past, alongside the often forgotten guiding principles of the current National Curriculum. The guidance seeks to help schools to create their own personalised driving principles for the curriculum by stating what it must and should do and the difference it could make for the future. It provides strategies to hook young people into the learning process. It does not seek to take planning into minute details. Over the years I have become firmly convinced that the size and degree of elaboration within planning documents is inversely related to the quality of action and learning. My advice at this stage is to be aware of the dangers of over-planning and lengthy documentation. Those restaurants with the longest menus don't tend to offer the best food because there is too much for the chefs to think about.

How to create an inspirational primary curriculum

As a consequence of the Rose Review new National Curriculum documentation was published and circulated to schools. However the proposals never became statute. When the Labour Party lost the general election in 2010 it was scrapped by the new coalition government. The whole process had cost several millions of pounds. The proposals stated that schools should have greater flexibility to create a curriculum that met local needs. The new government supports this stance and has stated that it wishes to pass more autonomy to schools to design their own curriculum. This chapter is designed to aid that process.

The first step in curriculum design is to begin with the end in mind. Every school leader should plan to leave a legacy that will change their school community for the better. Therefore the starting point has to be an understanding of the current advantages and disadvantages of growing up within a specific locality. An old African proverb says, 'It takes a community to raise a child.' However the reality is that some communities are good at it and others are less successful. This is reflected in the fact that a child's life chances are still largely determined by where and to whom they are born. The challenge becomes not only to build on the advantages of growing up in a particular community but also to seek to remove some of the disadvantages.

So if a school leader is to plan a legacy to enhance or transform a child's life chances for the future, they should start by asking the following questions:

- Who does well in our school?
- What do they do well in and why do they do so well?
- Who does less well in our school and what causes them to do less well?

This no doubt will trigger a host of follow-up questions that could include:

- Do the children come to school ready to learn and well-equipped to learn?
- Do the children come from homes where the use of oracy and the spoken word are actively encouraged?
- Do the children come from homes where learning is valued?
- Do the families have high levels of aspiration for their children?
- Do the children come to school able to build relationships and deal with conflict?
- Do the children have values and a sense of right and wrong?
- Do the children have a clear sense of identity with their community and understand its history and geography?
- Do the children work well independently and collaboratively?
- What is the faith make-up of our community?
- What is the cultural make-up of our community?

It's time for a bit of passion

After you have sought and found the answers to these and other questions about your school community you will have made significant progress towards shaping your own *personalised curriculum*. The next bit to add is the element of inspiration, and that is achieved by considering what drives you as an educationalist. I know a head teacher who has both a mischievous sense of humour and also a tremendous track record for appointing the right people to his staff. I once asked him about the secret of his success. He replied that he had two key strategies. First of all he jokingly said, 'When the application forms arrive split the returns into two equal piles and then put one of the piles straight into the bin because you should never employ an unlucky person. Secondly, when you actually meet the candidates forget about the interview questions and look for the passion in their eyes.' Overall his first strategy has little to recommend it despite its unerring logic, but the second has the potential to be very powerful. There is much research that clearly states that the first trait of a highly effective teacher is not having a larger than life or charismatic personality but an absolute passion for the task at hand. So in the context of curriculum design, what would you be passionate about? The prompts below could be helpful to you. Which ones do you read and say, 'Yes, that's what I really believe'?

- The children need to see the links that exist between the subjects.
- It is important that children learn to think for themselves.
- Children need to be taught to become enterprising.
- The children need to have an in depth knowledge of their locality.
- The children should take a key role in planning learning opportunities alongside their teacher.
- We must make sure children understand the nature of learning and strive to become better learners.
- The curriculum must help to make children socially responsible.
- There must be opportunities for children to actively explore the issues associated with growing up in twenty-first century Britain.
- The curriculum should be used to develop emotional intelligence and raise aspirations.
- There should be opportunities to develop creativity across the curriculum.
- Learning opportunities within humanities and the arts are essential and can also be used to raise standards in literacy and numeracy.

- Schools should actively create a sense of awe and wonder in its pupils.
- ICT is not a subject in its own right but should be used to develop deep learning across the whole curriculum.
- Much of the best learning takes place through the creation of high quality experiences that take place outside the classroom.

After the passion it's best to have a cup of tea

However whilst you are having a cup of tea you can start to contemplate the next two steps because you are now in a very strong position to create the *inspirational curriculum*. You have started to develop a clear understanding of the local community and this will have built up a desire to do the right things for them. You will also have considered your personal passions and drivers within education and these will provide you with a clear moral purpose which will be energising.

You will remember that one of the criticisms from the Cambridge Primary Review was that insufficient attention was given to schools for creating their own curricular aims and principles. I also suggested that it was necessary to begin with the end in mind and plan your legacy. So now consider the aims, principles and purposes behind the curriculum you are about to design. You will need to keep focused on the substantial difference you could make to the children's lives if you get it right. It is wise to keep this to a maximum of five key points because they need to be shared and remembered by all.

Curricular Aims, Purposes and Principles

We will be successful when:

1.

2.

3.

4.

5.

Tales of Inspirational Practice

The curriculum, school policies and butterflies

Amanda the head teacher was contemplating a very significant problem. The production of school policies and documentation takes a great deal of time. Sometimes the documents are drafted and redrafted until they are of the very highest quality. But even the best documentation can become very forgettable in the hurly-burly of school life.

The school had spent a considerable amount of time developing a clear understanding of what it was like to grow up in the local community. As a consequence they had devised a set of memorable statements that summed up their curricular aims, purposes and principles. This had been done in the manner described above. In an attempt to make everything aligned these had now been incorporated into the school's teaching and learning policy. The Ofsted Self-Evaluation Form had been rewritten to provide clarity about the locality and what the school sought to do as a consequence.

Amanda was now looking down at the statements once more time and thinking, 'I need a simple metaphor or symbol that will ensure that these principles are always at the forefront of our minds and guide all that we do.' She read the list of statements once again.

We will be successful when:

1. The broad, balanced, rich and vivid curriculum promotes a love of learning and high standards especially in literacy and mathematics.

2. The programmes of study equip the children with significant knowledge and understanding of what is right and wrong, fair and unfair and a set of values for life.

3. The children have a sense of identity with the local area.

4. The children understand the need to live harmoniously in their multicultural community, a multiracial Britain and an ever shrinking world.

5. The children understand the importance of emotional literacy, social aware-ness and the need to be enterprising.

She thought to herself that these could really make a difference. The phrase 'make a difference' brought back to her memory an article she had read about the 'but-terfly effect'.

The butterfly effect was brought to the world's attention by Edward Norton Lorenz and is based on the notion that small differences can lead to large varia-tions. Whilst the flapping of a butterfly's wing represents only a small change in local atmospheric conditions they could cause a whole chain of events leading to large scale alterations. Hence the theory that under certain conditions butterflies flapping their wings in Beijing today could transform the weather conditions in New York next month.

At that point Amanda decided that the metaphor that encapsulated the work of the school would be a butterfly, because it was the duty of all those working in the school to make small differences day by day. These changes are made in the belief that they will have a transformational effect on children's lives.

> The emblem was displayed throughout the school. The words of the school documentation may have become clouded over time, but the guiding principles remain.

In carrying out this process some of the schools I have worked with have adapted their core principles from the Royal Society for the encouragement of Arts, Manufactures and Commerce's (RSA) Opening Minds materials that were published in 1999. These suggest that the curriculum would be successful when children had developed:

- The competencies for learning, which include:
  - Understanding how to learn, preferred learning styles and how to manage future learning.
  - How to think systematically.
  - Understanding their own talents and how best to use them.
  - Learning how to enjoy learning.
  - Achieving the highest possible standards in literacy, numeracy and ICT.

- The competencies of citizenship, which include:
  - Understanding ethics and values and how they should be used to inform personal behaviour and how individuals should contribute to society.
  - Understanding the importance of active citizenship to society, government and business.
  - Understanding cultural and community diversity and why all groups of people should be respected and valued.
  - Understanding the social implications of technology.
  - Understanding the need to manage their financial affairs.

- The competencies relating to people, which include:
  - Understanding how to relate to people in a variety of contexts.
  - Understanding how to operate in a team and fulfil different roles.
  - Understanding how to help other people develop.
  - Developing competence in managing personal and emotional relationships.
  - Developing the competence to manage stress and conflict.

- The competencies for managing situations, which include:
  - Understanding the importance of managing time.
  - Understanding the need to manage change in a range of situations.
  - Understanding the need to celebrate success and manage disappointment and how this might be done.
  - Understand what is meant by entrepreneurial and initiative taking and the need to develop these.
  - Understand how to manage risk and uncertainty in a range of contexts.

- The competencies for managing information, which include:
  - Understanding a range of techniques for accessing and evaluating information.
  - Understanding the importance of reflecting when making critical judgements.

There is no doubt that the curricular aims, principles and purposes established by Amanda in the case study above (or the competencies listed through the Opening Minds curriculum) would fulfil the core purposes of the curriculum which were recommended by Sir Jim Rose. These were to create:

- Successful learners who make progress, enjoy learning and achieve.
- Confident individuals who are to lead safe, happy and fulfilling lives.
- Responsible citizens who will make a positive contribution to society.

These are admirable principles. They align with the statutory core principles of the secondary curriculum. If we are to provide our children with continuity, progression and the best chances of success I believe they should be adhered to. The next challenge is to place these aims alongside your own curricular aims, purposes and principles which were drawn up in the previous exercise and then consider:

- What attitudes, attributes and values do you wish the children to develop through the curriculum?
- What skills do you wish the children to have as a result of following the curriculum?
- What is the essential knowledge a child needs who is growing up in your community?

I have placed the questions in that order deliberately. During training courses I frequently ask the delegates to decide which of the following is the most important to equip the children with as they pass through the school:

- Will it be a bank of appropriate knowledge?
- Will it be a set of predefined skills?
- Will it be positive attitudes?

Time and time again teachers tell me that most important is a positive attitude, the second most important is the skills set and knowledge comes in third. However this exercise is very crude because they are all inextricably linked. Children cannot always develop positive attitudes or a set of values unless they have a sound knowledge about the world around them. Therefore we have to provide the appropriate knowledge that will allow the child to develop their personal qualities. Equally there is no doubt that if children learn the appropriate skills they will be able to gain knowledge and understanding for themselves.

The proforma opposite is designed to help you decide what you are setting out to achieve as you create a curriculum for the future. It provides you with the opportunity to list the key attitudes, attributes and values you are seeking to develop within the pupils. The second row asks you to identify the key skills you are seeking to develop and finally you will be asked to think about the essential knowledge you want the children to have in order for them to develop their own personal qualities and to be able to function well in twenty-first century Britain.

	List here	How well are we doing at the moment?	How will we need to change?
List the attitudes, attributes and values you seek to develop			
List the skills you seek to develop			
List the important elements of knowledge and understanding you seek to develop			

Tales of Inspirational Practice

The values curriculum

David was the head teacher of a very large inner city multicultural school. Twenty-two languages were spoken by the pupils on roll and twenty-four ethnic groups were represented. David was totally committed to the school and the local community. He was determined to make a difference to the lives of the students. He also knew he needed a unique curriculum for the very special community in which he worked. He had become particularly interested in the work of Dr Neil Hawkes who has devised a values led curriculum.[27]

As a head teacher in Oxfordshire, Dr Hawkes had worked with the staff and pupils of his school to devise a list of twenty-two values he wanted the children to have before they left school at age eleven. (More recently his ideas have been taken further forward by Independent Thinking Associate and head teacher Julie Duckworth.)[28] These values included respect, honesty, cooperation, freedom, thoughtfulness and trust. Following the identification of the values, the school then devised programmes to teach systematically one value per month over a two year period. (Now for those who are thinking why 22 and not 24 values, remember the children aren't at school during August.) The challenge was not to *model* the value but to *teach* the value through carefully constructed lessons.

David looked closely at this community and decided he wanted to narrow the range of values so that he could teach each one in greater depth. After full staff discussions and deliberation the school identified four key values. They were fairness, loyalty, cooperation and honesty. These values became a focus in all lessons. They were explored in a range of ways including stories, poetry, speaking and listening, the children's writing, studying famous people in history and the local community. As a consequence of this work there was one notable occasion when at a morning break a pupil came to his door and said, 'Our supply teacher today isn't demonstrating fairness.' David made a commitment to check out if this was true – as a consequence he sent the supply teacher home at lunchtime.

As you walk into the entrance of the school you will see four large glass jars containing different coloured beads. Each jar represents one of the four core values.

When the children are caught demonstrating the values they are given a bead to place in the jar. This provides school leaders with feedback on whether their work is effective, but more importantly there is a whole-school treat every time a jar is filled.

Andy, a neighbouring head teacher, went to see the school in operation and was moved by the way in which pupils cared for each other, learned together and played together in harmony. He decided to take the key principles back to his own school, including the beads and jars. However he added one interesting twist. There was also a set of four jars for the staff and when the pupils caught the staff demonstrating any of the four values they too were allowed to drop a bead in the jar. How about that for a new method of monitoring and evaluating!

There is one other unique feature of David's school that is worth mentioning. It is officially a 'no shouting school'. The rule is simply that no adult or child should shout at another adult or child, unless there is an emergency. If you were to apply for a job at the school, and be selected for interview, the final question you would be asked is, 'Do you realise that this is a no shouting school?'

If you were to walk into David's school, which is situated in a complex and diverse community, the caring and calm atmosphere would strike you instantly.

Doing the Ofsted WAGOLL

Those of you who are well-versed in assessment for learning terminology will know that the acronym WAGOLL stands for What A Good One Looks Like. Have you noticed that schools do certain things because they think Ofsted will like them and equally they don't do certain things because they believe Ofsted won't like them? It is as though the inspection framework has become a mantra for all of school life with Her Majesty's Chief Inspector sitting as the 'great mystic' passing judgement over all that we do. However the best school leaders do not set out to please the inspectorate. They do the things that they believe are right for their school community regardless of central diktats. They are clear on their rationale and they proceed with rigour to meet the clear success criteria they have set for themselves. They recognise that the inspection process is determined by outcomes rather than processes, and they trust that the Ofsted process will help them celebrate what they have achieved and give them a mandate for the future. Usually it works and their successes are appropriately celebrated.

In 2009 Ofsted carried out a survey inspection that looked at curriculum innovation in successful schools.[29] The inspectorate claimed that this was born out of a series of concerns, including allegations that schools wanted to provide a more exciting and stimulating curriculum but ... School leaders finished the sentence in a wide variety of ways. Some said they were fearful of what the local authority or inspectors may say. Others were concerned that standards could fall in the short term whilst practice became embedded. Another group quoted time restrictions that were caused by having to place an over-emphasis on literacy and numeracy in order to reach demanding targets. In the autumn of 2009 one head teacher said to me, 'I want to change the curriculum but I daren't and so I am going to carry on teaching the Vikings in Year 3 until someone tells me I can stop.' I told her she could stop, and she did!

The Ofsted survey concluded that underpinning our best schools was a clear philosophy for both the curriculum and learning, and whilst this philosophy remained the same the curriculum itself was constantly being refined or changed. In order to make this happen the staff in these schools discussed all issues relating to teaching and learning regularly and critically. There was a constant dialogue about how children were learning and the vehicles through which they were learning. This led to a rigorous and thematic approach to curriculum planning. Within this approach 'the basics' were taught in a traditional way but applied in more creative contexts. Learning was strengthened by real experiences within and outside the curriculum. They also concluded that our most successful schools assessed the things that they valued not just the levels achieved in English and mathematics. In the best schools the curriculum places a clear emphasis on meeting local needs and providing the children with a sense of identity with the locality.

A further Ofsted inspection survey in 2009 looked at *Learning Outside the Classroom*. It concluded that hands-on experiences in a range of locations contributed much to improvements in achievement, standards, motivation, personal development and behaviour. The survey was very clear that the place where the learning took place added value, and that memorable experiences led to memorable learning. Learning outside the classroom had a positive effect on all groups of pupils and especially the underachieving. A further advantage was that it helped children to learn how to stay safe.[30]

Tales of Inspirational Teachers and Inspirational Learners

Here's one that Ofsted liked

One day Joanne the deputy head teacher said, 'Come for a walk with me. I want to talk to you about the curriculum, and I do my best thinking whilst I am walking.' She had grown tired of teaching Florence Nightingale and the Great Fire of London to her Year 2 class. She also considered that there was an over-emphasis and a contentment with QCDA schemes of work within the school which was restricting the development of more innovative practices. We discussed the problems as we walked on a bright spring morning through the Yorkshire countryside. We turned and were suddenly faced with the full splendour of Wentworth Woodhouse, the former stately home of the Marquis of Rockingham. That's when the first revelation hit us. The curriculum had no sense of local identity. This location was just a short distance from the school, steeped in history and yet was not reflected in anything the school did. The school had bought into the government's one-size-fits-all model without ever questioning it.

From this point a series of meetings was planned in which the staff analysed exactly what it was like growing up on the streets around the school (in the manner described earlier in this chapter). The analysis of growing up in the community had revealed that many children lacked self-esteem and the confidence to 'have a go'. There was often a lack of aspiration from the families and therefore it was deemed important to develop the children as enterprising individuals. The pupils lacked a sense of identity with the community because there was an over-emphasis on national history and geography rather than the locality. The school also recognised there was a need to promote a lifelong love of reading. This led the staff to the conclusion that whilst it was important to provide the children with knowledge, the curricular content should be far more flexible and could and should vary year by year.

As a consequence it was decided that although the content was to become totally flexible, each of the six half terms within the school year would follow a particular theme which would give a clear sense of purpose to their learning.

- In a first half term the children studied an aspect of the locality that would create a sense of identity.

- In a second half term the children took part in a thematic topic based around a high quality piece of children's fiction.

- In a third half term the children had to plan and produce something for the wider school community.

- In a fourth half term the children undertook a business project which required using a budget.

- In a fifth half term the children used one of the Social and Emotional Aspects of Learning (SEAL) themes to help develop self-esteem and emotional intelligence.

- In a final half term the children took responsibility for improving a part of the school or the locality.

The school also recognised that it would be necessary to devise a system to measure pupil progress against the ideals it had set for itself. As a consequence a series of measures were devised for communication skills, critical and creative thinking, resilience, problem solving, team work and being a reflective learner. If you were to visit the school during any lesson the children would be able to tell you which of these skills they were working on and what their next target would be within that skill.

On the last occasion that I visited the school one class had just run a restaurant for the day. They had visited local restaurants, studied healthy eating, created an allotment and harvested the crop, studied the life cycles of plants and tracked down which parts of the world various fruits and vegetables come from. During the same week the school had been visited by Ofsted which judged the curriculum to be outstanding. The inspectors wrote: 'The curriculum meets the needs of the pupils extremely well. The energy the school has put into remodelling the curriculum to make it relevant, creative and alive for pupils has been instrumental in helping teachers to raise standards. Imaginative use of topics enhances pupils' experiences of the world.'

However there is one final thought: The initial ideas came during a walk, so when and where do you do your best thinking? It could be important to know if you wish to make significant changes for the future.

How should we organise learning: Making the pennies drop

The two reviews carried out on the national primary curriculum in England in the late 2000s had much in common. They both arose from millions of pounds of research and therefore schools should not discount their conclusions. They both demanded a curriculum that was more coherent and less prescriptive. Alexander and Rose both recognised the need for stronger continuity and progression. As a consequence the Rose Review laid out the programmes of study in three phases – early, middle and later. Both reviews stated that the focus on literacy and numeracy should remain important but there was a need to place far greater emphasis on speaking and listening and applying literacy and numeracy within a broad and balanced curriculum. Both reports stressed their expectations that children would use ICT across all areas of the curriculum. They both placed greater attention on the personal development of pupils and schools were urged to respond to local circumstances. There was a clear message that subject teaching should be supported by challenging cross-curricular studies. I believe our most inspirational schools already work in this way. Whilst teaching the key basic skills well through tightly focused and direct teaching, they take a thematic approach to the primary curriculum. Based on what we know about the human brain this is important.

There is a well-known phrase in Britain about when the penny drops. This is the magical moment when a person sees the link between one piece of information and another. It is like the feeling of satisfaction that comes from fitting the last few pieces of a jigsaw together. Over the last twenty years we have learned much about the development of the human brain. We know that it is wired up to seek links and that this is especially true of the primary age pupil who is filled with curiosity and trying to make sense of the world. He or she does this through creating new neural pathways. It can be useful to think of the brain as divided into two hemispheres joined by a bridge of fibres which allow both sides to work together. Each hemisphere serves a different function and processes information in different ways. The left hemisphere deals with linguistic issues. It is analytical and is therefore used extensively in problem solving activities or when sequential processing is required. If the left brain is analytical, logical, precise and time-sensitive then the right brain is dreamier and processes things in a more holistic way. It is also more emotional. It thrives on rhythm and music and learns well from images and pictures. When learning opportunities are created that link the two hemispheres of the brain together it has the potential to deepen learning – and help the pennies drop.

Many individuals tend to favour either the left brain or the right brain when processing information – a theory which has been confirmed by scientists using CAT scans. This has implications for every classroom because there will be pupils who prefer processing information with the left brain and those who prefer the right brain. It also has consequences for the way in which you teach. Teachers often interpret data, represent data and provide learning experiences based on that data in their own preferred way. The theory of left–right brain hemisphere dominance and learning styles has profound implications for education. Too often and without consideration our classrooms are largely geared to left-brained people, yet it is the right-brained people who are more likely to be creative and innovative. Equally right-brained people need left-brained activity if they are to bring order and structure to their sometimes chaotic minds. The best classrooms provide opportunities for both sides of the brain to work together. This might include the linking of subjects into new broader headings such as:

- Understanding English, languages and communication
- Mathematical understanding
- Scientific and technological understanding
- Human social and environmental understanding
- Understanding the arts and design

- Understanding physical health and well-being
- Religious education

This will allow our more inspirational teachers to make greater links and therefore allow even more pennies to drop.

How should we organise learning? What teachers can learn from *Coronation Street*

Fifty years ago Granada Television launched a new programme which was to be given a thirteen-week run. The show was called *Coronation Street* and today it goes from strength to strength hooking in millions of viewers each week. In 1989 Alan Bradley's demise under a Blackpool tram was watched by over 26 million people. This was almost matched by the 23 million people who watched Hilda Ogden leave the series in 1987. In December 2010 over 13 million people tuned in to watch the fiftieth anniversary show. It is now the world's longest-running TV soap opera and Britain's most financially lucrative television show.

I wonder if you have you ever considered why it is so successful? Its success represents a significant achievement on the part of the writers, directors and producers over five decades: for each episode that is recorded they have to pull in viewers with just twenty-two minutes of programme content. The appeal of the show lies in the fact that it hooks in people emotionally. *Corrie* and its stories become real. They love and cheer the good guys and hate and boo the bad guys. The feeling is so strong that when Deirdre Rachid (now Deirdre Barlow) was unjustly imprisoned in 1998 questions were asked in the House of Commons and a national petition was set up for her release. Teachers can learn much from *Coronation Street* by creating the same emotional hooks.

For years our most inspirational teachers have fully understood the need to make learning a process that stimulates an emotional reaction. Now there is research that backs this up. Daniel Goleman in his research into emotional intelligence concluded that intelligence is both cognitive and emotional, with the emotional ruling over the cognitive.[31] Therefore if intelligence is emotional then it makes sense to hook the emotions. Robert Coles' research shows that intelligence is composed of cognitive, psychological, emotional and moral realms.[32] If intelligence can be nurtured then the curriculum and learning environments must take this into consideration.

One of the most significant problems with education is that it can be very slow moving. Robin Alexander (he of the Cambridge Primary Review) writing in 2000 commented on how English education quickly tends to regress to very traditional models:

> English primary education in 2000 is the nineteenth century elementary education modified – much modified admittedly – rather than transformed. Elementary education is at its centre of gravity. Elementary education provides its central point of reference. Elementary education is the form to which it most readily tends to regress.[33]

He is right. There is much to suggest that the National Curriculum of 1988 and the subsequent rewrites is based on the Revised Code for Education which was produced in 1862. This recommended a subject-based approach to teaching and stipulated which subjects should be taught. The rationale behind the Revised Code was drawn up in the red-brick and ivy-clad universities of that era where vested interests clearly existed. Robin Alexander comments in the Cambridge Primary Review:

> It is a shame upon us all that, at the end of twentieth century, children in schools in England are following much of the same curriculum as at the end of the nineteenth. The current list of subjects is no starting point for the creation of a national curriculum for the twenty-first century.[34]

If we were to travel back all those years we would find that the dominant thinking in the nineteenth century was that an emotional involvement in learning was perceived as a nuisance to academic achievement. Any form of excitement would have been seen as potentially disruptive of learning. Emotions were regarded as distorting the purity and trustworthiness of dispassionate reason. As a result of this thinking the curriculum became dominated by dry scholarly lessons because anything else would retard the path of true learning.

We now know much better and maybe we always did. Is it a coincidence that the words emotion and motivation share the same Latin root *movere* which means 'to move'? Long before the discovery of the frontal cortex David Hume had declared that reason is the slave of passions. I certainly believe that our most inspirational teachers have achieved inspirational responses from pupils by intuitively creating emotional hooks.

Tales of Inspirational Practice

Invictus

Out of the night that covers me,
Black as the pit from pole to pole,
I thank whatever gods may be
For my unconquerable soul.

In the fell clutch of circumstance
I have not winced nor cried aloud.
Under the bludgeonings of chance
My head is bloody, but unbowed.

Beyond this place of wrath and tears
Looms but the Horror of the shade,
And yet the menace of the years
Finds and shall find me unafraid.

It matters not how strait the gate,
How charged with punishments the scroll,
I am the master of my fate:
I am the captain of my soul.

William Ernest Henley

Nelson Mandela spent twenty-seven years in a South African prison mainly on the grounds of the colour of his skin. When released he spoke not of revenge but of the peace and reconciliation that would be required to create a new South Africa. To coincide with the anniversary of the event, the film *Invictus* was released in 2009. The news broadcasts, as they had done twenty years previously, devoted much coverage to Mandela and South Africa. The release of the film also promoted worldwide interest. However it didn't seem to be reflected in the lessons taking place in many of our primary schools where they diligently maintained their studies on invaders and settlers, developing countries and how to make a carpet slipper. One school certainly did and they did so by creating a powerful emotional hook into learning.

Chris the head teacher was determined to take full advantage of the situation. The children studied key excerpts from the film on DVD and accessed film footage relating to life in the South African townships. They heard the inspirational speeches of not only Nelson Mandela but also other human rights activists such as Martin Luther King and Desmond Tutu. The children wrote biographies of these people, stories that could have taken place in the past, play scripts, poetry and letters, developed campaign leaflets and devised news broadcasts as well as exploring the issues of segregation through music and dance.

This was learning which quite definitely provided the children with knowledge. However it also potentially helped to shape the values and attitudes that the children will take with them through life. The studies promoted tolerance and respect and highlighted the negativity of racism. As one pupil explained: 'If you think about all the people in the world, they have lots of things in common with each other and there is very little that is really different.'

The process of creating an emotional hook into learning can be straightforward. Inspirational teachers have done it well for years. For example, at the medium term planning stage titles for thematic studies could change from:

- 'The Victorians' to 'Victorian heroes and villains' which could look at those reformers who promoted better living and working conditions for all.

- 'The Second World War' to 'The special qualities of people living through the Second World War' which could focus on bravery, loyalty and resourcefulness of the volunteers of the Home Guard or the Women's Land Army or the bravery of those youngsters who were evacuated or the commitment of those who received them.

- 'Britain in the 1960s' to 'What it was like when Grandad was a boy' which creates the opportunity to use real people to bring recent history to life.

- 'The journey of a river' to 'The story of the river ...' This is a similar example to the one used in the Prologue to Chapter 1. In addition to looking at the key geographical features of a local river the project consider how mankind uses and possibly abuses rivers.

- 'What happens when the earth gets angry' which could examine not only the geographical but the human tragedies of earthquakes. If appropriate this could make use of current news items.

Albert Einstein was famously quoted as saying, 'Education is what is left behind when you have forgotten everything you learned at school.' Inspirational teachers have long created emotional hooks which have endowed their learners with values that will see them through life and a passion to find out more, thus creating true lifelong learning. In his recent book *The Decisive Moment*, Jonah Lehrer wrote: 'The end result is that the uniquely human parts of the mind depend on the primitive mind underneath. The process of thinking requires feeling, for our feelings are what let us understand all the information that we can't directly comprehend. Reason without emotion is impotent.'[35]

Tales of Inspirational Teaching and Learning

Emotional learning journeys

Richard the head teacher wanted to make each of his Key Stage 2 classes take part in a memorable learning journey that would promote learning across the curriculum over the course of a year. He was determined that it would trigger an emotional response from the pupils and help to provide them with values, a desire to do the right things and aspiration to fulfil a full role in society. He was also adamant that the emotional hook would create a passion not only to write but also for pupils to express themselves in a wide variety of ways including art, dance and music.

The four journeys selected for the individual year groups were:

- Childhood through the ages, which examined what it was like to be a child growing up at various periods of history including the Industrial Revolution, the first compulsory education in the 1880s, an evacuee in the Second World War and the 1960s.

- People who migrated, which looked at groups who were moved compulsorily or felt the need to move including those who relocated from an agrarian to an industrial economy, the Pilgrim Fathers, slaves during the slave trade, deported convicts, those fleeing repression and the challenges facing those people who migrate to Britain.

- The period from 1900 to 1950 including the sacrifices made during both world wars, the Depression of the 1930s and the Jarrow Hunger March. The period also included a local mining disaster within the locality of the school.

- The period from the building of the Berlin Wall to the fall of the Berlin Wall. This may sound like a European-based topic but in reality it was much wider and included the work of peaceful protestors, the end of segregation and apartheid, fair trade, the miners' strike and the space race.

The work has had a very powerful impact on the pupils. On the last occasion I visited the school I walked into the Year 6 classroom about ten minutes before morning break. The pupils were taking part in a heated yet dignified debate about whether or not the use of nuclear weapons could ever be justified. The time moved very quickly and then the bell went for break. I moved aside expecting the children to grab footballs in order to start the 'big match' on the playground as quickly as possible. I was severely mistaken. The children merely sauntered past still engrossed in their conversations about whether or not it was ever right to use nuclear bombs.

Now let's consider the final stages. Imagine you are playing a card game of pontoon and so far you have drawn a seven, a four, a three and a two making a total of sixteen. It's a good hand ... but is it a *very* good hand? You could stick with the good hand or draw one more card and end up with a virtually unbeatable five-card trick. The guidance in this chapter will lead you to a good curriculum – but will you take one final risk and go for the twist?

Stick or twist?

As I recommended in my book *Leadership with a Moral Purpose*, if your horse has dropped dead ... dismount! You could have spent many years on a curricular journey riding across a barren and arid landscape of learning, having the dust sprayed in your face until you had no sense of where you were travelling, whilst using government steeds that are not really up to the job. You will have twisted and turned along the route but your journey will always have felt out of control. For over twenty years too many schools have operated on an 'outside-in' model of education where wave after wave of centrally controlled initiatives have been imposed which schools have felt compelled to follow because they fear the penalties if they don't. Over recent years I have spent much time writing and speaking about an 'inside-out' model of education whereby the school has a clear vision of the direction it is taking, based on the minds, hearts and souls of the school leaders. I remain convinced that our most inspirational and influential school leaders have turned their schools inside out. The proposals within the National Curriculum guidance provide the flexibility and encouragement to create an outstanding curriculum given the right support. The best support that government agencies can provide for the future is cash followed by silence. For the vast majority of schools their talented professionals should take full responsibility for shaping their own direction and destiny. The suggestions made in this chapter will help you along the route to creating a strong curriculum. However one final consideration is necessary in order to secure a powerful curriculum and that is giving it your own personal twist. So is it to be stick or twist?

So which twists – or drivers – would you want for your school curriculum in order to make it powerful to your community and totally unique? Some of the options are shown below but the list is not exclusive. Whilst all of them obviously exist in some form within the National Curriculum or its guiding principles the challenge is to pick out two or three that you consider it would be appropriate to emphasise.

Oracy	The arts
Citizenship	Thinking skills
Community cohesion	Global education
Knowledge of the world	Outdoor education
Enterprise education	Philosophy for children
SEAL	Physical education
Sustainable environments.	New technologies
Spiritual and moral	Diversity and beliefs

One head teacher who fully took hold of this opportunity was Richard Gerver. His book *Creating Tomorrow's Schools Today* describes how he built his school in the East Midlands into an exceedingly successful learning community.[36] The school had four key strands at its core. The first of these was communication, and whilst this had literacy at its heart it also drew on ICT, music, dance and drama. The second was enterprise, which had numeracy as a key driver but sought to apply these skills in problem solving and innovation. The third was culture which had science as its focal point, as the lifeblood for understanding our world and our place within it, but expanded to focus on the traditional cultural aspects of our heritage which are rooted in history and geography. The final component was well-being which sought to raise the importance of physical and mental health. Physical education was an important dimension but the work also encompassed citizenship, social education and emotional development.

Tales of Inspirational Practice

The focused mathematics curriculum

Carol is a mathematician and she loves her subject with a passion, but by the middle of 2009 she was getting increasingly concerned about its status within the wider curriculum. Yes, there was the daily mathematics lesson in which children learned a wide range of calculation strategies in a highly effective manner. However she also considered there were insufficient opportunities to develop mathematical learning across the curriculum. She knew that children should be using mathematics through map work, measurement, data analysis, probability, science, design technology, enterprise projects, investigating shapes and angles within the human and the natural world and through probability.

Carol was also convinced that far more mathematics should be taught in a practical way and through hands-on practical activities. In her mind the only way to study capacity was to be using real water and real measuring cylinders in a real context. She was worried that there was now a danger that mathematics was becoming an academic rather than a practical subject, and she knew that was wrong. She decided her school was going to put its twist on devising a new approach to teaching and learning in mathematics.

Carol had trained as a teacher in the early 1980s when the Cockroft Report had just been published. The report had stressed the absolute importance of practical mathematics.[37] Carol could remember how teachers had embraced this message with a passion and in many classrooms practical mathematics had become very high profile. The problem was that as a consequence the teaching of calculation often suffered. Carol was now puzzling over how she could bring the strengths of the two eras together and create something special. That was when she hit upon the notion of the 'Focused mathematics curriculum'.

From that point she decided that the daily mathematics lesson would focus solely on calculation and that all other aspects of mathematics would be taught through thematic cross-curricular studies. She set to work looking at teachers' planning looking to see if the idea might work, and quickly realised it could. However Carol also considered that the work needed some kind of special INSET and launch event so her ideas could quickly gather impetus. She leaned back in her chair considering what would really kick this work off and engage the imagination of staff and pupils alike. All of a sudden a flash of inspiration came and five minutes later she was dialling the telephone number of the local football league team and demanding to speak to the manager. After she had succeeded with that, she rang the local professional rugby union team and sought their assistance too. Carol was going to create a mathematics study relating to the two professional sports teams in the area and made sure that they were going to engage as partners in the project.

The ideas just kept pulsing through her mind. She scribbled them down as fast as she could. The thoughts didn't come in sentences. They came out like this: *attendances, programme sales, probability, league tables, goal difference, pitch dimensions, transfer fees, bonus payments, refreshment sales, how long to run 100 metres, how far can a ball be kicked, how fast can a ball travel, how far to the furthest away match, how far will the team travel each year, how many and how often can I get the players into school because they could inspire young lives, how often can I get the children to the stadiums ...*

The spring term commenced on 3 January. Carol walked into the Year 6 class where four professional rugby players were sitting with the different groups to support a calculation lesson (having undertaken a training programme relating to the mathematics framework), but the coach was also waiting because in forty minutes they were off to the training ground to study the mathematics of fitness!

Time has moved on and Carol's dream of having a high quality daily mathematics lesson which focuses on calculation, whilst the other aspects of mathematics are taught in a thematic way, has become a reality. The work with the sports team is remembered fondly by the pupils and staff. Although one thing has continued – the rugby players still support the daily mathematics lesson.

Projects like the one above or the other case studies in this chapter led to new and innovative practices from which we can all learn. However some educationalists argue that this has been frowned upon within the outside-in world of education that has existed over recent years. Robin Alexander writes: 'It is commonplace that historically, many system wide innovations have originated in specific localities and local authorities ... For over two decades this has not been recognised. I believe that in a climate where the local potential for nationally relevant innovation was acknowledged it would have spread faster.'[38]

A director of a local education authority vented his disdain for centralised outside-in models of education by writing: 'Some of the most interesting and powerful educational ideas and practices of recent years have come from the educational grass roots, but their later adoption by national agencies have been marred by an unwillingness to acknowledge their source, and even by plagiarism, for centralisation justifies itself by contrasting government omniscience with local ignorance.'[39]

To meet these ends the Cambridge Review suggested that 70% of available teaching time should be given over to the National Curriculum and the remaining 30% towards a 'community curriculum'. I believe that is right and proper. This is a strong endorsement for schools to take greater control over their curriculum and then add their own unique twist.

The notion of schools allocating a proportion of the time available towards placing their own twist on the curriculum is not new. Following Sir Ron Dearing's review of the primary national curriculum in 1993 he recommended that schools should decide which elements of the curriculum should be taught in depth and which would get lighter coverage. The Dearing Report also recommended that schools allocate 20% of their time towards creating their own unique foci.[40] At a later stage this initiative became discredited because too few schools took advantage of the proposals. However we must never forget that many schools did and they created an inspirational curriculum that helped inspirational teachers achieve inspirational responses from their learners.

As a head teacher during this era I allocated 20% of the time to developing genuine pupil creativity. This helped the school move towards higher standards and a judgement of outstanding by Ofsted. Since then I have spent time studying the twists used by our most inspirational teachers to drive their practice – and they unfold in the following chapters. However it will also be essential to set up highly effective assessment strategies and structures in order to measure what you value and not merely value what you measure. Whilst schools will continue to be assessed on achievement and attainment within the core subjects, they might also wish to consider measures relating to behaviour and attendance, civic participation, healthy lifestyles, personal learning and thinking skills or attitudes to self and school. Suggestions and guidance relating to assessment structures are made in Chapter 7.

A final thought

David Blunkett, on becoming the Secretary of State for Education in England just before the millennium, wrote, 'Within the next two or three decades the global society will have to face up to and make a set of decisions the like of which humanity has never before faced. I want these decisions made by people educated in the fullest sense of the world, i.e. highly knowledgeable, capable of understanding complex problems, highly skilled, talented in the art of communication, confident, working in teams, creative, and not least, capable of exercising moral judgement and taking a global perspective.'[41]

A decade has passed and been lost since those words were written. The national vision to produce the curriculum reform that was required to bring that dream to reality never occurred. The politicians were either too scared or too clueless to make the right and bold decisions. However some school leaders backed by inspirational teachers did take action and they are providing an exhilarating curriculum that is equipping children for the future. I hope you will want to do the same and that this chapter has sown important seeds in your mind.

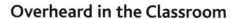

Overheard in the Classroom

Continued from page 30.

Pupil: Now we are in Year 5 will we be doing the Tudors? My brother and sister both did the Tudors in Year 5 and so did our next door neighbour and he is seventeen now.

Teacher: Children, we will have a fabulous time in Year 5. We will develop our thinking skills and solve problems. We will be creative and develop new ideas along the way. We will learn about honesty and fairness. We will learn to admire what is wonderful in our world and seek to change what is not. We will learn about our own strengths. We will work hard as a team and support each other, and on other occasions we will work alone, and when we do this we will celebrate each other's successes. We will work with pride and perseverance and together we will achieve great things.

Chapter 3

Some People Get Lost in Thought Because it's Unfamiliar Territory

How Inspirational Teachers Create Powerful Thinkers

One's mind, once stretched by a new idea, never regains its original dimensions.
Oliver Wendell Holmes

Overheard in the Classroom

Teacher: What are you doing, boy? You are not paying attention to me.

Pupil: I am thinking, Sir.

Teacher: Don't be so cheeky. I have been teaching for fifteen years and no one has ever had the audacity to say they have been thinking in my lessons before.

Philosophy for Children

That's for jessies

'Philosophy for Children, that for jessies!' proclaimed Wayne, who was just ten years of age. I am not quite sure what a jessie is but I am sure it was not a complement. Wayne also made it clear that he had no desire to watch a three-minute film, take part in a discussion or enter a Circle of Enquiry.

The world of education can be a very strange place. The teacher Thomas Gradgrind in Charles Dickens' *Hard Times* explained his educational philosophy thus:

> Now, what I want is, Facts. Teach these boys and girls nothing but Facts. Facts alone are wanted in life. Plant nothing else, and root out everything else. You can only form the minds of reasoning animals upon Facts: nothing else will ever be of any service to them. This is the principle on which I bring up my own children, and this is the principle on which I bring up these children. Stick to Facts, Sir!

We probably all know or have experienced teachers who have worked in this way and who have closed down minds because of their approaches to teaching. This is a great shame because the human brain is designed to think about new possibilities and consider not only what is but what might be. Our best teachers open up minds. They not only seek to make deep thinking desirable, they also make it contagious. So now let's return to Wayne.

Wayne had already decided that he was not going to participate in the planned activity. However his teacher had other thoughts and was determined to hook him into the lesson. Then she had a flash of brilliance. She told him that he could make a video recording of the discussions that were taking place before editing it so the class had a final product they could share in the future. Wayne decided that creating videos and ICT were 'manly' activities that could never be associated with jessies and therefore he agreed.

The class then started to watch a short film which showed a lonely youth ordering a 'cyberfriend' off the internet, and how he built a friendship before discarding it forever and ordering a new cyberfriend. The children raised a list of key questions to explore. These included: Is true friendship disposable? What makes a true friend? What does lonely feel like?

The children than moved into a circle ready to discuss the question: How do you create a friendship that lasts for life? Wayne was also standing with his video camera and was poised for action. He knew that he was the only one in the class with a real job to do and that all eyes would be on him. He prepared to become the centre of attention. He chose his camera angle carefully. Theresa would be the first child to speak and the viewfinder indicated that Wayne had her in full focus. He was ready to press record.

Theresa started to speak. She said that she had found the film quite worrying because she had looked across at her best friend from whom she had been inseparable since they had entered the foundation stage and thought how sad it would be if they fell out and were never friends again, and this had made her think about her Mum's favourite song which was 'Will You Still Love Me Tomorrow?'

The whole class fell silent momentarily because they had been moved by what had been said. Wayne put the video camera down on the floor and said, 'Theresa, you are missing the whole point of the film and this exercise. True friendship is something that will last forever, it's not something you throw away like an old tin can, but you do have to work at friendship and look after each other and that's what you two have been doing for the last five years. Friendships are something you have to really value. Well, that's my philosophy on it anyway.' Theresa looked up and said, 'I thought you said philosophy was for jessies!'

The moral of this true story is that an inspirational teacher can hook children into thinking deeply about a range of issues. Wayne may not have wanted to participate but he was in the hands of a skilful teacher who made thinking exciting and contagious. Our best teachers not only get children to think about literacy, mathematics, science and the subjects on the curriculum, but they get children to think about a whole range of issues including being a good citizen and the complexities of growing up in the twenty-first century. In fact, they just get young people to think. Period!

Some people believe there is a great mystique to developing children as creative thinkers or independent enquirers and that frameworks and systems are needed. They can be helpful and some will be referred to here. Others believe that only certain people are born as creative thinkers, and I am sure that some children are naturally gifted in this area. However when the climate for learning is right, where the stimulus is strong or the emotions engaged, children can develop very powerful thinking skills. This chapter explains how inspirational teachers create inspirational thinkers.

Thirty-five years ago many people in Norway earned their living from fishing in the North Sea. It was a harsh way of life carried out in very difficult circumstances. Then along came North Sea oil, which brought great wealth and changed lifestyles and aspirations. During the 1970s the Norwegian Government rewrote their national curriculum and placed a great emphasis on children developing thinking skills. The reason for this was that they recognised that North Sea oil would eventually run out and that future economic success would depend on seeking solutions through creative thinking. They stated: 'Education must demonstrate how creative energy and inventiveness have constantly improved the context, content and quality of human life.'[42] Around the same time the national curriculum authorities in Singapore dedicated 30% of curricular time to the development of thinking because they recognised that 'their future as an economy and a nation rested not on getting people to a high level in narrow fields but on developing creative individuals who were empowered in their creative thinking and their ability to create their own future'.[43] By way of contrast, in Britain's general election campaign of 2010, the then Shadow Minister for Education, Michael Gove, stated in an interview with

The Times: 'I am an unashamed traditionalist when it comes to the curriculum. Most parents would rather children had a traditional education with children sitting in rows learning the kings and queens of England, the great works of literature, proper mental arithmetic, algebra by the age of eleven. That's the best training of the mind and that's how children will be able to compete.'[44] Amongst the feedback on the newspaper's website were the words of a head teacher in an inner city school, who said she 'read the words and wept'.

Traditionalists or radicals?

Whilst the words of Michael Gove were from a then opposition spokesman for education, by 2010 government policy had already ensured that the children in our primary schools were the most tested in the world. The 2007 Unicef child poverty survey, which found England's school population to be the unhappiest in the industrial world, maintained that this was significantly related to a preoccupation with testing children.[45] The report elicited the following editorial comment in *The Independent*: 'The Government's favourite formula for raising educational standards has the merit of simplicity. We are now top of the European league table in at least one respect: our children are subjected to more national school exams than those in any other country ... Parents may comfort themselves with the thought that, however badly educated their children may be when they leave school, they will at least be able to do exams.'[46] I don't believe that the words and deeds of the politicians are necessarily traditionalist. They are more often the words and actions of those who are ignorant because they take little account of recent research into how children truly learn.

Sadly politicians from all Britain's political parties always seem to get pulled back to a dated model of education when it is under any kind of pressure. I refer you once again to Robin Alexander: 'English primary education in 2000 is the nineteenth century elementary education modified – much modified admittedly – rather than transformed. Elementary education is at its centre of gravity. Elementary education provides it central point of reference. Elementary education is the form to which it most readily tends to regress.'[47]

The reality of our classrooms

The children in our schools today recognise that they will need to solve many global problems. Therefore they need to study the right things and get into the right thinking habits as early as possible. Too often our schools fail to make this provision. This was confirmed in 2009 when Ipsos MORI carried out a survey entitled 'Understanding Learners'.[48] An initial part of the work was to establish the three main ways in which Year 6 pupils prefer to learn. From the survey of just under 2,000 pupils the highest score was from those who reported that they preferred to learn by thinking and learning alongside their peers in groups. The next highest were pupils who learned best by doing practical things. The next two highest scores were from pupils who preferred learning alongside their friendship group and those who preferred using computers. There is a strong commonality in this approach. These four favoured ways of learning are the ideal precursor to children working alongside each other and starting to think deeply about issues and to solve their own problems. Some direct teaching is clearly required but because discovery favours the well-prepared mind the outcomes of the survey show that children prefer to seek their own solutions by working alongside their peers – often using technology in a way that requires them to think deeply.

The same group of children were asked, 'Which were the three most common forms of activities carried out in the classroom?' The most frequent answer was copying from a board, book or worksheet. A staggering 55% of pupils thought that this was the most common method employed by teachers. The second most common answer was listening to the teacher for a long time. One third of pupils thought that this was the most common strategy used. The third most common answer was by having a class discussion. The fourth was taking notes whilst the teacher talked. Down at the bottom of the list were a range of strategies which are regularly employed by our most inspirational teachers. These include learning outside the school grounds, creating pictures and maps to help remember and taking responsibility for teaching classmates about something.

To fully understand the mismatch between the children's three most preferred ways to learn and the most common classroom activities consider the full set of information in the tables below.

In which three of the following ways do you prefer to learn?	Score
In groups	55%
By doing practical things	39%
With friends	35%
By using computers	31%
Alone	21%
From teachers	19%
From friends	16%
By seeing things done	14%
With your parents	12%
By practising	9%
In silence	9%
By copying	8%
By thinking for yourself	6%
At a museum or library	5%
From others	3%
Other	1%

Which of the three do you use most often in class?	Score
Copy from board, book, or a worksheet	55%
Listen to the teacher for a long time	33%
Have a class discussion	29%
Take notes whilst the teacher talks	25%
Spend time working quietly on my own	22%
Work in small groups to solve a problem	22%
Have a drink of water when I need it	17%
Talk about my work with a teacher	16%
Work on a computer	16%
Listening to background music	10%
Learning about things that relate to the real world	10%

(continued)

Which of the three do you use most often in class?	Score
Carrying out activities that allow me to move around	9%
Teach my classmates something	8%
Create pictures or maps that help me remember	7%
Have a change of activity to help focus	7%
Have people from outside to help me learn	4%
Learn outside for example in the school grounds	3%

Inspirational teachers creating inspirational thinkers

Why is it so important to get children thinking? The first one relates to our growing knowledge of how the brain works and goes something like this. We have billions of brain cells called neurons which give us the capacity to think and learn. For our brains to work properly these neurons have to connect with one another so they can pass electrical impulses from cell to cell. As we grow and experience the world the neurons become coated with myelin which helps the transfer of electrical impulses. The more opportunities for stimulation and active exploration the child has, the more new connections will be formed, and when a child is required to use previous learning it will lead to the myelination of existing connections. Once the neurons start connecting pathways are formed. The more they are used the more they become a permanent part of our brains, thus increasing our thinking power.

Neuroscientists may tell us that the brain is not actually designed for building up banks of knowledge but for getting things done quickly and fluidly in situations that matter. We are built for real-life learning rather than scholarship. This could actually lead us to the view that schools are therefore irrelevant and being an effective teacher is an impossible task. We should not get too depressed, however, because we all know teachers who do it brilliantly and so becoming an inspirational teacher is learnable and teachable. Our brains are wired for imitation as a key form of learning. There are identifiable ways of teaching which will develop the ability to pay attention, to wonder, to construct imaginative learning and to love learning. Sadly being an ineffective learner is also learnable and teachable. Some teachers open minds but others close them down.

Overheard in the Classroom

Mrs Jones: Mr Smith, you have only been head teacher for five minutes and you come here criticising my classroom practice and saying that I work in a classroom where teacher talk dominates. You seem to forget I have thirty years of experience at this school.

Mr Smith: No, Mrs Jones, you have one year's experience repeated thirty times.

The second reason why it is important to get children thinking is because the human mind is enormously elastic and when it is stretched it is capable of brilliance. This fact is of far more interest to our inspirational teachers. They know that the mind is like a muscle and if it is worked and exercised hard they will get responses that create a warm glow of satisfaction for learners and teachers alike.

Inspirational teachers have always recognised that effective learning requires deep thinking. In short, they recognise that children have to think hard to really learn. Many of our best teachers have done this intuitively in the past. However increasingly we all have a wider and fuller understanding of what the thinking process involves and are therefore more able to develop learners as well-rounded thinkers who will be resilient and flexible in the real world. Our best teachers do not see themselves as the traditional font of all knowledge; instead they create deep learning and understanding by:

- Reflecting upon themselves as thinkers and learners and modelling effective thinking and learning habits for their pupils.

- Recognising the importance of not only providing opportunities for thinking within traditional academic subjects but also through exploring issues that exist outside the classroom and in the real world because their learners need to fulfil a full role in an increasingly complex society.

- Believing that without creating deep thinking opportunities we will be limiting understanding and the opportunities to apply their learning.

When these three factors come together children develop the capacity to make big jumps in their learning.

'Spoon feeding in the long run teaches us nothing but the shape of the spoon.'[49] or The need to make big jumps in learning.

The most effective people regularly demonstrate the capacity to make big jumps in their learning and they do this repeatedly throughout their life. You can check this out by observing life within a school. If you are a teacher the next time you are sitting in the staffroom take a look around you. Focus in on the most effective practitioners. These will be the people who drink up their continuing professional development opportunities and are always looking to progress. They bring in new ideas and make improvements in their practice annually. Now look at those who are less successful. Are these the people that fail to significantly adapt their practice year by year; work in classrooms where teacher talk dominates and probably teach in the style in which they were taught? Similar situations will exist in other professions and walks of life. Based on this analogy we need to equip learners to make big jumps.

Learning in our schools often comes from carrying out finely graded activities. Teachers work hard to ensure that lessons are built around children making and taking very small steps. However this does not reflect life in the real world where people do not experience a gentle and smooth learning curve. Large strides and hard work are required – and we need learners to rise to that challenge. Our best teachers model this within their practice. They know that children like the challenge of getting stuck into substantial – but not demoralising – problems because this helps real and deep learning to take place. There is nothing wrong with children learning to think hard in a wide variety of ways.

Our best thinkers

Our challenge as educationalists is to create the thinkers of tomorrow. The most exciting classrooms I have visited strike a balance. Yes, there is direct teaching that takes place in a relatively formal context. There is clearly a requirement for subject content and a need to teach knowledge. However the challenge is to provide the appropriate content in a context that promotes deep thinking and genuine understanding. Therefore there will be other times when formality feels a million miles away. On these occasions the classroom is a place where learning takes place in an atmosphere that rewards adventure and risk taking – which inevitably leads to mistakes being made. Our best classrooms will also be a place where children learn about great thinkers who have sought solutions to significant problems and had the resilience to see these solutions come to light. Then, pitched at an appropriate level, the children need to have the opportunities to bring their own ideas to a successful conclusion. Pupils should have the chance to start from taking part in their own messy and unstructured creative thinking, which might lead to flights of fancy, and then towards a solution that will only be achieved when they demonstrate such qualities as risk taking, perseverance and resilience.

If we are to make these kinds of classrooms the norm rather than the exception, the next question has to be: In what ways do inspirational teachers get children to think?

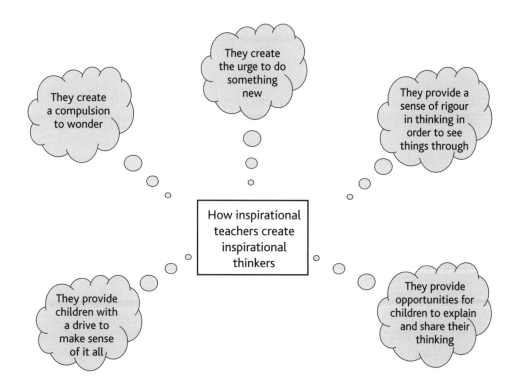

There are clearly links between each of the five areas identified in the diagram on page 77. On some occasions within the classroom each area will stand alone and on others a number of areas will become interlinked or even represent a form of progression (because you have to complete your thinking in one sphere before moving on to the next). I have had the privilege of seeing many inspirational teachers who have achieved inspirational responses from their children by creating a desire within them to think deeply in the range of situations identified. Some of their stories follow. I have selected one from each of the scenarios above. Where appropriate these have been cross-referenced to specific areas of research. The ideas and techniques are adaptable to other classrooms. I am sure you will spot the links between the areas of thinking identified.

Inspirational teachers help learners to make sense of it all

Why is thinking so important in our classrooms? Susan Cowley provides the answer. Inspirational teachers who promote inspirational thinking from their students will develop the skills of:

- conceptualising
- empathising
- developing morality
- common sense/emotional intelligence
- concentration and focus

whilst developing an understanding of the big issues in our world today.[50]

The following case study covers all of these aspects.

Tales of Inspirational Practice

Hairspray

This is the story of a flash of inspiration that hit Richard the head teacher just after he had picked up his golf club to play an extremely tricky high pressure shot.

But first imagine the tension. If he missed this he would lose the match and, as he was playing a far younger player, his dignity. He needed to time his shot perfectly. It was vital that the ball passed under the water wheel and climbed the hump that followed to preserve his crazy golf record which had remained intact throughout his holiday on the Yorkshire coast. Just as he pulled the club back his opponent suddenly asked, 'Anyway, Dad, what is so important about Barack Obama becoming President of the United States of America?' Richard missed the shot, lost the match and with it his dignity.

He did, however, answer the question by pointing out that Barack Obama was black, to which his son replied, 'So what!' From that point Richard gave his son a potted history of events in the United States over the last seventy years. To which his son replied, 'It's a bit like *Hairspray* then,' and that is when the idea started to take shape.

For a while Richard had been toying with the notion of how he could create high impact assemblies that really engaged pupils – leaving the children wanting to learn more about the real and complex world in which they live. Richard was also a musician first and foremost and music was often the starting point to his thinking.

He knew that if he could build a series of assemblies around the musical *Hairspray*, which currently had cult popularity amongst the children, it could have a tremendous impact. He played the music, taught the children some of the songs and used segments of footage from the film. Whilst the overall story is about a person with a love of dance, he knew that by concentrating on the subplots, imagery and song lyrics he could explore such issues as stereotyping, racism, segregation in a divided US and the importance of people having dreams and ambitions. They explored the derogatory way in which language is used towards certain groups of people. The assemblies also covered the lives of other significant individuals such as Nelson Mandela, Rosa Parks and Martin Luther King. The children looked at the origins of different genres of music in the United States in the 1950s.

When I was a head teacher I would sometimes say to the children: 'What was assembly about this morning?' I could see them trying to recall the information from what were often mundane starts to the school day. Sometimes they responded with 'Was it about God?' This was not the situation at Richard's school.

On the day that I visited the children were watching the scene in *Hairspray* where people are marching through the streets of Baltimore campaigning for integrated rather than segregated dances. The scene faded in and out mixing in real film footage from the news archives showing black people marching during the Montgomery Bus Boycott. These children could recount every single moment of the assembly and they understood that the different groups of people that make up our world have a great deal in common and there should be very little that divides them.

Inspirational teachers create the urge to try something new

There have been a whole host of books written about the qualities possessed by highly successful people and those who have had the courage to try something new and succeeded. There are often common factors in their success stories and the qualities that these individuals possessed. Firstly, many of them had to overcome elements of disadvantage caused by parenting or the community in which they were growing up. Secondly, there was a need to work hard. Many writers cite the 10,000 hour rule, which is based on the principle that to be truly successful at anything 10,000 hours of practice or training will be required. Thirdly, there is a belief that working hard will actually lead to experiencing lucky breaks. The case study below shows how one head teacher sought to equip his learners to succeed by modelling these traits.

Tales of Inspirational Practice

Peter's story

I was walking down the corridor of a primary school recently and a Year 4 child was walking towards me carrying a musical instrument. He looked up as we passed and said, 'Hello Mister, I'm learning how to play the trumpet.' I told him that I was very pleased and would look forward to hearing how he was progressing when I next visited the school. When I returned four weeks later I tracked him down and asked how well his trumpet lessons were going. He looked up and said, 'I packed it,' which was the local terminology for saying he had stopped the lessons. This was so disappointing. He had wanted to try something new and had been allowed to fall at the first hurdle. It made me think about an inspirational head teacher that I first encountered a number of years ago, and our paths seem to cross periodically.

I meet Peter every three to four years. It isn't planned, it just happens. One of us walks into a room somewhere and the other is already present. The first time we met was when we were both training to be Ofsted inspectors. We were both looking around the room at the other people present – I think we were trying to imagine if they had ever been any good in front of a class of children. One thing is certain: neither of us stuck with Ofsted for long. Peter left the local authority he was working for and returned to headship, but not before he had started to tell me his inspirational tale.

The first thing Peter did when he became a head teacher was to remove the sign on his door that said 'Headmaster'. However he did not replace it with the obvious sign that would have said 'Head Teacher' but with a sign that said 'Head Learner'. He then picked up a set of bagpipes and set off for his first assembly.

He stood in front of the assembled school tussling with the various tubes and pipes; eventually he got them in almost the right place and proceeded to blow – making a sound like a stuck pig. He then said to the children that this was the first time he had ever picked up a set of bagpipes and he didn't have any idea about how to play them. At that point he made the children a promise that by the last day of the school year he would have mastered the bagpipes, and he would bring them back and play 'Scotland the Brave'. The reason he did this was that he wanted to demonstrate to the children the importance of accepting new challenges and constantly seeking self-improvement. He told them that along the way things would get difficult and he would need willpower and resilience and sometimes he would need to practise when he really didn't want to. He was trying to model to the children the challenges of what a real learner has to do.

When I next met Peter he was still working in this same way. Each year brought a new challenge, and on that occasion he was learning to play the didgeridoo. On the last occasion we bumped into each other I simply looked at him – I didn't need to say anything. He said, 'Ballroom dancing ...'

Inspirational teachers create an urge to wonder

Howard Gardner once said, 'If pupils don't learn the way we teach, perhaps we should teach the way they learn.'[51] The reality is that most children don't learn best sat behind a desk nor does such a position create an urge to wonder. The reality is that the best learning often comes from one or more of the scenarios listed below:

- Watching other people do things, especially if they are a role model, and then adapting what is seen.

- Seeking time on their own to practise a new skill or piece of learning in order to improve.

- Asking their own questions at the time they need to and of the people they think will be able to help them most.

- Making rough-and-ready notes and diagrams to help them think and plan, knowing that these will never be seen.

- Developing strange or bizarre ideas and possibilities and then starting to try them out on people who can be trusted.

- Running through ideas in their head imagining how different scenarios would work out.

- Imagining being able to do something better than they do now by creating their own set of images in their mind to help them practise.

The case study below is an example of some of these possibilities. Albert Einstein once famously stated, 'Imagination is more important than knowledge.' Many great thinkers have been driven by a curiosity to wonder how the world could become a better place for people in the future. However this normally involves the use of spiritual and emotional intelligences rather than the mathematical intelligence demonstrated in the story below. It involves the learner creating his own set of questions, making his own rough-and-ready notes and considering the different scenarios that could exist – and it all came from a mathematical problem.

Tales of Inspirational Practice

Sixteen years and the wrong set of balls!

I remember the date well. It was Friday 18 November 1994 and the time had just reached 2.25 p.m. I was a head teacher at the time and I'd just had the privilege of observing a superb mathematics lesson, and you don't tend to see too many superb mathematics lessons in schools on a Friday afternoon. The session had started with direct teaching about the properties of square numbers before moving towards a more open-ended investigation. The mixed ability class were asked to identify the first six square numbers using a variety of strategies. The children were then required to find a way of predicting how many square numbers existed between 0 and 100, 100 and 200, 300 and 400 and so on, and find a way of seeking the answers. Some children explored patterns, some reached for calculators, others used squared paper and peg boards. You may be wondering why the date became etched on my mind.

The following day would make history as the first ever National Lottery draw would take place in the UK, and just before the end of the lesson Robert Thompson turned to me and said, 'You should have those first six square numbers for your lottery ticket tomorrow!' and then he added, 'I wonder how likely you are to win?' Then, like so many teachers, I saw a learning opportunity opening up before me and simply said, 'You could find out about my chances and what the implications might be.' Now Robert was a very good young mathematician and his fellow pupils had also spotted another significant trait he had. The children said that Robert always had spending money left at the end of the week which suggests that he was shrewd with money as well. As the school closed for the weekend Robert was still thinking about the challenge he had been set. He went home wondering about those six lottery numbers and whether or not they had the capacity to change my life.

On Monday Robert came to school and asked me if I had purchased the lottery ticket. I replied in the affirmative and told him I had lost. He then went on to say that if I selected the same numbers every week and a different combination of balls were selected every week it could take as long as 13,983,816 weeks to hit the jackpot and cost as many pounds. This might also require me to live to the age of 268,959. He then informed me that if instead I concentrated on saving £100 per month (which should be perfectly manageable on my salary because he had checked out the teacher pay scales!) in a regular saver account I would be able to afford a very nice medium-sized car in eight years' time. Unfortunately, some sixteen years later, I am still using the same numbers and do not possess a car that is either medium sized or very nice.

In carrying out his research over the weekend Robert used a framework that had been introduced to him in school. It came from Edward de Bono's Cognitive Research Trust (CoRT). The technique is called PMI. Whatever issue is being explored the person thinking identifies, in turn, all the positive (P) points, minus (M) all the negative points and any other interesting (I) thoughts or scenarios on the subject on a grid like the one below. This has been partially completed to demonstrate how it works.

Plus points *of buying a lottery ticket*	Minus points *of buying a lottery ticket*	Other interesting questions and scenarios
I might become a millionaire	I am very likely to lose my money	How much would I make if I invested the money in a bank?

In the scenario described above Robert voluntarily exhibited five key thinking skills. He *processed the relevant information*, he used *reasoning*, he asked the relevant questions as he *created his enquiry*, he created and *generated his own ideas* and *evaluated his findings*.

The school had also invested considerable energy in getting the children to use 'could be' language. This – rather than 'is' language – was important in the context of Robert's challenge. He set out to discover the implications of buying a lottery ticket rather than the chances of winning the lottery. By asking what is 4x5 you risk getting the answer 20 and very soon minds will close down. By asking what

4x5 could be you open up a host of other answers including the numbers of play-ers in a football match if two are sent off, two dozen with four missing or a good hand in pontoon. Try it and watch the minds open up.

Inspirational teachers create a sense of rigour in thinking

At the start of the 1960s the producer of Decca Records rejected The Beatles saying that the era of beat groups was over. By the end of the decade they were judged to be the most successful pop group ever and hailed by many as geniuses. The reality is that they were not geniuses but they honed their skills over hours of practice in the formative stages of their career. This was often done in challenging circumstances performing for hours at a time in Ham-burg's shadier nightclubs.

Children need to develop the resilience to see things through. Too often in my career as an adviser/inspector I have seen half-completed tasks and good ideas that never quite come to fruition. Skilful and inspirational teachers do not allow this to happen. They are not afraid of longer-term projects because they provide opportunities for true learning and understanding, but they also know about the range of support strategies that will be required to bring a meaning-ful task to a successful conclusion, as the following story illustrates.

Tales of Inspirational Practice

Playgrounds, graffiti and thinking hats

Margaret Mead once famously said, 'Never doubt that a small group of thought-ful, committed citizens can change the world. Indeed, it is the only thing that ever has.'[52] The words are very true. This story could read: 'Never doubt the capacity of a group of small people to change the world because in this scenario they did.'

The children in Nick's Year 5 class were not necessarily looking forward to their lessons on the Ancient Egyptians. It had been taught as a historical topic in this year group ever since the advent of the National Curriculum in 1988 and therefore had become somewhat predictable. Just before the study was about to commence the class got the news that the children's play area outside the school was to be scrapped. In many ways this was not surprising as it had become a target for vandalism and an area where drug abuse had become a regular evening occurrence. A four-letter expletive was sprayed across the roundabout which made an ear-piercing shriek if anyone tried to turn it. The school now knew the playground was to be scrapped in order for a new municipal office to be built, because they had been informed that new entrances were to be made to the school site. It was around 4.45 p.m. and Nick turned off his laptop from which he had been downloading lesson plans for his forthcoming literacy work which related to letter writing for a purpose. He looked across the vandalised site and then the idea of using the playground hit him. He felt angered because the recreational area had been built for the benefit of children and he thought that it should remain that way. Those reflections led to a sudden change of thinking. In a stroke the Egyptians were ditched and a project involving a full campaign to build a new play area was put into full swing.

The children wrote letters expressing their concerns to the council, local newspapers and radio stations. They set up petitions. They consulted with parents and other children about what the new playground could look like. They asked the police about how it could be made safe at night. They asked if they could speak with students at the secondary school about helping to look after the site. They created their own website and set about creating their own media campaign. The local council elections were imminent and they set out to make it an issue in the eyes of the electorate.

Then the children were informed that a small group of councillors were to meet with them to discuss implementing the plans they had drawn up. Nick drew the class together and told them they could be either poised for success or they could lose their battle, and the play area would be lost forever. He said they had to prepare a watertight argument so they could answer any question they were given with well-reasoned thinking. It was at this point that he introduced the idea of Edward de Bono's Thinking Hats.[53]

Edward de Bono believes that in order to help people take different approaches to thinking they should wear six 'mythical' hats. By putting on a specific hat the wearer engages in a form of mental role play. Each hat is a different colour and none is more important than the rest, nor is the order in which they are worn important – you just have to work through all of them.

When children wear the white hat they are being neutral and are collecting information without presenting an argument. The playground was designed for children but was vandalised, dangerous and not used for the purpose it was intended. Coupled with this a new municipal office was needed.

When children wear the red hat emotions and feelings become involved. Red is the colour of fire – it is at this point that feelings start to become visible. An injustice was being carried out and children were being robbed of a space that was their entitlement.

When children wear the black hat objectivity is brought back through a logical but negative argument. Significant problems are pointed out and it could be that what comes out is that the argument is not worth pursuing. The playground was not being used any more by young children or even for a constructive purpose and the new council offices would not be the eyesore that the play area was.

When the children wear the yellow hat a logical positivity is restored leading to forward and constructive thinking. The hat is yellow because the sunshine is yellow. This brings in a mood of optimism and a more positive assessment. Investment could lead to a new play area being provided that could be well-used by the children. At this point concrete proposals and suggestions are made.

When the green hat is worn the thinking becomes truly creative and the green shoots of the idea start to take hold. New ideas are introduced. Secure fencing and lockable gates are added to the site along with surveillance cameras and the children will involve the neighbours in a Playground Watch Scheme and suggest changes to the duties of Community Police Officers.

Finally the blue hat is worn and now control and organisation takes place. The hat is blue because we move from blue sky thinking to taking a cool and controlled look at what needs to happen next and directing the thinking for the future. At this point the cast-iron plan for the new play area is presented.

Prior to the visit by the council members the children used a further strategy promoted by Edward de Bono's CoRT and this involved doing an OPV (collecting Other People's Views). This exercise allowed the children to develop objectivity and empathy. If residents expressed concerns about the play area being misused it allowed the children to offer counter views, and when local citizens stressed the need for the new municipal offices it allowed the children to suggest other possible sites.

Three members of the local council duly arrived along with two local government officers and members of the press. They listened carefully to the proposals. But that was the last the children saw of the delegation and press – until of course Nick and his class officially opened a new, safe and secure play area six months later.

Another of the key features of highly successful people is that they make the most of the time they are living in. Schools and inspirational teachers can help this process by opening children's eyes to what is going on around them, and that is precisely what Nick did.

In addition to the Six Thinking Hats identified above, Edward de Bono, never one to let a good idea go unworked, also identified Six Action Shoes. The shoes represent different kinds of actions. They help a person or group of people to decide what they should do next as a result of thinking. I have seen many inspirational teachers use the model to help children decide how to proceed with a plan or to check if it is coming to fruition. The action shoes are detailed below. You might want to try them in your classroom – remember that you are allowed to mix the shoes and wear different coloured shoes on each foot.

- **Navy formal** shoes are associated with systems and routines. These should be worn when you need to know if things are proceeding to plan.

- **Grey sneakers** are for when the mind is in a fog. Grey represents the mist and sneakers represent exploration and investigation. You would wear them if you need to forage for new information.

- **Brown brogues** are for when the tough get going. Brown represents earth and mud and you would wear them when the terrain is rough and undefined. Put them on when practical action is needed to reach a solution or bring a plan to fruition.

- **Orange gumboots** are to be worn in emergency. These boots are worn by firefighters so wear them when the immediate safety of others is your primary concern.

- **Pink slippers** suggest warmth and comfort. They are associated with femininity and tenderness. You would wear them when you need to show compassion and kindness.

- **Purple riding boots** represent power and position. Purple is the colour of Imperial Rome. Wear them on those occasions when you need to be in control and take charge (perhaps when Ofsted are coming).[54]

Inspirational teachers encourage learners to share their learning

Politicians are always telling us how concerned they are about the economy. They are also always telling us how concerned they are about educational standards and the absolute need to focus on the basics. So schools and teachers concentrate more on the basics and less on the creative aspects of the curriculum. Politicians tend to pontificate about these issues and sound awfully wise. Their wisdom is often false because they fail to take into account that the creative economy usually grows at twice the speed of the rest of the economy. Therefore the message they should be giving is to invest more in creativity to help build a secure economy for the future. One simple way of doing this is to provide children with creative opportunities to share their work with each other. This can be readily done in all subjects, including mathematics and science, as the example below shows.

Tales of Inspirational Practice

A story of digital images and decimal fractions

Teacher: And now, children, here is some paper to record your work.

Pupil: Who says we need paper?

The American educationalist and cultural critic Neil Postman once described text-books and worksheets as anti-educational. He famously defined them as 'instruments for promoting dogmatism and trivial learning'.[55] Whilst modern textbooks for primary aged pupils may have colourful graphics and try to engage the interests of hard-to-reach boys by looking at things like football scores they often contain closed and unimaginative tasks. The same can be said of many worksheets especially some of the published ones. I once saw children completing a worksheet entitled 'Through the Classroom Window 7' which was allegedly a geographical investigation of the locality and, yes, there had been a previous six worksheets with a similar title. There will be more on that story later, but suffice to say that the children would have gained far more by walking out through the classroom door rather than looking out through one classroom window, let alone seven.

Patrick believed that wherever possible children should take full responsibility for their work from start to finish without feeling constrained by following a pre-scribed route. He also recognised the need for children to help each other in order to shape their learning and celebrate their successes.

The first day I met Patrick he was just starting to let loose the whole of a Year 5 class on a mathematical investigation relating to decimals. The children had got a set of red, green, yellow and blue 'learning links' that hooked together to make a chain (these are available from many educational suppliers but Centicubes or Unifix cubes would serve the same purpose). The children were told that the different coloured links each had different values:

Each red link was worth 0.3
Each green link was worth 0.4

Each yellow link was worth 0.5
Each blue link was worth 0.6

The children were told in their groups that they had to find eleven ways of making chains that would total 2. However they had also to understand that four red links and two green links, regardless of the order they were put together, was only one answer to the problem. The children were also asked to devise their own ways of presenting their work which would then be assessed by their peers. The success criteria for the presentation included pride in presentation, uniqueness of thought and evidence of children thinking individually and working collaboratively.

The children proceeded purposefully. They developed their knowledge of place value. Some groups used algebraic phrasing such as 3R+1Y+1B=2, kinaesthetic learners used the links, auditory learners tossed them to one side and discussed solutions, and visual learners reached for coloured felt-tip pens. Hypothesising and testing took place.

The children's recorded work was carefully and sometimes beautifully presented. Some used plain paper, some used squared paper and some used no paper. There were charts, diagrams and illustrations. There were written accounts, some of which incorporated digital photographs. There were PowerPoint presentations and Flip videos recording the solutions. The children mixed up their groups to share their answers. They provided feedback to each other using the 'three stars and a wish' system (if you are not aware of this technique, it involves praising three elements of the work and suggesting one way in which it could be improved).

And how long did this process take? Just one hour.

The above are examples of practice I have witnessed in primary schools over the last thirty years. Although in recent decades neuroscientists have done much to help educationalists understand how the brain works, great thinkers, philosophers and educationalists have actually been getting it right for centuries. Sadly some of those who control our education system have closed their ears, leaving it to inspirational – and brave – practitioners to shape the best practice.

Tales of Inspirational Lives (and Deaf Ears)

Socrates, Rousseau, Einstein

Over the years great minds have told us about the importance of developing the art of thinking in children, and for just as long the people responsible for our education system have not taken due account of the advice given.

I like to think this story about the ancient Greek philosopher Socrates is genuine. When the people told him, sometime around 400 BC, that he was a great thinker and the wisest and most intelligent man in all of Greece, he thought, I'd better go and check this out. So he set off into the streets of Athens where he found men and women who were great thinkers. However he discovered they thought in a variety of different ways which gave them differing intelligences. Firstly he found those who were great *academic* thinkers who could store huge swathes of knowledge in their considerable minds and bring it to the fore when required. He knew that these people would be ideal team members to have with him on the pub quizzes in the bars and tavernas of the city. Socrates then found those people who had developed a great *practical* intelligence, who could solve problems relating to plumbing and heating systems and could design and construct impressive temples. Socrates knew he would want these people alongside him if he was constructing great buildings or a new home. Next he found people with a great *emotional* intelligence, who could use resilience and willpower to overcome the problems that lay in front of them. Finally Socrates found people who had a great *spiritual* intelligence, who asked weighty questions and sought solutions to the meaning of life and the importance of society. From this point Socrates devised a method of working though a series of questions to find reason and truth.

Let us now skip forward several centuries to the life and times of Rousseau in the late eighteenth century. He was keen to tell the educationalists of the time that the child is not a mini-adult and therefore they have different needs to adults. He thought childhood should be celebrated in its own right and should be characterised by experience rather than knowledge, and sensation rather than reason. Through these experiences and sensations the child would learn to think and make sense of their world. He also considered that studying from books and initiation into academic discipline should occur when the child is mature enough to benefit from them. Prior to that, the creation of quality experiences is what counts, as this will promote thought and thereby children will start to appreciate right from wrong and be equipped to lead fuller lives.

Moving further forward in time once more, Einstein famously said the important thing is to create learners who never stop questioning. He stressed the significance of teachers doing the right things and opening up minds by making children think when he said: 'Most teachers waste their time asking questions which are intended to discover what a pupil does not know, whereas the true art of questioning has for its purpose to know what the pupil knows or is capable of knowing.' My favourite Einstein quote is:

> The most beautiful thing we can experience is the mysterious. It is the source of all true art and science. He to whom emotion is a stranger, who can no longer pause to wonder wrapt in awe, is as good as dead, his eyes are closed.

Perhaps too many schools may have found the teaching of thinking to be a mystery. However countless great minds have put their substantial talents towards aiding this process. For example, Edward de Bono has spent considerable time promoting direct teaching of thinking as a skill in our schools. His Six Thinking Hats, Action Shoes and some of his CoRT strategies have already been mentioned previously. He has written eighty-two books which have been translated into forty-one languages and his thinking is clearly evident in the national curricula of twenty countries around the world. However his anger and frustration when the UK government scrapped plans to introduce thinking skills into the National Curriculum was very evident when he wrote on his website:

> It seems that the Minister for Schools in the United Kingdom has chosen not to 'impose' thinking skills on schools. This is unfortunate. We know that teaching thinking increases employment opportunities. We know that teaching thinking reduces criminal convictions amongst the violent by up to ninety percent. Teaching knowledge by itself does none of these things. Knowledge does not increase self esteem or allow youngsters to take charge of their lives. There is a need for the teaching of thinking tools to those who make decisions in education. Around the world there are an increasing number of countries who have made this teaching a mandatory part of the curriculum.[56]

What were the National Curriculum thinking skills?

Just exactly what was Edward de Bono complaining about? Proposals had been made to make the teaching of thinking more explicit within the curriculum. Five key thinking skills were identified to be incorporated into the life of every classroom:[57]

1. **Information processing:** which required learners to locate and collect relevant information, sort and classify, compare and contrast, analyse whole to part relationships and sequences.

2. **Reasoning:** which required learners to give reasons for opinions and actions, draw inferences and make deductions, use precise language, explain thoughts and make informed decisions and judgements.

3. **Enquiring:** which required learners to ask relevant questions, pose and define problems, plan what to do and how to research, predict outcomes and anticipate consequences and to test conclusions and improve ideas.

4. **Creating:** which required learners to generate and extend ideas, test hypotheses, apply imagination and look for innovative outcomes.

5. **Evaluating:** which required learners to evaluate information, judge the value of what had been read, learnt or done, develop criteria for judging value and to have confidence in the judgements they had made.

How inspirational teachers promote thinking without national frameworks

This is a fine list but I don't fully share Edward de Bono's concerns. It is not a list that will create a new generation of imaginative or inspirational teachers who can hook children into learning. I have seen what has unfolded previously when a centrally imposed initiative arrives. The big publishers will move in with their quick-fix books of 101 thinking activities, or thinking is given a one-hour slot in the curriculum on a Tuesday afternoon at 1.30 p.m. so that Ofsted can tick the appropriate boxes on the evaluation schedule. The list may be very good for monitoring purposes and I would urge school leaders everywhere to walk their school looking for evidence of these skills in classrooms. However there is something far deeper than a national curriculum list of thinking skills that pervades the classrooms of our most inspirational teachers. There is something special in the heart and soul of everyone within the room. These classrooms are places where thinking, questioning, predicting, contradicting and doubting are actively promoted. Our best teachers recognise that the best learning will take place when children become the active creators of their own knowledge. Inspirational teachers create regular opportunities for sequencing and sorting, classifying and comparing, making predictions, relating cause and effect, drawing conclusions, generating new ideas, problem solving, testing solutions, taking decisions and making sense of the complex world in which we live.

The inspirational teacher who can create inspirational thinking in their classroom is a confident individual who removes any barriers to thinking and intuitively models the thinking process. They are happy to embrace risk taking. This comes in two forms. They personally model risk taking but also encourage pupils to take risks or seek alternative solutions. They challenge bias when they find it but equally they will allow children to challenge their thinking as teachers. They are not afraid to own up to the fact that they don't know everything and model that it is alright not to succeed first time or every time, and build into their pupils the notion that failing is an essential part of the learning process. Finally they are open to new ideas especially those that come from the learners.

The inspirational teacher also chooses their language very carefully. The use of 'could be' language rather than 'is' language has already been discussed. The inspirational teacher phrases and rephrases questions carefully, allowing plenty of time for learners to process their thoughts – and importantly are comfortable with silence as the children think, without jumping in to 'rescue' them. They use paired and group work in order to allow collaborative thinking. The language used in questioning alongside carefully designed visual tools, diagrams and charts enables children to create conceptual connections in order to link prior knowledge to new learning. They allow children to develop temporal connections so that events can be placed in a chronological sequence. They permit children to develop an understanding of similarities and differences within situations. They also help children to see cause and effect links.

Whilst the best thinking takes place within the subjects and aspects that make up the curriculum, there is a very small and influential book that can be used to allow teachers to develop their language skills when posing questions and follow-up questions, when instigating thought processes and also to help learners develop their thinking mind. This is *The Little Book of Thunks* which was written by Independent Thinking founder Ian Gilbert. A Thunk is allegedly the noise made by the brain when it has to work hard.[58]

Tales of Inspirational Practice

The Little Book of Thunks

Amanda and Paula are two head teachers who have used Thunks as a way of developing deep thinking. However they have used them in slightly differing ways. For those who are not connoisseurs of Thunks they can be described as 'a beguilingly simple-looking question about everyday things that stops you in your tracks and helps you start to look at the world in a whole new light'. Such questions include:

Is there more happiness than sadness in the world?
If I pick up a pen by mistake is it stealing?
If all the books are borrowed from the library is it still a library?

One of the head teachers introduced a Thunk as a thought for the week during Monday morning assembly. She especially focused on those that created a moral dilemma or were topical. For example, on the shortest day of the year she picked the question: When does night turn to day? She took some responses from the children and also used it as a time to prompt further thinking and discussion. However the thinking did not stop when the children left assembly. Large pieces of paper and chunky felt-tip pens were positioned around the school so that children could continue giving their responses. At the final assembly on Friday afternoon there was a celebration of the whole school's thinking around the thought for the week.

The second school approached the task differently. The Thunk was still introduced in a whole-school assembly but then each class pursued their own thinking using the more traditional Circle of Enquiry techniques from Philosophy for Children, which is carried out in a similar manner to Circle Time but with the teacher maintaining the option to extend thinking by providing additional prompts.

Inspirational teachers creating inspirational learners in inspirational classrooms

So finally you might like to consider how you as a teacher, or your school, matches up to the best practice. The following checklist explores the relationship between inspirational teaching within literacy and the arts, how it impacts on learners and what the best classrooms look like. You could score each element out of 5 and then select areas for improvement.

Inspirational Teachers	Score
In the inspirational words of Lilian G. Katz: 'If teachers want to have robust dispositions to investigate, hypothesise, experiment and so forth they might consider making their own such intellectual dispositions more visible to children.'[59]	
The work is planned to encourage adaptability so that children can transfer learning from one subject area to another	
The teacher provides a balance between closed and open ended activities	
The teacher extends the ability of those children who show exceptional ability within their thinking (regardless of prior academic attainment)	
The teacher ensures that children are encouraged to take risks and that they feel supported on these occasions	
The teacher has accessed in-service opportunities in order to promote high quality work within thinking skills and problem solving	

Inspirational Learners	Grade
In the inspirational words of Carol McGuiness: 'Developing thinking skills is supported by theories of cognition which see learners as active creators of their own knowledge and frameworks of interpretation.'[60]	
Children regularly respond to problem solving challenges with enthusiasm	
Children welcome new ideas and situations	
The children persevere in order to find solutions	
Skills and techniques are used in unusual ways	
Children enjoy working with others to solve problems and also working through their ideas alone	
Children evaluate and refine the ideas of others	
Children regularly carry out mathematical investigations in a creative way	
Children carry out their own scientific investigations	
The children use ICT to help them solve problems or refine their thinking	
The children carry out high quality design technology work	
The children express their ideas orally	

Inspirational Classrooms	Grade
In the inspirational words of Oliver Caviglioli and Ian Harris: 'Pupils need a toolkit of thinking strategies that will enable them to become independent thinkers – so that they can continue to learn when the teacher and the classroom are no longer there. Unless these strategies are made explicit we cannot really claim to be teaching pupils to become effective, independent lifelong learners.'[61]	
The learning environment provides a secure basis for risk taking	
Children can readily access appropriate mathematical resources	
The classroom has a suitable range of science resources	
The classroom allows for large-scale construction, play, designing and making	
The classroom has interactive and thought-provoking displays	
The interactive whiteboard is used to develop thinking skills and problem solving in a creative way	

Overheard in the Classroom

Teacher: You see, your Jordan is no better than you were when I taught you all those years ago. He needs to settle down and listen.

Jordan's Dad: I have thought about that a lot over the years. On that day you told me to 'shut up and listen' you might well have said 'stop learning now'.

Chapter 4

Not Everyone Will Be an Entrepreneur, but Everyone Needs to Be Enterprising

How Inspirational Teachers Create a Sense of Enterprise in Their Classrooms

It is a grand thing to rise in the world. The ambition to do so is the very salt of the earth. It is the parent of all enterprise and therefore the cause of improvement.

Anthony Trollope

Overheard in the Classroom

Teacher: Michael, you are not doing your mathematics properly! What on earth are all these workings out for?

Pupil: Please, Sir, I was using the information about percentages to find a way of making my spending money go further!

Teacher: And do you think that is a suitable thing to be doing in a mathematics lesson?

The Prologue

Zero to hero

Eddie was a loner. He was not unpopular, he just didn't seem to have any special friends. It would be hard to say if he was unhappy when all the other children got invited to birthday parties and he seemed to miss out. It just seemed to pass him by. Eddie was not good at group work or activities that required the children to function as a team. He was certainly very bright and usually preferred to work alone. He was certainly artistic and he drew tremendous cartoons of his elderly grandmother riding a Harley-Davidson motorbike. Sometimes he even made up stories to go with the pictures.

One spring morning the teacher stood before the class and told them about a new enterprise project they were going to be involved in. Each member of the class was to be given £5. However they had to find a way for the money to grow over a period of half a term by creating a business opportunity. Children were quickly discussing a range of typical activities such as setting up a car washing business or making and selling smoothies. Eddie the Loner sat apart from the other children and was clearly thinking about this very deeply.

After a while he asked the teacher if he could purchase some card and felt-tip pens from the school and also have access to the laminating machine. He then purchased a bag of cheap magnets and set about his project. Within two hours he had made a dozen fridge magnets in a very unique design. The first one on the production line was a picture of a very hairy man stood outside a cave. The wording around it said, 'My secret friend is called Tom and he is 150 years old and lives in a cave and this is his e-mail address.' So not only did you get an extremely fine fridge magnet but you could also e-mail your new found secret friend. Within hours of launching his new product it became the must-have item within the school. Temporarily Panini football stickers were yesterday's news and Eddie's secret friends were the 'in thing'.

The orders were rising by the day. There was only one thing for Eddie to do: he needed to expand and recruit new staff who could follow his design formula, assemble products and answer the glut of e-mails that were now flooding in from his new found secret friends. When asked about the success of the project Eddie said he had created his network of secret friends because he thought it would help everybody to get on with each other. After Eddie had sold his three hundredth fridge magnet he moved on to make bookmarks in his 'Motor Cycling Grannies' range.

Eddie was clearly very enterprising:

- He knew when to work in a team and when not to
- He knew when to take the lead
- He could negotiate and influence
- He was a risk taker
- He had ingenious and unique ideas and could spot opportunities
- His product was designed to create a happier environment.

Young children are naturally enterprising but only our most inspirational teachers use enterprise education as a way of promoting deep learning across the curriculum.

If you want to know more then read on!

Enterprise: To boldly go where no man has gone before

I was sitting on a stainless steel bench in the centre of a northern town. It had barely got above freezing point all day. The coldness of the steel seemed to penetrate my clothing. The scene was bleak. On one side of the street was a boarded-up Woolworths. There were half a dozen empty shop units on the other. There were a few shoppers, mainly in the lunchtime queue at Greggs buying hot sausage rolls and soup. Four charity shops were in view. The full impact of the credit crunch was clearly evident. In the distance an elderly woman was walking in hunched-up style towards a block of flats with bulging carrier bags. It looked like a scene from Eastern Europe before the fall of the Berlin Wall. Four youths emerged from a pub shouting expletives that were not a good advert for the National Literacy Strategy.

A newspaper blew under my feet. I picked it up and glanced at the headlines. The Confederation of British Industry was complaining once again that the youngsters leaving our schools did not have the skills they required in the workplace. This is no surprise because the CBI makes the same complaint every year. The next article pointed out that young people in the United States were twice as likely as their counterparts in England to set up their own business. Just 16% of English citizens aspire to running their own business.[62] Now that made me recall an article I had been reading the day before about 'zippies'.

What is a zippy?

The existence of zippies was first identified in an Indian magazine called *Outlook* but it was later picked up by Thomas L. Friedman in his book *The World is Flat*:

> Zippies are the huge cohort of Indian youth who are the first to come of age since India moved away from socialism and dived headfirst into global trade and information by turning itself into the world's service centre. *Outlook* described zippies as a young city or suburban resident between 15 and 25 years of age with a zip in the stride. They can be male or female, studying or working. Zippies ooze attitude, ambition and aspiration. They are cool, confident and creative. They seek challenges, love risks

and shun fear. Indian zippies have no guilt about either making money or spending it ... They are destination driven not destiny driven, outward looking and not inward.[63]

The zippies were certainly not evident in the scene that I was witnessing, but for me the important question was, why not? In Chapter 1 I told you how my experiences in primary education tell me that young children are naturally enterprising and how six-year-old girls would turn their front room at home into a restaurant, shop, theatre, radio station or possibly even a school. (Did you realise that as a teacher there are young children in your school who go home and play at being you?) In these role-play situations roles and responsibilities are ascribed, rotas and timetables produced, advertising leaflets distributed, resources made and furniture moved to create the right ambience. Equally young boys hooked into football devise their own tournaments, decide how many players to have in a team, how long a game will last, how many points for a win and they may even have their own transfer system. So why does this sense of enterprise from a role-play situation not materialise in creating young enterprising individuals?

Q: Why do businessmen drive BMWs? A: It's the only car they can spell.

The truth is schools don't sufficiently exploit children's natural enterprise skills as a form of learning. Whenever I am at a conference and speaking about the need to build such opportunities for children I can guarantee that at the interval someone will sidle up to me and tell me a story about their son (or occasionally daughter) who got into trouble at school for setting up some sort of business during playtimes and lunchtimes. Their trading possibly took place behind the bike sheds or another remote part of the school. Inevitably they got ticked off and possibly learned that their ingenuity and business acumen was something to be ashamed of. I wonder how many entrepreneurs of the future learn that education is not for them. James Caan, the famous businessman from BBC Television's *Dragon's Den* described his education thus:

> I was in the top stream and did just enough to get by. I didn't have the drive for university and excelling in my grades; I found

watching my father growing his leather garment business was more rewarding. From the age of 12, I felt my future was going to be entrepreneurship. I went to school in one of my father's jackets, a different one every week, and I would sell them. In one transaction I was doubling my pocket-money of £1.50 a week. I think Dad must have cottoned on to the fact that I was taking a cut because he asked me what I'd sold it for. I was a bit nervous that I'd done something wrong but he laughed. He was absolutely delighted that I was showing a bit of initiative.

I didn't stay long enough to take the O-levels; you could leave at Easter after the mocks. No one from the top stream had ever left early but I knew what I wanted to do; I was going to run my own business some day, so what good would a handful of O-levels do me anyway? I seem to have done OK.[64]

When I read quotations like this I simply ask, why haven't schools taught people the skills of entrepreneurship? To be enterprising in its broadest context is one of the key skills people need in life and it always has been. Enterprise education is not a concept of the twenty-first century – it has been endorsed as a significant form of learning in the past. In 1935 the Board of Education, in promoting the economic value of school gardening, wrote:

The primary object of school gardening is not the production of food. Food is however produced and must not be wasted. There is no reason why some or all of the vegetables and some of the flowers and fruit should not be sold, but no teacher should ever have to feel that, for the purpose of recovering the whole or even a large part of the expenses, the course of instruction is restricted to the growing of produce that will sell readily. However any profits from sales should normally be expended on the further development of the garden.[65]

The message about enterprise is clear, but the truth is that teachers and schools have always been drawn back to a model where they are there simply to transmit knowledge to the learners. This is a great shame because enterprise education can be an inspirational way of providing knowledge whilst developing important skills and attitudes.

Enterprise, real learning and the 'industrial revelation'

As a result of following the National Curriculum, children will learn that the Great Fire of London was in 1666, the Grampians are a mountain chain in Scotland, rivers rise in the mountains and follow their course to the sea and Henry VIII had six wives. I am sure that I once heard a teacher tell her class that in the middle of the eighteenth century an 'industrial revelation' occurred when thousands of men up and down the country realised they could send women and children to work in factories and coal mines for ten hours a day. Schools have relentlessly focused on teaching such information, something I refer to in Chapter 1 as 'just in case' learning. This means the children learn something just in case they need it at a later stage. Real-life learning is most effective when it takes place for a clear purpose and just at the right time. In short, the learning is just in time and not just in case.[66] In many classrooms a good deal of learning lacks that sense of timing. However many inspirational teachers have linked the concept of just in time learning with enterprise education. Here is an example.

Tales of Inspirational Practice

Museum for the day

Ray had become increasingly frustrated as a Year 5 teacher. He really didn't want to teach the Tudors yet again. But the reality was that he worked in a school where they had taught the Tudors in Year 5 ever since the Primary National Curriculum had been introduced twenty-one years ago. He knew that at least thirteen pupils had older brothers or sisters in the class who had done the Tudors previously. He was concerned that it was all becoming stale and lacked the level of spontaneity that should exist within a primary school. He had already carried out a Circle Time with the pupils and they had expressed certain views about learning in the school. Typical responses included:

- We want to make more decisions ourselves within our work.
- We want to develop real skills that will help us for the future and not just write stuff for our topic folders.

- We want to spend more time working with each other – we spend too much time working in groups but alone.
- We want to use more ICT.
- We want to learn more outside the classroom.
- We want to be supported and encouraged rather than told what to do.

Ray was now stood in front of the class next to a flipchart containing a blank piece of paper. He said to the assembled group, 'I have listened to all that you have told me. Now next term we have to study the Tudors but at the end of the term we will run a Tudor Museum for a day. In the museum there will examples of your writing and we will make some Tudor artefacts. We will also need a Flip video film about the Tudors and high tech PowerPoint presentations. I want some Tudor music and we need to include some drama. And finally we are going to have a shop selling Tudor goods.

'Now, children, we will plan this together. What do I need to teach you? Where do we need to go? What resources will we need? Who needs to do what and when do we need to do each of these different things?'

Frantically Ray wrote on the flipchart the ideas that were almost bursting out of the children.

The children had a truly memorable time. Their Tudor Museum was superb and was opened to the whole school community and its invited guests at a red carpet event. The children learned huge amounts of information about the Tudors using just in time methodology. They developed positive attitudes because everyone contributed and they also developed many of the key skills of enterprise including team work, risk management, negotiating and influencing, communication skills, innovation, taking initiative, organising and planning, leadership, managing decisions and product and service design.

When Sir Jim Rose was conducting his review of the National Curriculum during 2009–10 it was impressive how the team collected and collated the views of learners. They provided strong and clear opinions. The first was that they were tired of the same old topics being recycled year after year using the same resources and the same educational visits. The learners know that as a generation of pupils they will have significant problems to solve as they see many of the world's imperfections. These include harnessing new energies, living in an increasingly technological world, creating cohesion in communities with increasing social complexity and being a skilled and flexible worker in a rapidly changing economic climate. A recent analysis of job adverts in *The Guardian* newspaper revealed that employers were looking for a workforce with the following qualities:

- Capacity to motivate others
- High quality communicator, negotiator and networker
- Ability to thrive in a fast-paced environment
- Confidence within a team
- Flexibility to react to external circumstances
- Confidence, resilience, with superb communication, interpersonal and social skills.
- Ability to think creatively and strategically
- PR whiz, media guru, manager, leader and team player all rolled into one (the starting salary for this post was £27,500).

A new 3Rs is emerging

British primary schools have long focused on a basic curriculum of the 3Rs and it is absolutely right that we strive to ensure that our learners reach the highest standards in the key skills of literacy and numeracy. However our youngsters are now giving clear messages that an inspirational curriculum should focus on a new set of 3Rs and they are very precise on how this should be delivered.

Real things	Learners are recognising that too many lessons and themes simply get recycled on an annual basis. They complain that lots of schools lack any form of spontaneity. They claim that they want to be more involved in studying real and relevant problems in the twenty-first century. They want increased problem solving opportunities where there are clear solutions.

| Responsibility | Learners believe that overall they receive far too many closed tasks that require them to use a confined method of working and recording. They want greater choice in how they organise learning and are asking for increased opportunities to work in collaboration with their peers, rather than working alone. |
| Respect | Learners say that if they are to become greater partners in the learning process by taking increased ownership for constructing their learning, then their ideas must be treated with respect. They seek less teacher talk and more open-ended tasks where they will be supported, guided and encouraged, rather than being over-supervised. |

Why enterprise education is a solution

Before we proceed further it is probably necessary to dispel the myth that enterprise education is about money and making profit. Whilst it may be a key element on some occasions it doesn't have to be. It is simply about turning young people into enterprising individuals. The second great myth is that it is a 'bolt on' element to the curriculum. It can be used to bring real-life learning and the skills of enterprise to any cross-curricular topic just as Ray did in the scenario described earlier in this chapter.

Inspirational teachers have always added an enterprise element to their lessons. A class studying food can run a restaurant for a day. Rather than doing one-off newspaper accounts as an academic exercise children could produce their own newspapers. Children can design and run their own allotments as part of a study of seeds, growing and healthy eating. Learners can plan and produce their own shows, videos or assemblies in which they share their skills, knowledge and understanding with others. The scope is tremendous. However the inspirational teacher knows that their role is to step back and allow the children to make their own decisions and provide support only where necessary. They fully understand from the examples above that the best enterprise work is done for a far wider audience than simply the teacher. This approach has many advantages including:

- Providing a clear sense of purpose
- Raising an awareness of the needs of other audiences
- A wider sense of accountability
- Building the capacity of pupils to be both part of a team and to lead a team
- The opportunity to receive feedback and potentially praise and encouragement from a broad range of people.

The examples of practice mentioned also show that the inspirational teacher recognises that such projects require considerable time to be invested. The words of Gilbert Highet probably sum up their thinking: 'anything worth learning takes time to learn and time to teach'.[67]

What will children learn from taking an enterprising approach to learning?

So let's just do a recap. Inspirational teachers do not just see enterprise education as just another subject to add to an already overcrowded curriculum. They seek ways to teach key programmes of study in an enterprising way. It presents an opportunity for children to take up roles and responsibilities in a manner that is highly enjoyable. It helps children to create their own learning through a truly memorable experience. As a consequence learning becomes deep and leads to high levels of understanding. Here is another example.

Tales of Inspirational Practice

Restaurant for a day

Kate looked at her National Curriculum documentation, scratched her head and thought there had to be a better way of teaching about plants and healthy eating that would have the children buzzing with excitement and in a manner that would celebrate the adventures and joys of childhood. That's when she stumbled across the idea of her seven-year-old children running a restaurant for a day. She nervously explained her ideas to the pupils who were wondering if she had lost her senses (something I find is always the sign of the start of an inspirational lesson).

Before long the children were bouncing on their seats contributing new ideas. The customers could be grandparents or some of the senior citizens in the community. They knew they would need to research what kind of food they liked. It would be important to visit a restaurant to clarify the roles and responsibilities each child would have to take up. Then Brett, who seldom contributed to class discussions, said 'I don't know if you have thought about this, but the most successful restaurants only use fresh vegetables so what you need is an allotment and you have to ring the council to get one of those.' Ten minutes later Brett was on the telephone to the local council trying to secure the short-term lease of an allotment. Not only did he succeed but he also negotiated a discount deal.

By the time Brett had returned to the classroom, Bethany was describing how her Grandma used to go to tea dances at Atkinson's Restaurant where there was a Palm Court Orchestra. Kate had decided this was probably an idea that really was out of reach when the peripatetic violin teacher walked through the door. Five minutes later the Palm Court Orchestra had signed on the bottom line. 'Hang on,' said Lee, 'does this mean we need to learn the dances as well?' But that was soon solved because Darren's Aunty taught ballroom dancing.

Then Elsa raised the issue of money and pointed out that all of this could be very expensive and the main purpose of a restaurant was to make a profit and businesses wouldn't be able to survive for long if they didn't. It then became obvious that a business plan was essential and advice needed to be sought from a reliable source. She also pointed out that it may be necessary to take out a short-term business loan because that was what her Mum had done before she opened her sandwich shop.

The project grew to be a great success. The children succeeded in reaching the level descriptors in many key National Curriculum attainment targets. The strange thing is that the project took place seventeen years ago and the story of the work was told to me by a newly qualified teacher during a conference. She had been a pupil in the class at the time and could remember with clarity all that had happened. This was a clear example of how an inspirational teacher can create memorable experiences. However it was more than that. It was an example of how an inspirational teacher can create life-transforming experiences because it was the moment that Elsa (she who suggested the business plan) decided she was going to become a primary teacher.

When an inspirational teacher takes this type of approach key life skills should develop that will equip children well for the twenty-first century. They will be able to both seek solutions and open up opportunities for themselves because they will be enterprising by nature. The diagram below outlines the key skills and attitudes that will develop from such a project.

Team work

Skills: The ability to plan and organise in a team and develop a clear understanding of the roles and responsibilities including the responsibility of leading the team.

Attitudes and values: Loyalty, cooperation, respect

↓

Negotiating and influencing

Skills: As the team moves into action it is inevitable that they will be required to negotiate with and influence others both within the team but as time moves on with a wider audience. This will develop the confidence to communicate with different people.

Attitudes: Fairness, empathy, awareness

↓

Creativity and ingenuity

Skills: As the team proceeds with their plans they will be seeking creative and unique solutions or seeking to produce innovative product designs. This brings in another key element which is risk taking and the ability to identify and manage threats and opportunities.

Attitudes: Positivity, resilience, aspiration, application

↓

Financial literacy and making decisions with an economic dimension

In certain projects it may be necessary to effectively manage a budget and understand the implications of failing to do this effectively. In some projects it may be necessary to make a profit.

Attitudes and values: The importance of valuing money

↓

The moral and ethical dimension

Many projects include an ethical dimension and teams will have difficult questions to answer such as: 'Is this a good product to make/design/sell?' or 'Should a school sell sweets?' or 'How do we make the project environmentally friendly?' or 'If we are to make a profit what is a reasonable price to charge or profit to make?'

Attitudes: Caring for others, fairness, an understanding of right from wrong

---

Tales of Inspirational Practice

The power of an end product

Sue and Liz were school leaders who had a serious problem with writing – not their own, their children's. Standards were not high enough and the scores consistently lagged behind those for reading and mathematics. However there was something worse than this. They knew that the children simply didn't enjoy writing. You could almost hear them groan with despair every time they were required to pick up their pens. The more writing they seemed to do the more the loathing developed in the pupils.

One morning in late spring the sun was shining through the windows and glinting off the trophies and awards that the school held. As Sue looked up the light was shining directly on the school's Enterprise Award – and that's the moment when she really did see the light and rapidly set about scribbling ideas on a piece of paper.

Within forty-eight hours she had met with other senior leaders, the school staff and the pupils and set about curriculum reform. The school thought about the different genres of writing that needed to be covered and then considered how to teach them in highly creative and stimulating ways. The school hit upon the idea of creating a series a short cross-curricular 'learning journeys' that always started with an exciting first-hand experience which stimulated writing within the target genre(s) and ended with some form of production or enterprise event which had to be shared with a wider audience.

Within weeks the whole school was hooked into this as a way of learning. The Year 3 children went to Sherwood Forest in search of Robin Hood (and you'll never guess what ... they actually found him). They then went on to plan and build their own woodland shelters so they could hide from the Sheriff's men. In another year group the police descended on the school and enabled the children to study a day in the life of a detective and solve a spoof crime. As a consequence they performed their own whodunit play. Another class took part in a visit to a local jeweller which led to a project called 'Bling' whereby the children held a fashion show at which they sold their own handmade jewellery. Children designed vehicles and held their own Grand Prix. Children studied what the impact of an alien invasion might be through *The War of the Worlds* and provided their own recordings of the story with background music they had composed. Each learning journey lasted just three or four weeks but the children always had to use the skills of enterprise to plan a final event.

But what of the writing I hear you ask? The prime purpose of the approach was to improve children's attitudes to writing (and note, the first step to improve attitude) by providing rich experiences that would stimulate writing within a particular genre. Progress accelerated. There was evidence of greater pride and perseverance. The school used pupil interviews as part of a monitoring and evaluation process. The children loved the learning journeys – but wouldn't totally admit to enjoying writing. Maybe it would not have looked 'cool' to admit to such a thing.

Sue and Liz know however that it needs to be kept fresh. If the same learning journeys are repeated year after year the spontaneity that led to their success will disappear.

Those who say that money can't buy happiness don't know where to shop

Now, having said that enterprise education is about creating enterprising individuals rather than promoting economic awareness or making money, it is important to stress the significance of financial literacy. The links between an adult's economic well-being and their emotional well-being have been well documented. Adults and families will be placed under far greater stress when there is a fear that bills cannot be paid or mounting debts lead to income being spent on excessive interest repayments. In schools we provide high quality learning within sex and relationships education. We promote social and emotional learning through the SEAL programme. We raise awareness of the dangers of drug and alcohol abuse. We provide lessons on healthy eating and the need for exercise. The missing link, however, in many schools is helping children to understand a range of issues relating to personal finance.

It all starts off very well. Children in the foundation stage and Key Stage 1 regularly role-play the part of shopkeeper and customer. During these activities goods are purchased by young children and change is given. However a significant question needs to be asked: Is there sufficient progression from this point or do children quickly get exposed to academic mathematical tasks and exercises *about* money rather than fully understanding the world *of* money? Only the inspirational teachers take the challenge further by providing opportunities to:

- Set up school businesses and business meetings where there is a responsibility to look after other people's money or achieve value for money.
- Take responsibility for a class budget over the course of a year.
- Raise funds towards key educational opportunities such as school visits or creating a class allotment.
- Understand other forms of payment such as credit cards and debit cards.
- Look at real life financial issues such as interest rates and taxation.
- Establish what might constitute a good investment and a poor investment.
- Encourage the children to operate a school bank.
- Talk about money in a way that develops both financial literacy and speaking and listening skills.

When schools and teachers plan and teach personal finance relevant to students' lives and needs it will enable youngsters to have the confidence, skills and knowledge in financial matters that will allow them to participate fully in society.

> The relevance of economic understanding is that it may be a means to an end. The end is not the consumption of beef burgers or the accumulation of television sets, nor the vanquishing of some high level interest rates rather than an entitlement to mankind's feeling of well being. Economic things matter only in so far as they make people happier.[68]

Overcoming the Matthew Effect

For unto everyone that hath shall be given, and he shall have abundance: but from him that hath not shall be taken away even that which he hath.

Matthew 25:29

What does this quotation mean? Does it mean that the strong get stronger and the weak get weaker? Does it imply a sense of unfairness? Malcolm Gladwell uses it in that context when he introduced the idea of the 'Matthew Effect'.[69] The principle could imply that life chances are simply determined by where you are born and to whom you are born. We all recognise that this is the era of the internet and free information for all. As a consequence the kid wearing blue trainers from Bash Street Primary School should be able to excel. Sadly too often they don't. In 2008 the Sutton Trust reported, 'It is appalling that young people's life chances are still so tied to the fortunes of their parents, and that this situation has not improved over the last three decades.'[70]

So what could be done to change this situation? Well, I certainly believe that inspirational teachers can play a significant role. Gladwell identified five key factors that led to success in life. I have added how the inspirational teacher can have an influence:

The inspirational teacher creates a sense of aspiration and a desire for success. They open the door to life's opportunities.

The inspirational teacher gives children a sense of self-belief and shows them the benefits of taking risks and this helps them to make lucky breaks. Many people have observed that you make your own luck in this world.

Inspirational teachers open the world of the twenty-first century to the children so they understand and can make the most of the time they are in.

Inspirational teachers focus on developing uniqueness of thought, originality and creativity so that children learn to spot the unique opportunities that exist.

Inspirational teachers build a strong work ethic in the learners and qualities such as perseverance and resilience. Malcolm Gladwell refers to the 10,000 hour rule of hard work. The Beatles practised for this amount of time in a Hamburg nightclub before they made it big. In the words of violinist Pablo de Sarasate, 'I have practised for fourteen hours a day and now they call me a genius.'

Meanwhile back at the park bench ...

Enough of all this pontificating. You will recall that I was sitting on a metal bench in the middle of a northern town and the chill is now starting to rise up my spine. I looked once more at page of the newspaper that was blowing around my feet. It was from *The Times* dated 3 February 2010. The article was entitled 'How to Recognise Opportunities in Business'. With a little adaptation it offers a mantra for an approach to enterprise education in schools.

1.	**Observe the world** Budding entrepreneurs are encouraged to carry around a notebook and record everything that 'bugs' them in the world. This book has already argued that a prime purpose of primary education should be to understand what is right and what is wrong and what is fair and what is unfair. The minute children start to recognise a need to change something they have taken the first step along an enterprise journey.
2.	**Focus on your passions** Anthony Robbins argues that the first trait of a highly effective person is their passion for the task at hand.[71] Jim Collins in his book *Good to Great*, an analysis of American businesses, proves that the most successful companies have something at their heart that they are passionate about. Inspirational teachers can ignite a passion within children and focus that passion through an enterprise journey.[72]

3.	**Look at what is in front of you** Whilst it is important to have a clear long term goal or clarity about what you are trying to create, you also need to break it down into smaller next stages and proceed in a systematic and strategic way.
4.	**Understand your customers** The best enterprise projects are always produced for a far wider audience, group or client base than the teacher. Therefore it is important during an enterprise journey that learners always spend time researching their needs of the target group.
5.	**Don't reinvent the wheel** Whatever product or service you seek to provide always make sure it has your unique mark on it. When I wrote my first book, my editor gave me just one instruction and that was to make sure I wrote the book that only I could write. It was at that point that the fog lifted and I felt empowered. A product or service might build on a previous model but never simply copy it.
6.	**Be thorough** Plan and prepare meticulously at all stages. When you are about to take a risk be aware that if it can go wrong it will go wrong! Therefore try to alleviate any weaknesses as you move along within a project.
7.	**Rediscover your imagination** Creativity and using your imagination to solve problems are fantastic ways of opening up opportunities. Did you know that the man who invented the ring pull on a can got the idea from peeling a banana?
8.	**Pair up** Never try to do anything totally alone and always be prepared to take advice – being a member of a multi-disciplinary team will always pay dividends.
9.	**Leave your comfort zone** Get used to taking risks as it will make you stronger and always remember that the fear of failure will never be as bad as the feeling of regret.
10.	**Take advantage of the current climate** Be aware of the opportunities that only exist at the current period of time.

Tales of Inspirational Lives

Being enterprising: Is it a set of skills or a state of mind?

Multimillionaire Richard Reed thought his entrepreneurial career was over at the age of twelve because of his experiences at school. Today he is the co-founder of Innocent Drinks which is the UK's fastest growing food and drinks company and the number one smoothie brand in the country. At the age of eight he was running his own car washing business but in the latter part of his primary education he found himself in trouble for setting up a business buying and selling Smurf stickers. Having been discouraged by his teachers, it was only when he took up a summer holiday job packing dog biscuits that he realised that he wanted to work for himself.

Multimillionaire Ben Way fared even worse at school. At the age of seven he was brutally told by his teacher that he would never read or write or make anything of himself. He claims that these words haunted him over the following years. Ben became one of Britain's first dot-com millionaires making his fortune in digital technology. He formed his first company at the age of fifteen and had amassed business interests of £25 million before the age of twenty.

Multimillionaire Jamie Oliver left school at the age of sixteen with no qualifications whatsoever. He moved on to study catering at Westminster College but quickly started to spot business openings. His personal wealth now stands at £65 million. He is an international television celebrity and owns a string of restaurants. Throughout his schooldays he had struggled with reading and writing. He is now the author of twenty top-selling books.

The list of school failures who have become influential in the world of business extends far further than the individuals above. There is no doubt that each of these highly successful people made good despite failing at school. I'm not criticising schools for what they did, but for what they didn't do. The question has to be asked how many others, with the same aptitudes or even greater, slipped through the net because the curriculum simply didn't cater for their aptitudes, meet their needs or allowed them to develop their unique talent? For some being enterprising is a state of mind. For others it will need to be taught by inspirational teachers who can spot, develop and create talents in their learners.

The Rose Review and its subsequent proposals for a revised National Curriculum concluded:

> To enjoy healthy, active and fulfilling lives children must learn to respond positively to challenges, be enterprising and handle risk and to develop self confidence and physical capabilities. This area of learning lays the foundations for long term wellbeing and contributes to children's wellbeing, social, emotional, economic and physical development. It is central to their development as confident individuals.[73]

However maybe the following is an even more powerful argument for the cause.

Tales of Inspiration

We are the people we have been waiting for

If you have followed the arguments made in this chapter and need just one more prompt to believe that we need inspirational teachers who will produce a new generation of inspirational and enterprising learners, then go to your computer and type in 'we are the people we have been waiting for'. It will take you to Lord David Puttnam's brilliant film about education in the twenty-first century. Here is an extract from the film:

> The world is facing huge challenges and they are growing daily in severity, scale and complexity. It is no exaggeration to say they are not going to go away. Indeed they will get worse unless we start to find solutions and find them soon. If we are going to survive we need the next generation to be smarter and better prepared than any generation before. Our only chance is to improve the way we teach our young and make the most of their talents in a way that will help them meet the challenges of the modern world. So the question is does our current education system work?

> Schools are steeped in static knowledge and fail to take into account the here and now. They don't prepare for contemporary society or the realities of the

world we live in. They fail to prepare young people for the emerging issues of our time.

How is this helping our children prepare for what they are going to be as adults in twenty-five years time? How adaptable are they going to be and how confident are they going to be? Students starting in our schools today will retire around 2065, but we can't predict with any certainty what the world will be like in ten years time. Therefore the very best we can do is to prepare children for a rapidly changing social and technological environment. They will need to be the most flexible, adaptable, resilient creative generation that has ever been.[74]

In short they will need to be enterprising. Bring on those inspirational teachers who will bring out those inspirational responses from our youngsters.

From the 3Rs to the 5As

I have had the privilege of observing many inspirational teachers achieve inspirational responses from their learners by constructing an enterprising approach to the themes being studied. In addition to the genuine deep learning taking place, the children develop in five broad areas:[75]

1. **Aspiration:** Inspirational teachers provide opportunities for children to feel that they can succeed and make a difference and aspiration is raised. By linking learning to earning through exploring entrepreneurial opportunities inspirational teachers raise ambitions.

2. **Application:** Inspirational teachers give meaning to their subject by exploring it through the creation of projects with an end product or through the world of work or business. This requires all learning to be applied in a meaningful manner.

3. **Active:** When children are required to make an inspirational response as a result of the teacher taking an enterprising approach to learning they will

actively co-construct their own learning and the risks they take will add intensity to learning.

4. **Awareness:** Too much learning in our schools merely consists of pupils completing academic exercises. This does little to raise awareness of what it is like to function in the real world or how to work in genuine partnership with others.

5. **Achievement:** The inspirational teacher who develops his or her pupils as an inspirational and enterprising learner will raise achievement within academic subjects but also start to build a skill set that will be essential in life.

Tales of Inspirational Practice

Late sports news

We interrupt this chapter to bring you some late sports news. The World Cup is almost at an end and Jane the head teacher is at her wits end. Not because of the World Cup as such. She had already decided that Portugal had the best-looking team. Her issue was more to do with the football stickers the children kept bringing to school and swapping, and this was leading to disputes and arguments. Sometimes the children were looking at them when they should have been doing their very interesting work on nouns and pronouns. So she made the decision that they were going to be banned and a message was duly sent around the school.

An hour later there was a knock at the door. It was Eddie (of the fridge magnet fame). He nervously said: 'There is an alternative solution to the problem with the football stickers. The children should be allowed to attend a properly organised club where the stickers can be traded, bought and sold. The school fund could claim 10% of any cash changed.

'Not only that but we could get Mr Wood to do some really exciting mathematics work with them. We should find out the minimum cost of completing the album and then a realistic cost of completing the album. We should look at the probability of getting repeat cards if you buy five packs or ten packs at a time or even try to find out if they make the same number of each of the cards. We could find out which country has had to travel furthest to play in the tournament and I am sure there are loads more things we could do especially with geography. You're a teacher, perhaps you might have some ideas?

'Oh and finally I could take some of the information from the cards and create a Top Trumps pack, because to be honest, it's all fallen a bit flat on the fridge magnet front. In return for all of this I am sure the children will agree not to get into any further trouble with the cards.'

Well, go on dear reader … You're most likely a teacher. What would you say to Eddie's proposition?

Jane thought for a while looking up at the ceiling. Eddie thought she was going to erupt in anger. Then she turned to him and said, 'That's brilliant, but forget Mr Wood and count me in!'

Inspirational teachers creating inspirational learners in inspirational classrooms

So finally you might like to consider how you as a teacher or your school matches up to best practice. The following checklist explores the relationship between inspirational learners who are taught by inspirational teachers within enterprising classrooms. You could score each element out of 5 and then select areas for improvement.

Inspirational Learners	Score
In the inspirational words of Leonardo da Vinci: 'Knowing is not enough; we must apply. Being willing is not enough; we must do.'	
The children get regular opportunities to plan and present their own work to a wider audience	
Children show high levels of independence, pride and perseverance within the process of a task in order to reach a successful conclusion	
Children work well in collaboration with each other by using team work and negotiation skills	
There are sufficient opportunities for children to fully develop their own unique ideas in an individual, original and imaginative way when producing and presenting their work	
Children regularly develop and refine the ideas of others	
There are opportunities for children to feel a strong sense of ownership in their work	
Children get to learn to take responsibility for finance and budgets	

Inspirational Teachers	Score
In the inspirational words of the QCA: Schools need to encourage pupils to 'handle uncertainty and respond positively to change ... Innovation, risk management, a can-do attitude and the drive to make things happen'.[76]	
Teachers and pupils often plan work together	
Teachers plan to engage pupils so that they become enterprising and this takes place across the curriculum	
Teachers have high expectations that allow pupils to take full responsibility for planning and presenting their work in a range of creative ways	

(continued)

Inspirational Teachers	Score
Teachers regularly encourage children to share their ideas in learning	
Genuine time is allowed for children to develop and modify their ideas	
The teacher encourages and supports the children in taking risks in their learning	
Teachers provide genuine opportunities for pupils to learn financial literacy	

Inspirational Classrooms	Score
In the inspirational words of the Department for Children, Schools and Families: 'Learners need enterprise capability, supported by financial capability and economic and business understanding'.[77]	
The classroom is a creative place where pupils regularly present and exhibit their work in an imaginative way	
The classroom is designed for and encourages meaningful pupil collaboration	
Displays in the classroom reflect both individual and group work	
Examples of process are displayed such as photographs, sketches or draft copies that show the learning processes used by the children	
These classroom displays are sometimes planned by the children and reflect the learning processes they have gone through	
Displays and exhibitions of pupils' creativity are labelled so that children, parents and governors are aware of the processes within the strand	

Overheard in the Classroom

Ofsted Inspector: Does all this stuff on enterprise education get in the way of learning real things?

Ten-year-old pupil: No, it is the way we learn the real things that will take us through life.

Chapter 5

The Supreme Art: Awakening Joy in Creative Expression

How Inspirational Teachers Embrace Literacy and the Arts to Achieve Spectacular Results

Many great civilisations managed without the wheel,
but none managed without stories.

Ursula K. Le Guin

Overheard in the Classroom

Teacher: Now, Year 2, let us continue with our analysis of *Cinderella*? Who else can find evidence of direct speech?

Pupil: Please Miss, could you just read it to us again … It's really good!

The Prologue

Opening doors

I wonder if in your teaching career you have ever come across anybody with an absolutely incredible talent. I have and I will tell you about three of them. On the third day of my first headship I wandered into the school hall. An expressive dance lesson was taking place. My eyes were immediately drawn to twin boys who moved superbly. They had poise, agility and dexterity. At the age of nine the way in which they expressed themselves was absolutely breathtaking. What was even more frightening was that I knew I was scheduled to teach the class PE over the forthcoming weeks. During these lessons I seemed to keep repeating 'Well done Dale, well done Darren' and they smiled at me most politely, for the two boys were already on the road to considerable success.

Dale later won a string of dance titles before moving to the United States to work as a top choreographer. He has now come back to the UK where he runs a dance studio. His brother Darren Bennett is regularly watched by millions of viewers who tune in to the BBC television programme *Strictly Come Dancing*. He also regularly sells out theatre and arena venues with his performances.

Edward Hogg was another significant talent. He filled the school stage with his presence. His acting ability was phenomenal. Words were spoken with feeling and clarity with never a strain in his voice. He went on to study at the Royal Academy of Dramatic Art in London. He now has a string of successful theatre, film and television appearances behind him and was named British Shooting Star in 2010.

Dale, Darren and Edward had something in common apart from attending the same primary school. They had strong support which helped them to achieve their success. By the time I first met Dale and Darren they were receiving dance lessons. Edward had tremendous parental backing too.

All over this country behind the closed doors of housing estates or down country lanes there are other budding dancers and actors, but they may never set foot on a stage. There are budding musicians and writers and orators and artists but the door of opportunity may never open for them, because they will not receive the same support as Dale, Darren or Edward.

How can this inequality be addressed? One of the answers is through the provision of a rich and vivid curriculum for literacy and the arts. Through this essential aspect of the curriculum children learn the skills of communication, representation and expression in its widest variety of forms. In the hands of an inspirational teacher inspirational responses will be achieved and potentially new talents will be unleashed. This chapter highlights some of the significant challenges facing our schools and provides guidance on some of the best ideas that will equip children for the challenges of the twenty-first century.

The supreme art

Albert Einstein claimed that the supreme art of the teacher is to awaken joy in creative expression. Sadly our primary schools regularly fail to make full use of literacy and the arts in order to develop communication, representation and expression amongst our youngsters. For example, it sometimes seems as though primary school teachers have become solely and obsessively preoccupied with writing. It is as though it is the only effective form of communication available to us. I understand the significant challenges faced in raising standards in writing but I am worried we may be failing to get an essential balance right.

I was speaking at a conference recently and witnessed two long lost female college friends being reunited. After excited shrieks, smiles and hugs and the exchange of a few basic pieces of information, they didn't discuss what had happened to them over the intervening years. They went straight into a discussion about what this year's writing assignment would be in the Year 6 tests. It is true that writing is the hardest aspect of the curriculum to ensure the children make expected progress in; therefore teachers do more and more writing. This is because they believe that the sheer weight of writing will resolve the problem. Then they find that doesn't work so they do yet even more writing. It would also be fair to comment that too much of the writing produced is unimaginative and relates specifically to an academic task rather than exciting real-life experiences. However we probably all know inspirational teachers who manage to get writing of a phenomenal quality and sensitivity from pupils. Have you ever wondered about the secret of their success?

I believe the challenge is to use communication, representation and expression in its broadest form. Our ability to communicate in a wide variety of ways is what differentiates us from other species. To function as a human being you need to be able to give and receive information. The reality is that it can be done in many forms and this has the potential to give richness to life. However too many schools fail to do literacy and the arts justice. Consider these words from comedian Lenny Henry:

> I gravitated towards the teachers that encouraged or pushed me – that made me laugh. My science teacher Mr Brooks made us smile with his diagrams and witty remarks. He let a school friend and myself go into his back lab with a tape recorder and make stupid radio shows for our friends. He didn't know it at the time but Mr Brooks was sowing seeds. I think I desperately needed to be told I was an OK kid.[78]

What we seem to have here is a magical relationship between a teacher and his pupils. Was Mr Brooks an inspirational teacher who possessed a form of pedagogical brilliance? Did he recognise that if Lenny Henry was going to learn science effectively he had to help him to find a unique and original way of communicating it that would lead to a deeper sense of retention and under-standing? Did he also recognise that by helping Lenny Henry to find unique ways of communication he would be raising his self-esteem and developing his emotional intelligence? Alternatively Mr Brooks could just have been doing what intuitively seemed right.

Inspirational teachers recognise that in education it is essential to provide opportunities for young people to express their own ideas, learning, values and feelings in unique ways. More often than not, children express their learning through writing and less often through the spoken word. However when communication, representation and expression takes place through drama, dance, music, art or visual literacy, it can take learning to new heights.

Some schools placed a tremendous emphasis on this way of working in the past. However the critics argued that the main advantages were therapeutic rather than academic. These detractors were wrong. Imagine a class of children who have experienced their first trip to the coast and seen stormy seas crashing against the cliffs whilst the wind drives into their faces. If the children then explore stormy seas through dance or music, different words and phrases will be running through their minds. These could then be used to help structure children's writing whether it is a story setting, poetry or newspaper account. In short, it is now a dance, music and literacy lesson all rolled into one. The inspirational teacher recognises this opportunity and knows that the merging of these opportunities is likely to create an inspirational response from pupils in a wide variety of forms, all of which are important.

In 1999 the UK Government seemed to recognise the absolute importance of this approach when the National Advisory Committee for Creative and Cultural Education wrote:

> Our primary perceptions of the world are through the senses: through light, sound, shape, texture, smell and movement. We do not only experience these in different ways we think in them too. A person painting a picture is thinking visually; a musician is thinking in sound. Dancers think in space and movement. These are not substitutes for words; they illustrate the rich diversity of human intelligence and the many different ways in which we think and communicate. A painter is not producing images of ideas that could be expressed equally well in words or numbers. He or she is presenting visual ideas. Musicians are expressing ideas that can only be fully understood through music. Conventional education tends to emphasise verbal and mathematical

reasoning. These are vital to the intellectual development of all young people but they are not the whole of intelligence.[79]

So what happened to this government commissioned report? It was filed away to collect dust. Instead teachers were made to focus on National Frameworks and Ofsted inspectors were sent to check up on them. The then Prime Minister Tony Blair warned his political colleagues and civil servants that their education policies must be acceptable to the readers of tabloid newspapers. However the brave schools refused to follow the government's script. This chapter analyses the work of our most courageous – and finest – practitioners and how they make the best use of literacy and other key aspects of the arts, communication, representation and expression in order to bring learning to life.

Literacy: The theft of enjoyment

Is it me or is the educational climate in which children are growing up and making sense of their world going mad? Imagine that you were thumbing through your favourite newspaper and you stumbled across headlines like these: 'Multi-Million Pound Literacy Strategy Kills Off Reading' or 'Bedtime Stories Down to One Minute'. Yet both headlines are ludicrously true.

The National Foundation for Educational Research has examined the impact of the National Literacy Strategy since it was introduced into English schools in 1998. They concluded that it was true to say that the standards achieved by pupils at the end of Key Stage 2 have risen. It would also be fair to say that this has reached a plateau over more recent times, and since then gains have been only modest. However over the same period of time the pleasure children derive from reading has fallen dramatically. In 1998 70% of boys expressed a love of reading and by 2003 this had fallen to 55%. Whilst it held up for girls during the start of the Literacy Strategy, their enjoyment of reading is now in line with boys.[80] These sad events have happened despite the phenomenal success of the *Harry Potter* books which led to children and parents queuing at shop doorways for the latest editions or conspiring to get hold of copies before the official release date. Guy Claxton discussed this problem further by asking the following question: 'Is this collateral damage to the pleasure of reading something that we can afford to bear?'[81]

The Progress in International Reading Study (PIRLS) is a huge project monitoring the standards of literacy that are achieved worldwide. Evidence from the PIRLS survey in 2006 showed that reading for pleasure outweighed every social disadvantage, including parents' income, in the future success of the child.[82] They showed that children's chances of success in life depend not on whether they can read but on whether they do and if they derive enjoyment from doing so. Guy Claxton further comments: 'So current practice in England is not just damaging the disposition to read because it deprives young people of the pleasure of curling up with a good book: it shoots the fundamental purpose of education in the foot.'[83]

The demise of children's enjoyment in reading has now taken another turn for the worse. US and British websites selling children's books are now advertising the book *One Minute Bedtime Stories*. The Disney organisation has brought out a book called *3-Minute Bedtime Stories*, and this is the sequel to their series of *5-Minute Bedtime Stories*. The books are cleverly advertised as being suitable for the children of 'busy business parents'. One of the problems we face today is the pressure placed on families by the 24/7 world of work. Too many adults in the UK work long hours only to bring even more work back in the evening whilst also running the family home. Sleep deprivation amongst British adults is now recognised as a serious problem. One of the consequences is that the quality time children need with their parents is diluted. Clearly, those close moments of curling up with your young child to share a story are often a victim of this situation. The review of *One Minute Bedtime Stories* on Amazon declares it is 'the best bedtime storybook ever!' This is because when the child asks for another story, you can say 'just one more'. There is further good news for time-pressed parents. When they have completed their *One Minute Bedtime Stories* they can move on to *One Minute Fairy Tales* and even *One Minute Greek Myths*. This hardly promotes a love of books and literacy. Parents and carers have a critical role to play in reversing this trend and wherever schools can they should urge parents to:

- Make reading visible by having books available in the home.
- Share books as often as possible.
- Make sure that boys see that reading is something men do.
- Talk about books.

- Sit and listen to their child read – turn the TV off and not do chores around the reader.
- Respect their choices. The child is much more likely to become a better reader if they are interested in what they are reading. Therefore comics and special interest magazines are allowed!
- Introduce children to different types of books: classic fiction, short stories, joke books, poetry and non-fiction.
- Read them the book that was your favourite when you were a child.
- Read slowly with expression. Try to use different and funny voices for characters.
- Follow the words and read the story using the pictures to help understanding.
- Talk about what is happening and what might happen next.
- Leave stories on a cliffhanger.

It seems that somewhere along the line the government, schools and parents have been charged with taking the fun out of literacy. We may already consider the politicians guilty as charged; to some extent they have already admitted their guilt. When then Secretary of State for Education, Charles Clarke launched *Excellence and Enjoyment: A Strategy for Primary Schools* in 2003 his speech included the statement that, 'As a government we have been charged with taking the enjoyment out of education and this is the birthright of every child.' Little has changed since that time and there is a need for inspirational school leaders and the teachers who will recover this situation.

The real challenge facing inspirational teachers is to bring literacy in its broadest context back to life and prominence in the classroom. Many of us will be able to remember and identify books from childhood that were special. We will recall those moments in which something burst right out of the pages of a story, gripping us with an unprecedented emotional force. Maria Tatar argues that 'books impart knowledge and ignite a desire for knowledge that goes way beyond the book. The author's wisdom, cast in the form of supreme beauty kindles our imaginations sending us out into the real world – or other imagined worlds – as enchanted hunters.'[84] Our best teachers will harness that power to create exciting learning opportunities.

The power of literature

If one of the fundamental purposes of education is to help pupils to understand right from wrong, what is fair and what is unfair, what is beautiful and what is not, then high quality children's literature has a key part to play. The truth is that good literature will transport children to other places, worlds and times which are often filled with brighter colours, deeper textures and sharper contours. In these worlds they meet characters who are adventurous, talented, principled, intellectually empowered and stimulating in ways that many of the people they meet in real life are not.

The inspirational teacher recognises this power and makes the best use of stories set in the past, the present and the future. They make the best use of stories that take us to other parts of the country and to other parts of the world. They make the best use of traditional stories and fairy tales and the best use of science fiction. They use poetry that will make us laugh and make us cry. They use stories that make us marvel at the beauty and richness of language. They sometimes use extracts that can bring the subject they are studying to life, but most of all they regularly use full texts rather than extract after extract.

One of the features of the literacy strategy has been the over-use of extracts that are too often taken out of context. Teachers use these passages for the analysis of linguistic features – such as the use of exciting connectives or complex sentences – rather than simply the richness of the text. As far back as 1974, a government report on the teaching of English language in this way stated: 'such approaches afford no opportunity for the generation of language ... What we are suggesting is that children should learn about language by experiencing it and experimenting with its use.'[85] George Bernard Shaw was also concerned about an over-concentration on the technical features of language as far back as 1907 when he wrote a letter to *The Times*:

> There is a busy body on your staff who devotes a lot of time to chasing split infinitives. Every good craftsman splits his infinitives when the sense demands it. I call for the immediate dismissal of this pedant. It is of no consequence whether he decides to go quickly, or quickly to go or to quickly go. The important thing is that he should go at once.

If a child is required to flit from text to text without the opportunity of enjoying the full story, poem, play script or whatever, it is inevitable that they will feel a sense of frustration. Nor will they feel the attraction of immersing themselves in literature. The inspirational teacher recognises this. I believe that our best teachers love reading fabulous stories to children and sharing books with them. If I had the ear of the Secretary of State for Education (or even an arm, behind his back preferably) the first thing I would be campaigning for would be the return of daily story times in every primary classroom. The best stories stimulate all the senses and make the listener tingle with expectation and excitement. They are led by teachers who know and love the text they are reading. They bring the story to life through clever use of the voice and intonation. The children will be gathered around in close proximity to the teacher. An electricity will be in the air and the teacher will have planned exactly when to snap the book shut in order to keep the children hanging in suspense.

A few years ago I had a moving experience when I came across a newly qualified teacher who had been a former pupil of mine when she had been ten years old. She said, 'Do you know what I remember most about you? (Whenever I hear a question like that I know it will never be a wonderful algebra lesson or a lesson on forces ...) I remember sitting on the carpet engrossed listening to you read, *The Wierdstone of Brisingamen*, whilst my best friend Deborah plaited my hair.' That experience had clearly lasted ten or more years, and I walked off feeling the warm glow of contentment (as well as my age).

True books

Do you know what a 'true book' is? The writing of a fourteen-year-old child introduced me to the concept of true books. If you want a definition read on.

In the Words of the Inspirational Learners

True books

Good novels include 'you' in their stories,
Wrap themselves around you, won't let you go.
The description so specific, detail so precise,
gives you images, so clear you can see them,
sounds so definite, you can hear them.
You can't put the book down.
All outside life is blocked out, only the story remains.
Your mind full of people, places, sounds.
To the point where you become part of the story.
A story so gripping, funny, sad, scary, true to life, romantic, horrific.
A book with all these qualities is worth reading and reading over and over.
This is a true book.

Macaley Smith (age 14)[86]

How many true books do you know that would have the power to totally engross and absorb children? Imagine the potential to extend learning if each school had a list of books they were going to read and share with pupils. It could be a list that is drawn up by both teachers and pupils. The use of high quality literacy by inspirational teachers can reverse the recent trend that has seen a decline in children's enjoyment of reading. The list of true books should be a collection that not only inspires a love of reading but also extends knowledge, creates positive attitudes and potentially transforms the direction of a young person's life. The skilful teacher will know exactly how to use a text to create a deep, rich and meaningful learning experience.

Extending the learning opportunities from true books

Imagine the power of the following list of true books:

- *Goodnight Mr Tom* by Michelle Magorian – which explores issues of evacuation during the Second World War.

- *The Boy in the Striped Pyjamas* by John Boyne – which recounts the horrors and heartbreak of the Holocaust.
- *Street Child* by Berlie Doherty – which is about children fighting poverty in Victorian Britain.
- *The London Eye Mystery* by Siobhan Dowd – which is an adventure story set in the capital city but explores the complexities of twenty-first century life including racism.
- *Fly, Eagle, Fly!* by Christopher Gregorowski – which is about a farmer in South Africa.

Now imagine the power of a talented teacher not only skilfully reading the stories to the children but building a thematic topic around the book over a period of time. A historical novel can not only develop the pupils' knowledge and social understanding of the period, it might also open a range of other learning opportunities. The diagram below shows how this could be developed using the six broad areas of learning that exist within the primary curriculum.

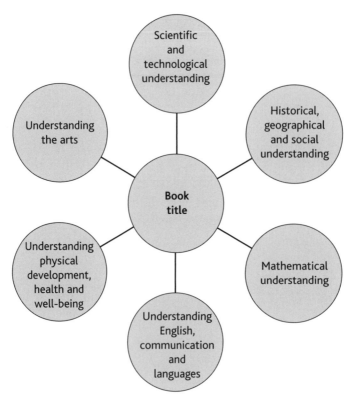

An inspirational and skilful teacher who knew his or her texts well could introduce relevant learning in these different areas at exactly the right time just as the story unfolds. For example, if the text was based in Victorian times, a key focus might be the Victorian 'villains' who exploited cheap labour and the Victorian 'heroes' who sought reform. This would open up a whole range of exciting literacy opportunities. Children could extend their scientific knowledge and understanding by learning about steam and water power. They could carefully produce observational sketches of Victorian artefacts and buildings. They could find out more about killer diseases such as cholera and how healthy lifestyles were essential in preventing them. Children could compare and contrast the geographical setting of the historical novel with their own locality. This would help them to understand how their environment changed during the Victorian period thus helping them to create a clear sense of identity. These are just a few possibilities. The power of the true book is phenomenal.

Grow your own inspirational teachers

I wonder if you are a school leader who has ever wished he or she could grow inspirational teachers. Well, maybe you can. The starting point would be to tell teachers not to spend so much time looking at the National Frameworks but to absorb themselves in a high quality piece of children's literature. Here's why ...

In 2004 the Centre for Literacy in Primary Schools launched a project called The Power of Reading. The scheme grew from the belief that true books played a transformational role in changing children's attitudes and achievement. Sainsbury and Schagen, writing about the evaluation of the project, wrote that 'Books are special because they allow children to experience through imagination other worlds and other roles.'[87] However it was found that many teachers were unfamiliar with the range of children's literature available including award-winning books. Teachers were then encouraged to absorb themselves in high quality texts and consider how they could use them in a creative way with pupils. As a consequence of this work, there was a marked increase in reading aloud, 'book talk', drama and role-play, storytelling, art work, drawing, mapping and writing including poetry in cross-curricular studies. What was reported next is phenomenal. The project developed teachers' confidence and enjoyment of teaching and their sense of autonomy:

> Alongside specific changes to teachers' practice we found a strong shift in teachers' attitudes to the teaching of literacy and their sense of themselves as skilled practitioners. Responses indicate that teachers had greater confidence in their own professional judgement and gained more enjoyment ... Teachers describe feeling re-energised through teaching more creatively and seeing the positive effect it has on children.[88]

So there you go. If you are a head teacher and are aware that some teachers in your school are stuck in their practice, tell them to go home and read some true books! A good start would be to select some award-winning children's literature. The teachers may need some convincing but if they enjoy the text and look for the possibilities they will begin a journey that may transform their practice.

So far I have focused on teachers but you will recall that this chapter initially focused on the problem of children being 'turned off' reading. So now let us consider the impact on them.

The true impact of true books

The real winners of building thematic studies around children's literature will be the children themselves. The need for this work has never been greater. Martin, Mullis, Gonzalez and Kennedy first highlighted a significant issue in 2003 when they reported that whilst children's attainment in reading was the third highest amongst the countries surveyed, children's pleasure and involvement in literacy was relatively low.[89] One year later a survey conducted by the Prince of Wales Arts and Kids Foundation found that within the seven to fourteen age range 24% of boys and 16% of girls did not have enough experience of reading to name a favourite book unprompted.[90]

Now consider the evaluation of the Power of Reading project which found that the inspirational use of true books in an inspirational, thematic and cross-curricular manner in the classroom led to children:

• Choosing to read more often in school and/or at home.

- Talking more about books including their liking of particular books.
- Showing an increased desire to talk about books to their teacher.
- Beginning to read at greater length or with greater focus.
- Being confident in browsing and selecting books.
- Showing an increased willingness to seek out deeper meaning in texts.
- Taking greater advantage of classroom contexts and provision for reading.
- Sharing books more readily and more often with other children.
- Showing greater enjoyment and raised achievement in writing.

Tales of Inspirational Practice

The Jolly Postman

Many of the schools who fail to achieve the government's national targets join the Improving Schools Programme. Whilst it has a proven track record of improving test scores it is intensive and demanding. The pressure to keep accelerating pupil progress can prevent schools from looking at more creative and dynamic ways of teaching. These schools often feel constrained and complain of a world of compliance and fear – especially the fear of the penalties of failure. They are often located in areas of social deprivation which brings further tensions. Schools in these circumstances sometimes feel they have lost their autonomy.

However this sense of powerlessness does not have to be the case. This is the story of a group of inspirational schools and teachers in the programme who set out to counteract this situation alongside the teaching and learning consultants within a local authority.

The project was targeted at children in Year 2 and 3 classes and was based around the very popular children's story *The Jolly Postman* by Allan Ahlberg. The fun (and the children had huge fun) started when a CD-ROM arrived at school from the Jolly Postman who sadly informed the children that he had lost his sack full of letters. He told them that he knew who the letters were for and what he thought the content was about. The Jolly Postman informed the children that he would be grateful for any support they could offer. Before long children were in regular e-mail conversation with the Jolly Postman and writing replacement letters in a variety of genres to the characters in the book, whether it be Jack's postcard to the giant, the letter from Hobgoblin Supplies to the witch in *Hansel and Gretel* or Goldilocks' letter to the three bears. The children immersed themselves in the traditional tales, developed their own skills as storytellers and in one case wrote a Christmas play inspired by the project.

Just as it was all coming to an end, and the Jolly Postman was declaring his gratitude, things took a turn for the worse. Burglar Bill burst on the scene and confessed to stealing the Jolly Postman's bag. He was taken to the school and interviewed by the children who had now become crime reporters. They told the story of the crime in newspaper accounts and news broadcasts. (I am not sure if Burglar Bill had been CRB checked and therefore the schools may have broken safeguarding procedures.)

If it is not immediately obvious, the schools either persuaded willing – or coerced unwilling – adults to take the part of the Jolly Postman and Burglar Bill. However the children (some of whom were in areas of considerable deprivation) had become immersed in a world that fully celebrated the magic of childhood. They were totally hooked and rose to the challenge inspirationally. Furthermore it led to accelerated progress in reading and writing. Funny that.

Here's another example of how a child who has become absorbed in a high quality children's story alongside rich educational experiences has had the emotional 'hook' into writing needed to produce exciting results.

Tales of Inspirational Practice

Children of Winter

If you were to travel to the picturesque village of Eyam in Derbyshire's Peak District and then stand on streets amongst the stone cottages you would guess that there was a sad story to be told. The village is usually hushed, passers-by pause and read plaques placed on cottage doors listing the names of people who died a horrible death in the village hundreds of years ago.

In 1665 a tailor lodging in the village sent for some fabric from London at a time when the plague was sweeping the city. The material was delivered containing the germs of the Black Death, and before long the death toll started to rise. However the brave villagers took a courageous decision: rather than fleeing and risking the possibility of spreading the disease far and wide they decided to stay and contain the plague. Nobody left the village and nobody visited it until they were convinced there was no further danger.

The bravery and spirit of the villagers is captured in the brilliant children's book *Children of Winter* written by Berlie Doherty. Many children visit the village each year to trace the story. However only a few inspirational teachers find the time to immerse the children in the book. The following extract comes from one child in an inner city school who had enjoyed the book. It is in the form of a love letter and it captures the heartache superbly, not to mention demonstrating how the child is working with considerable perseverance to recreate the language of the period.

My Darling Roland,

I really love you, but I can't meet you at the boundary stone any more because my little sister has caught the dreadful plague. She has a cough, big red rashes and big awful spots. My Mum and I have been nursing her, Mum has caught it too and I fear I might have.

I shall not be able to meet you. I mean this Roland, don't enter the village! If you do I will want you to go back and you might not be able to because you could die of the plague and that would make me very upset because I love you.

I don't think I shall be able to come to Stoney Middleton and marry you as I promised, but if I haven't got the plague and the plague finishes, if it does, I shall come to Stoney Middleton and become Mrs Torre.

I love you Roland so don't come to Eyam. The whole of Eyam is a silent place, and many are dying. It is such an unpleasant sight. The whole village shall not go to the river to get water in case they catch the terror or they spread it to anyone.

No one shall stay in comfort or is calm. They are frightened of their death but proud of their sacrifice. Our vicar William Mompesson, said we should have our church services in the open fields so that if anyone has got the plague then it will not spread because everyone can stand separately. That doesn't work because after a day or two, someone who went to the church service died of the plague. This plague is just a mystery that I think will never be solved.

At school my sister was called to the teacher's office. When she went she was told that the school was shut from the next day because of the plague.

Some people think that the plague is sent by God to kill the bad but the innocent are also dying.

I have dreams about groups of children singing this rhyme:

> Ring a ring a roses a pocket full of posies,
> A tishoo a tishoo we all fall down.

Fear walks around the village. We want our country to be saved by our sacrifice, and we are making it for the whole of England we are proud. But we also shed tears for our family and friends who have made this sacrifice by letting themselves expire of the plague.

We were such a happy village until the plague came to us, to be our murderer and kill us with pain. No one wants to step in the village where everyone wanted to make their home, so all the time the village is shut down and quiet.

As I write this letter I cry tears for my village. The reason that I write this letter is to make sure that you know not to enter the village or come close to me until the plague has finished. I do not say this because I don't love you but I say it for your own safety, so that I don't spread the plague on to your village. I don't want Stoney Middleton or the rest of England to suffer the plague at all. I want our country to stay healthy and that is why I can't meet you.

Love,

Your girlfriend,

Emmot Sydall.[91]

A short while ago I had the privilege of leading a training day at one of England's leading public schools. It was a privilege because I love talking about teaching and learning and have a passionate desire that all learners receive a high quality and memorable education. However these opulent surroundings were very different to the area where I normally work. The parents didn't buy the teachers a gift mug from the local high street, they bought tennis courts and science labs. During the training some teachers expressed concerns that their students were not sufficiently active learners and often chose not to respond in question and answer sessions. I asked more and then suggested there could be a better alternative to using 'hands up techniques' when posing questions. I think some of them thought I had lost my marbles.

In November 2010 the cabinet members of the coalition government which included 22 millionaires and many ex-public school students devised their blueprint for education for the rest of the nation. By now I had returned to my work within schools in the super output areas of South Yorkshire. Before you get the wrong idea about super output areas can I tell you they are the localities within the 30% most deprived postcodes in England. On the day the White Paper[92] was published I was visiting a delightful school which was fully focused on providing an education fit for the twenty-first century. Well-behaved children shared positive relationships with their teachers and were engaged with a highly creative curriculum based around literacy and the arts. The head teacher read the press release with tears in her eyes.

The politicians had used public platforms in the weeks before the White Paper to clumsily insinuate that every school in a socially challenging area was a failing school and needed a takeover. The White Paper raised the national floor targets placing an even greater strain on schools in deprived areas. Reading tests were to be introduced for six-year-olds. Ex-military personnel would be fast-tracked in the teaching profession in order to sort out poor behaviour. The strange thing here is that I don't see much poor behaviour in schools and nor does Ofsted. I think this is because teachers have become very skilled in behaviour management. However if they were to adopt more direct confrontational techniques anarchy could quickly take place. The White Paper called for a return to basics, traditional subjects, the removal of coursework as a means of assessment, harder formal examinations and the reintroduction of blazers and ties in schools. At a recent conference I attended in Malaysia I was asked by a delegate why British politicians always look backwards when it comes to education?

At the time of the White Paper's publication educationalists up and down the country were campaigning for a new and inspirational era for primary education, where literacy and the arts would play a significant role. The independent Cambridge Review under the direction of Robin Alexander severely criticised central control and an over-emphasis on testing. Others were complaining about dull and over mechanistic approaches to teaching. For example Anthony Seldon writing in *The Observer* called for a new great debate on education because it has become over formulaic and mechanistic. He complained that our learners are over drilled and undereducated and he called for schools to become places of delight where teachers relish their jobs and can display their own individuality.[93] So what did the government's plans look like. Surely they would pick up on the massive concerns about children's reading or that school libraries were falling into disarray or being were being replaced by computer suites. Take a look at the words below.

So what is the significance of the words above and the way in which they are presented. The government White Paper was couched in the deafening language of outcomes, accountability and delivery and failed to do justice to the life affirming importance of education. The document was prepared by my Independent Thinking colleague, Ian Taylor and the words above are presented in relation to the number of times they are mentioned. Can you find references to creativity the arts and literacy? What about inspiration, which according to Nelson Mandela, is 'the difference between a person reaching their potential and exceeding their potential? Perhaps you could look very hard and see if the government has plans to develop inspirational schools. Never mind though. Let's accept that politicians are unable to deliver the goods and look elsewhere for our own inspiration.

Inspirational Tales

I'm just a backwoods Barbie in push-up bra and heels

So sings Dolly Parton about herself. She was the fourth child of twelve and was born into grinding poverty in Tennessee, the daughter of a sharecropper. She regularly jokes that when she and her brothers and sisters were growing up they were so poor that even people on welfare gave them stuff. She described her family's poverty in another famous song, 'Coat of Many Colors'. The family lived in a poorly built, dilapidated, one-room cabin near the Great Smoky Mountains. It had neither water nor electricity supplies. They lived in a devout Pentecostal region where the Bible was the key book – often the only book – in all homes. Whilst she had little material wealth the Bible helped Dolly to develop a love of stories and reading. The books she managed to loan and read as a child transported her to other worlds and developed her imagination, which gave her the hope and aspiration to use the talents she was blessed with to create a new and better future.

However she never forgot the impact of books on her when she was a young child. In 1996 Dolly Parton launched an exciting new project that would benefit the children of her home county in East Tennessee. Dolly wanted to foster a love of reading amongst pre-school children and their families. She wanted them to experience the magic that stories can create and to create a passion for books that would take them through the rest of their lives. Moreover she could ensure that every child would have books regardless of their family's income. She called her project the Imagination Library. Under the scheme she would send a new age-appropriate book to every registered child under five years of age every month.

The children became hooked and waited in anticipation for the new book to arrive at their doors and then share it with their parents. The experience proved to be a tremendous success and soon neighbouring districts were clamouring to be part of Dolly's Imagination Library. Initially she feared that it might grow to such a proportion that it could not be sustained. However she also knew of the absolute importance of children developing a love of books from a very early age. Consequently in March 2000 Dolly Parton stood on a national stage and declared she was going to put her money where her mouth was, and that as she had a 'pretty large mouth that would be a substantial amount of money'. As a consequence a new foundation was set up in association with Penguin Books to provide books for children under five in Branson, Missouri and Myrtle Beach, South Carolina.

From that point Dolly Parton's Imagination Library has continued to grow and develop with the support of local business communities. In 2008 it arrived in parts of England and all registered children under the age of five years now receive an appropriately stimulating free book every month of the year.

Let's hope they use this tremendous gift to develop a lifelong love of reading.

Whilst there is no doubt that books in the hands of inspirational teachers can transform children's lives, it is very important to remember that books are not the only form of literacy.

Visual literacy

Here's a thought for you:

> Young people learn more than half of what they know from visual information, but few schools have an explicit curriculum to show students how to think critically about visual data.[94]

The use of visual images and data as a form of communication is rapidly increasing. Children are surrounded by images and constantly responding to visual communication. The typical ten-year-old will be hooked into computer games, go home to numerous television channels, take and receive digital photographs by mobile phone and see vivid advertising images on hoardings, in magazines, on the sides of taxis and the backs of buses. Visual imagery is fast becoming the most predominant form of communication. But is this recognised in our classrooms? The answer to this question is too often no.

Have you ever witnessed a youngster who seems to keep watching the same film or television show over and over again and been tempted to ask: Why do they do that? Some people might argue it is out of boredom but I believe our youngsters have a very low boredom threshold. Therefore other factors must exist. I do not doubt there will be a sense of contentment derived from watching a favourite story, event or piece of information unfolding again and again. However it is also true that at each viewing additional information is taken in and much of this happens in a visual manner. Therefore should we also ask: When a child watches familiar images unfold before him/her are they learning from a study of facial expressions or body language, from settings used, from the use of colour, light and shade, or the impact of special effects and even the use of camera angles?

Inspirational teachers believe the answer is yes. They also believe that children will pick up further information from verbal clues around the imagery which may help them to spot more subtle aspects of the plot or additional factual information.

Visual imagery is a key part of popular culture in the twenty-first century. Televisions, computers, DVDs, YouTube, the transmitting and receiving of digital photographs all play a central role in the lives of youngsters. Inspirational teachers recognise this and harness the power of communicating through visual images to create inspirational learning opportunities. The effective use of television and film images can be used to explore important issues such as right from wrong and fairness and unfairness. Examples of this are demonstrated elsewhere in this book, such as the use of *Hairspray* and *Invictus* in Chapter 3 and *Dad's Army* in Chapter 6. The range of visual images used does not have to be restricted to film and television – how about pieces of art work, sculpture, photography and advertising.

If you want to know more about the power of visual literacy then consider this. In 2004 a project was set up called Raising Boys' Achievements in Writing to examine the continuing gaps between the attainment of boys and girls.[95] It sought to obtain clear evidence on the use of visual stimuli such as videos/DVDs and still images to increase pupil motivation and accelerate progress. The project lasted just three weeks but in that brief period of time the impact was powerful. It concluded that a focus on visual literacy can result in:

- increased quantity of writing
- increased quality of writing
- wider use of vocabulary
- greater use of imagery
- increased fluency
- more adventurous writing
- improved attitude to writing
- greater engagement with writing
- greater commitment to writing
- improved motivation, self-esteem and enthusiasm.

Billy Elliot, Les Misérables and some old Jacobean painting – or the wider use of literacy and the arts

So far this chapter has looked at how books, stories and visual imagery can provoke an emotional response from children that triggers new learning across the range of subjects within the curriculum. However our inspirational teachers know that when the humanities and the arts come together they bring a real richness to learning.

If you want to know more about the links, do what I did and take a look at the *London Theatre Guide*. I see that crowds are still flocking to see *Billy Elliot*, which explores the complexities of growing up in a mining community in the North East of England during the miners' strike. *Blood Brothers* is celebrating twenty continuous years of exploring the issues of class and life chances in recession hit Liverpool in the early 1970s. Both *Les Misérables* and *The Phantom of the Opera* take you back to nineteenth-century Paris and *Oliver!* will allow fans of the theatre to travel back to Dickensian England. All of these shows bring the audience to their feet night after night as they emotionally hook their viewers into the issues being explored. As I thumb through the review section of *The Observer*, I see that many of the current best-selling books are set in key periods of history, fascinating locations or explore the problems of society. Finally I read that a Jacobean painting has been discovered which is giving a new and fascinating insight into everyday life in that period (although I did skip most of that article because it didn't quite do it for me).

The links between the arts and the humanities are obvious and inspirational teachers seek to exploit them with their pupils to create inspirational responses that lead to deep learning. When this works well teachers can create memorable and life-transforming experiences that remain with the child forever. The diagram overleaf explains the links and helps teachers to consider powerful starting points.

Which do you remember best – your first secondary school geography lesson or your first kiss?

The first time a youngster sits in their new secondary school it should be an exciting experience that leaves children with a thirst for learning. The learner feels that they are on the point of entering a fresh and exciting world. The reality is usually that the new world fails to materialise. As a youngster I was always intrigued by maps and human geography and I remember sitting in my new state-of-the-art secondary school waiting for my first geography lesson. A sense of expectation ran through me. In practice I was soon colouring in maps and copying down notes and diagrams that I had no hope of understanding. I regularly work with an inspirational colleague from Independent Thinking called Simon Cooper-Hind who asks delegates to describe either their first lesson at secondary school or their first kiss. (Strangely, they usually describe the latter including every graphic detail.) I often ask, why is that? The truth is that it was memorable because it engaged the senses and emotions and you really do feel like you have entered a brand-new world.

If successful life-forming experiences depend upon engaging the senses, then we had better look at the ways in which inspirational teachers link humanities and the arts to create inspirational responses from children.

You can start from vivid, rich and meaningful experiences
in the humanities (such as a visit to a historical location,
the coast or even the locality of the school) and then
develop deep learning through the arts.

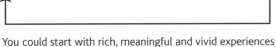

The humanities provide the learner with:	The arts provide the learner with:
An understanding of historical struggle and conflict	Vehicles to express their true understanding of historical struggle and conflict
OR	**OR**
A geographical understanding of the locality, the country and the world	Vehicles to express their understanding of the locality, country and world around them
OR	**OR**
An understanding of their society as well as other faiths, cultures and societies	Vehicles to celebrate diversity and similarity
AND	**AND**
An understanding of what is beautiful and what is not, right from wrong, good and evil and what makes a responsible citizen.	Creative forms of expressing their knowledge of right from wrong, good and evil and what is beautiful and what is not.

You could start with rich, meaningful and vivid experiences
from the arts (such as a picture, film, story or music) and
then seek to develop deep learning about a period of
history, location or issues that affect society.

Humanities and the arts

The links are obvious and yet so often overlooked. The humanities are those fields of academic learning that are concerned with understanding human culture. They include history, the study of languages, religious education, aspects of geography and social studies. When they are taught inspirationally they have a tremendous impact on creative and cultural education. Firstly they broaden and deepen children's understanding of the world around them: its diversity, complexity and traditions. Secondly they enlarge their knowledge about what they share and have in common with other human beings regardless of their background. Thirdly they provide a critical awareness of the society and times in which children live.

The arts are concerned with representation, expression and communication. Through creative approaches to writing, music, dance, visual art, drama and other media we can develop true understanding from our learning. It develops empathy, feelings and perceptions that create an emotional response in us as humans. The arts can help us to form a deeper understanding of ourselves, others and different periods of time. It is through the arts in all their forms that youngsters experiment with and try to articulate their feelings about their own sense of cultural identity and belonging. Historically it was assumed that academic learning would be enhanced if it was divorced from emotions. Intellect and emotions were considered to be distinct and separate. However we now understand much more about the brain and it is now known that where there is emotional involvement learning is enhanced, which leads to higher levels of understanding. However far too much work in the arts is done in isolation and teachers do not connect the learning to other areas or intelligences. Inspirational teachers understand that the arts provide the opportunity for children to make the most vivid expressions about human culture.

Many experienced teachers will recognise this as a key way of working before the advent of the 'prescriptive' National Curriculum and the concomitant over-emphasis on testing of primary school pupils. During the 1970s and early 1980s some educationalists believed that work within the arts was essential because of its therapeutic qualities. This view should not be discounted. It is essential for education to provide opportunities for young people to express their values and feelings. In recent years there has been a real recognition of the vital importance of what Daniel Goleman calls 'emotional intelligence' – the ability to express and use our feelings and intuition. One of the key ways a school can do this is through the effective teaching of the arts. There is no doubt that composing or playing music, writing poetry or performing dance may be driven by powerful emotional influences, but there is more to it than that. It is also about bringing learning to life by giving it form and meaning, leading to a far deeper knowledge and understanding. Florence Beetlestone in discussing the importance of the arts in developing deep learning writes:

> The three Rs dominate classroom life in primary schools and
> have done for several decades. Yet despite this there is a call for
> more work on the basics, as if mere quantity will solve national
> or local shortcomings in literacy and numeracy. Many teachers
> argue that approaches to the latter have been too narrow and
> have failed actively to engage children in learning, and what is
> needed is a qualitative approach based on an understanding of
> the way in which creativity can enhance literacy, numeracy and
> learning.[96]

There may be a view that linking literacy and the arts favours more extrovert
children but that does not have to be the case. An inspirational teacher will
leave pupils fired up by a challenge but not threatened or excluded by it. A balance of approaches will allow both extrovert and introvert pupils to shine. It
can help introverted pupils to develop important extrovert qualities and vice
versa. Children who turn to performing through dance, drama or music may
be naturally extrovert. However many performers draw upon an inner world
to support their performance and they can immerse themselves in a role to
the extent that they become unaware of themselves. The more occasions are
provided for reading aloud, oral storytelling or playing instruments, the more
it becomes an everyday part of life and confidence grows. This is especially the
case when the opportunities take place in an environment where all children
support each other and celebrate their successes. As a head teacher, the weekly
celebration assembly where children shared their best work with the rest of the
school was a significant event. Often pupils would say that they didn't want
to read their writing out loud. I always tried to persuade them to do so and
usually they did. Afterwards I would praise them for overcoming their fear and
asked them if they were pleased with the way they had completed the task.
Usually they answered in the affirmative, and the handful of children who
asked me to read their work for them possibly regretted it.

Those children who are naturally introverted will relish opportunities for quiet
contemplation and reflection. Writing poetry or creating story settings can be
the time to practise very private skills that do not always need to be shared.
That said, I fervently believe that children should be given more opportunities
to share thoughts and write together because many spend too much time writing alone. Similarly painting and sketching are other key skills which require

deep personal concentration. For example, for many inspirational teachers close observation is a technique much used to enhance drawing and painting skills, and this is transferable to other areas of the curriculum. It heightens perception, enables children to focus sharply and helps them to assimilate fine detail. All classrooms should provide time for creative activities that require children to express themselves through quiet independent activity which has a sense of privacy where they can create their own works of beauty that recreate and represent their inner vision.

Tales of Inspirational Practice

Take one picture

Just as you can create a cross-curricular study from high quality fiction, you can do the same from a piece of music, photograph or painting. The National Gallery recognised the power of this when it launched the Take One Picture initiative.[97] Many local authorities and networks of schools now run their own version of the project. It works like this.

In the project run by the National Gallery one picture is selected as a national stimulus. However if a small group of schools or even an individual class is operating its own project there is the opportunity to select an image with a strong local flavour. The challenge is to use the image in unusual ways across the whole curriculum. It is at its strongest when staff collectively brainstorm their ideas and think strategically about how the picture can be used to extend learning within other schemes of work and areas of the curriculum, and also to plan which high quality resources will be needed if genuine deep learning is to be achieved.

It is essential at the planning stage that the focus is not simply on building knowledge but also on extending existing knowledge and developing new skills and positive attitudes. In addition schools and teachers will need to decide whether the work is best carried out within a dedicated week or over a longer period of time such as a half term. The paintings could include those set in a particular period of history and sometimes it may be possible to use a historical painting from the local area. For example, the works of Lowry can be particularly evocative of twentieth-century life in England's northern industrial towns. Alternatively paintings could be used of a contrasting location or of wildlife.

The work is at its most inspirational when it engages the wider school community and ends with an event organised by the children. Whilst this could be an art display, it could also be a celebration assembly such as a drama production or dance performance.

Creativity without rigour is crap

Lord David Puttnam once proclaimed these words above at a conference that I was attending. He is right. How many teachers do you know who have set off to carry out some form of creative work within the arts, only to be deeply disappointed with the outcomes? The best creative work is not about simply standing back and letting the children express themselves without support and encouragement. Work of this nature takes the greatest planning of all. Our most inspirational teachers have very high expectations and low tolerance of underachievement in their learners. They recognise that if it can go wrong it will go wrong, but they work exceedingly hard to make sure it doesn't. Consider the stories of the two teachers below.

In classroom A the teacher has decided to have a more creative afternoon, and as promised I return to an earlier example. The children have been following a geography unit of work based on the locality called 'Through the Classroom Window'. It has been largely based on published low-level worksheets (and yes, I have seen a teacher do a topic on the locality without leaving the classroom). However on this particular day the children were taking in the autumnal scenes by looking at the trees that skirted the school fields. The children were simply asked to do an autumn picture using materials available in the classroom. These included coloured pencils (half of which were broken and the full range of colours unavailable), wax crayons, blocks of paint in quite garish colours, tissue paper and felt-tip pens. The children set off busily at first but showed little inclination to look carefully or develop any true level of pride and perseverance. A sense of frustration kicked in with the resources that had been provided. There was no support or direct teaching of techniques from the teacher, although on a couple of occasions she did do part of the work for the children. She didn't notice that some children had good ideas that could have been developed or shared with others. Before long there was quite a lot of wasted paper and mess. Several children laughed at the work of others.

In classroom B the teacher is also using the autumnal conditions to develop communication, representation and expression. When school started at 8.30 that morning the teacher took the children out in the mist. The dampness created a hushed atmosphere. They were asked to spend ten minutes alone completing a sensory walk and then write powerful sentences about what they could see, hear, smell, touch and what autumn tasted like on their lips. Pupils kicked up the fallen leaves. They felt them crinkle between their fingers. The smelled the bonfire coming from the brazier on a nearby allotment. The teacher then challenged the pupils to come up with a 'wow' word or powerful adjective for each letter of the alphabet. The children rose to the challenge in twos and threes (and yes, they did find the letter X difficult). Then they used their sketchbooks and pencils to complete a draft close observation of leaves, fungi or pieces of bark. The children then returned to the classroom to turn their draft into a final piece of artwork they could be proud of. Whilst completing this they were urged once more to consider key words and phrases in their mind and to note down their thoughts on a piece of paper. As they were carrying out their work the teacher moved around the different tables discussing each child's ideas, listening, supporting and questioning. The children felt supported and encouraged. There was regular praise and the pupils knew their work was valued and therefore they were valued. This created an atmosphere where the learners had a clear sense that only the best was good enough.

One seven-year-old child scribbled down the following words by his sketch:

> Serrated bark like crocodile skin.
> Speeding rocket leaving earth
> Bent branches like someone's arms
> Ancient oak tree.

The first teacher gives this kind of work a bad name. The lesson is not sufficiently planned, has insufficient input or direction and scant regard has been given to resources or fitting them to the task. The lesson results in mess, wastage and questionable learning experiences, and children are discouraged because their efforts are not valued. The second teacher brings this form of learning to life and receives an inspirational response from her pupils.

The best use of literacy and the arts can have a significant effect on children and learning, as Tim Brighouse observes: 'The arts are quite simply a magic key for some children. Not only do they open the mind of the learner, they then reveal a vast cornucopia of endless delight, challenge and opportunity.'[98]

However this cannot be achieved by teachers taking a laissez-faire approach to teaching. Often it appears in the best and most creative lessons where children rise to the fore there is an apparent lack of planning. However this is not the case. This high quality approach to teaching and learning takes the greatest planning of all. The inspirational teacher in classroom B brings literacy, the humanities and the arts to life by demonstrating:

- Commitment
- Subject knowledge
- Knowledge of techniques and skills
- A full involvement in the task
- The ability to give guidance
- A clear sense of direction and focus
- Sensitivity and awareness
- Active listening
- The ability to make pupils feel positive and protected from disparagement and ridicule
- A recognition of when real effort will lead to an inspirational outcome through further encouragement
- A climate where innovative thinking and creative ideas are fostered.

Inspirational teachers creating inspirational learners in inspirational classrooms

Finally you might like to consider how you as a teacher or your school matches up to the best practice. The following checklist explores the relationship between inspirational teaching within literacy and the arts, how it impacts on learners and what the best classrooms look like. You could score each element out of 5 and then select areas for improvement.

Inspirational Teachers	Score
In the inspirational words of Gervase Phinn: 'By exploring the world through their own writing children are able to strengthen their self expression and more readily understand how others live and feel.'[99]	
The teacher creates opportunities through language and other forms of communication such as art, music and dance to share information, ideas, thoughts and feelings	
The teacher uses stories and poetry to create deep learning within thematic learning	
The teacher ensures that high quality story times are held on a regular basis	
The teacher has a good knowledge of high quality and up-to-date children's literature	
The teacher makes good use of visual literacy and popular culture to enhance learning	
The teacher promotes learning through the inspirational use of language, literacy and the media	
When working within the creative arts teachers fully explore the links with literacy	
The teacher regularly plans to ensure that the links between the arts and the humanities are used to create an inspirational response from pupils	
Teachers create opportunities for children to combine different art forms imaginatively in complementary ways	
The teacher models a love of literacy and the arts to all pupils	
The teacher seeks to stimulate all the senses and makes full use of natural phenomena such as the weather	

Inspirational Learners	Score
In the inspirational words of Maria Tatar: 'Children need to make words out of their world and worlds out of their words.'[100]	
The children regularly enjoy listening to stories, music and the views of others	
The children read widely for pleasure	
The children have many opportunities to express their imagination (e.g. storytelling, drama, writing)	
The children regularly communicate in a variety of ways including the spoken word, a range of writing genres, art, dance and music to evoke moods, thoughts and ideas	
The children develop close observational skills that focus on fine detail in artwork	
The children develop spoken language and writing skills alongside observation	
The children use a good range of vocabulary in order to express ideas both verbally and within their writing	
The children regularly draw upon a wide range of experiences in their work	

Inspirational Classrooms	Score
In the inspirational words of Jeremy Strong: 'Creative writing is probably the most exciting form of the written word. It can dazzle and dance. It can bring you tears or make you fall off your chair laughing. It can change the way you see things and even change your life.'[101]	
The classroom has a rich range of resources, which aid the development of high quality language work	

(continued)

Inspirational Classrooms	Score
The classroom promotes a love of books	
Children get the opportunity to work with authors, playwrights, poets, musicians, dancers, painters, sculptors, etc.	
Examples of creative writing are shared with pupils and are well displayed within the classroom	
There is a wide range of children's art and 3D work that is well displayed within the classroom and where appropriate this is linked to literacy skills	
Where appropriate there are well-developed role-play areas encouraging imaginative interpretations (including Key Stage 2)	
Resources such as clay are provided to stimulate the imagination	
There is sufficient space, time and commitment for potentially noisy or messy creative activities	
There are also quiet times when children can reflect deeply upon their work and develop strategies for self-improvement	

Overheard in the Classroom

The best moments in reading are when you come across something – a thought, a way of looking at something you thought special, particular to you – and here it is set down by someone else, a person you have never met, maybe even someone long dead. It's as if a hand has reached out and taken yours.

From *The History Boys* by Alan Bennett

Chapter 6

Emotionally Friendly Classrooms and Emotionally Triggered Learning

How Inspirational Teachers Create a Sense of Awe, Wonder, Spirituality and Wisdom in Their Pupils

The more children know that you value them, that you consider them extraordinary people, the more willing they will be to listen to you, and afford you the same esteem. And the more appropriate your teaching is, based upon your knowledge of them, the more eager the children will be to learn from you. And the more they learn, the more extraordinary they will become.

M. Scott Peck

Overheard in the Classroom

Part one

Teacher: What is that you are holding?

Ryan: Sir, it's a World War Two medal. It's very special. My Grandad earned it in the war and he said I should bring it to school and see if my teachers can tell me what it is worth. Do you know how much it is worth?

Teacher: You know you are not supposed to bring things from home. Anyway, I am far too busy. Don't bring it again.

The Prologue

Fred

It was April 1987 and the first day of my first headship. The clock had just ticked onto 9 a.m. and I sat back thinking to myself, 'Well, what do I do now?' The school secretary pointed out that my predecessor usually had coffee at this point and so I did. Then I started to thumb idly through the filing cabinet. The files were immaculately labelled and had all the obvious titles, and then I found an intriguing file simply labelled 'Fred'. I opened it up to find a short story on a single piece of A4 paper. There was no indication by whom or when it had been written. The text was profound. I keep that piece of paper to this day, and I will share the story with you because it captures the spirit of this chapter.

> About a hundred years ago there was a young boy called Fred and he lived on an island with his father and mother and nearby lived his uncle and aunt. His father kept pigeons and bees and a garden of flowers and vegetables. His uncle was a forester and planted acre after acre of trees in rows. The boy did not go to school because there wasn't a school on the island, but his mother taught him to read and write, and she also recited poetry to him and sang to him when he was little and took him on shopping expeditions to the mainland. He helped both his father and his uncle.

Every year he went to stay with another uncle who lived in York who had a passion for history and he loved to tell Fred about the history of the city as they walked the ancient walls and entered its churches and looked at the items of history they contained. The uncle also took his nephew to see the limestone scenery at Malham and Gordale Scar in the Yorkshire Dales and told him about its geography and geology. And the young boy grew up with an understanding of many things.

Then one day a learned educationalist visited the island and met the boy and was astonished at his understanding and knowledge and the intelligence and wisdom which he had developed around these things. The educationalist said to himself: How wonderful it would be if every child in the land had the same learning built around the simple experiences Fred has had with the bees, pigeons, flowers, vegetables, forestry, and the visits to York and Malham. The learned educationalist was amazed to find out how well the boy spoke, mainly because his mother read and recited poetry to him and because he himself had read much about these personal interests.

And the learned educationalist reasoned thus: It is impossible for every child to lead the life that this boy has led, and to develop the knowledge, intelligence and wisdom which this boy's way of life has given him. But what we can do is give all children all the knowledge this boy has had but without the experiences.

First of all we will look at the numerical and mathematical ability which he has gained from reckoning areas from odd shaped bits of land and working out the numbers of trees that could be planted, and from his mother's shopping expeditions and from the measuring which he has had to do in making pigeon lofts and beehives, and we will reduce these to symbolic formulae and tables and make the children learn a lot of them very quickly.

Then we will take the boy's speech and writing which is so good and subject it to careful analysis. If we teach other children whose speech and writing is not so good how to construct what they say and write to this kind of analysis they will realise how badly they speak and write and will promptly set about trying to improve.

Then, said the learned educationalist, we cannot provide every child with the bees and pigeons, and the flowers and the vegetables which have taught this boy so much, but we can cause books to be written and force them to learn what is in these books. We will have books written about all that has happened in the City of York and all that is known about the geography and geology of Malham and Gordale Scar. Then we will make all boys learn these facts and then they will have the same understanding of our original boy who had lived with his father and mother and his uncle and aunt on the island.

So the learned educationalist went home and divided out the boy's knowledge into parcels which he called subjects, and he called together a lot of publishers and handed them a parcel of knowledge and told them to write a book about the parcel.

And then he went into schools and he said: 'I have met a very remarkable little boy called Fred who has derived great understanding from his bees and his pigeons, from shopping with his mother and listening to her reciting poetry and from seeing and finding out about all the ancient buildings in York and from trips to Gordale. His understanding of these things has led him to read about them and derive great knowledge and wisdom from them. What I want you to do is reverse the process, give your children the knowledge that you will find in the books we have published and when you give them this knowledge understanding will follow.'

And so it came about that all over the land children were assembled in groups of thirty and made to learn facts set out in these books.

And then the learned educationalist began to entertain a horrible suspicion that the reverse process did not work. In other words, whereas the little boy called Fred grew in understanding because he started with the experience and read to feed the interest which derived from it, those who started with the reading failed to develop understanding because the interest was not there. The learning was in a vacuum, unrelated to the context of the lives that absorbed them.

And so the learned educationalist decided to do something very very important. But what would it be ... (to be continued)[102]

Fred had built up a wisdom because he felt valued. His experiences created a sense of awe, wonder, spirituality and wisdom beyond his years. This chapter aims to take you on a journey that shows you how inspirational teachers can create their own generation of Freds through a focus on developing emotionally literate learning environments and creating a sense of awe, wonder and spirituality in children. This will lead to factual knowledge and academic learning but also a sense of intelligence and wisdom that equips them to do the right thing at the right time in the right way. I hope you enjoy the journey.

The magical mystery tour starts here: All you need is love

Do you believe in Father Christmas? I do hope so, because if you believe in magic you are still living a magical life which probably started in your childhood. A magical childhood should be the birthright of every learner in our schools. Inspirational teachers set out to achieve this ideal daily through a number of key strategies. The inspirational teacher recognises that emotions play a significant part in being an effective learner. There is an old saying that your schooldays are the best years of your life. However there are far too many adults who associate their schooldays with fear (not to mention boredom). The reality is that successful learning is far more likely to take place when the learners experience the healthy emotional well-being that comes from being in an inclusive classroom, where everybody feels confident to participate and respond because they know their contribution will be valued. The classroom should not be a place that is dominated by either the teacher or by certain pupils. In the best classrooms, adults and children work together to support each other and celebrate each other's successes. This chapter highlights why and how our best teachers make this happen. It shows how they make their learning environment into an emotionally intelligent classroom where everyone feels they can achieve great things and can help others to achieve great things. However it will go further than this and stress the importance of creating a sense of awe, wonder and spirituality in learners that provides a special form of intelligence and wisdom.

In 2008 Independent Thinking Associate Dr Andrew Curran wrote, 'From my ongoing study of how the brain works, perhaps the most surprising message for me looking through billions of dollars of research is that the most important thing you can do for yourself and for others is to love yourself and others for who they are, because by doing that you maximise the brain's ability to learn and unlearn.'[103] I have tried to read many books on how the brain works but usually give up after three or four pages because it is too hard for my simple mind. I know different parts are used for different purposes and there seems to be a load of chemicals and a whole pile of circuitry that can be adjusted, changed or remodelled in order to make it all work better. I love the simplicity of this quote because I understand it. It gives a clear message to teachers that they need to teach children to understand themselves, others and our place within a far greater but increasingly complex world. However with the drive to generate the next few percentage points on the test results these thoughts become either lost or relatively low profile. In 2006 the Primary National Strategy introduced the SEAL resource into English primary schools. The resources were of a high quality and were written from the stance that educational standards would rise if schools focused on these important aspects of the learning process. The materials were extensive but in too many schools they had been disregarded within a year because a new revised framework for teaching literacy and mathematics had been introduced (so they all rolled over and one fell out). The SEAL resource, though used, was never truly given time to become embedded into the curriculum of primary schools.

Overheard in the Classroom

Part two ... later the same day

Teacher: What is that you are holding?

Ryan: Sir, it's a World War Two medal. It's very special. My Grandad earned it in the war and he said I should bring it to school and see if my teachers can tell me what it is worth. Do you know how much it is worth?

Teacher: Well, we are busy today Ryan ... Perhaps another day.

The journey to emotional literacy

Some educationalists have stressed the absolute importance of teaching emotional literacy in schools. Howard Gardner argues that the brain has a number of intelligence centres and the key to effective learning lies in unlocking all of these centres. Most of these intelligences have been reflected elsewhere within this book. However it is now appropriate and important to focus on two specifically, with a third to be introduced later in the chapter. The first of these is *interpersonal intelligence*. Our best teachers not only model how but also teach their learners to:

- Relate to others
- Work as a team member
- Lead a team
- Empathise with others and demonstrate care
- Adapt roles to suit social situations
- Be discerning and respond sensitively to subtle changes of mood, behaviour, motivation and intentions in others.

The second of Gardner's intelligences relevant to this chapter is *intrapersonal intelligence*. Inspirational teachers equip learners to:

- Understand their inner self
- Make sense of thoughts, emotions, values and beliefs
- Be sufficiently 'in charge' of themselves to be able to act on those understandings and change the way in which they learn, behave and relate to others.

Gardner argues that, from a very early age, children are placed into a normal distribution curve of ability often based on a narrow range of testing which focuses on verbal-linguistic and logical-mathematical traits. Teachers and schools rightly place a considerable emphasis on disturbing that curve of distribution in order to produce better academic results. However we all know that academic excellence does not guarantee success in life and that the qualities of interpersonal and intrapersonal intelligence are important if our youngsters are to grow into successful adults.

Therefore all teachers should ask themselves the following questions:

- Am I fully committed to helping the children in my class to become competent adults who are able to follow their own goals in life?

- Do I believe that the classroom should be about far more than just delivering programmes of study from the National Curriculum or National Frameworks?

- Do I want to provide genuine high quality learning experiences that will provide the children with knowledge, skills and understanding and prepare them to lead a full and active life in which they believe they can and will achieve?

- Am I prepared to do something about it, no matter how much it will make me feel that I am going against the grain and may get into trouble?

Any teacher who answers yes to these questions will recognise the role that emotional literacy plays within the inspirational classroom. Emotional literacy can be defined as the ability to recognise, understand and appropriately express emotions. It matters because it enables individuals to achieve their best and make a greater and more fulfilling contribution to society. It has been claimed that EQ is more important than IQ for predicting lifelong success in both the workplace and personal relationships. Teachers who promote emotional literacy in their classrooms contribute significantly to the emotional well-being of pupils. This is essential if successful learning is to take place. Children need to feel safe from harm whether it be physical or emotional. They also need to feel valued as an individual, empowered by belonging to a caring community and succeed through challenging but achievable learning activities.

Inspirational teachers recognise that:

- The best learning is an emotional experience which involves risk taking but should also build confidence.
- Emotional well-being can either help or hinder learning.
- When there is an emotional involvement in learning it will motivate pupils.
- Positive emotions within a classroom influence learning skills including concentration, memory and problem solving.

- Through supporting the emotional needs of all children the most vulnerable will also be supported.
- The emotional climate of the classroom is extremely important as it will promote creativity, risk taking and innovation for both teachers and pupils.

Tales of Inspirational Practice

Classrooms that sustain a positive state of mind

Daniel thought he was a good teacher *and he was*. He thought he was creative and could come up with original ideas *and he could*. He thought he took risks *and he did*. He was a good teacher who was dedicated to his work. He planned meticulously. But Daniel wanted to do better because at this stage he was not an *inspirational* teacher. Then one day he read an article which claimed that saying five positive things to a child each day had a profound effect. This made him read and research further and he realised that he was failing to take full account of how the brain worked. Daniel started researching the concept of sustaining a positive state of mind within his classroom. As a consequence he started to change his practice. In addition to his usual meticulous planning he took a set of prompts into the classroom each day which became a mantra for his classroom practice. The prompts included:

- Make sure that positive statements outnumber any form of criticism by at least four to one.
- Speak to each individual by name and making eye contact.
- Through conversation find out more about learners, their lives, hobbies and interests.
- Ensure that regularly changing displays demonstrate how you value children's work.
- Constantly model and communicate high expectations, a sense of purposeful pace and challenge children further in a positive context.
- Catch the learners who are doing well and celebrate it immediately.
- Ensure all learners receive positive constructive feedback that provides affirmation.
- Allow children to affirm their own successes and celebrate the successes of others.

Daniel didn't find this challenge easy. Maybe he had the features that are sometimes typically associated with males and didn't easily engage in emotionally based conversations. But over the period of a term he persevered until all those elements were regularly in place in his classroom. The responses he was receiving from the pupils got better and better as the confidence levels within the classroom grew and grew. However he still did not regard himself as the inspirational teacher he wanted to be. So during one summer holiday he decided to think again and went back to the key research. He then drew up his own set of professional development objectives for the following year. These included:

- Developing a new set of criteria to differentiate the outcomes of children's work using a technique called Must-Should-Could. In telling his class what he was looking for in any task he told them of the elements it *must* have to be an acceptable response to the challenge. Then he told them what it *should* have to be a good response. Finally he asked them to consider what else they *could* add that would make their work unique and exceptional and stand out from the rest.
- Ensuring that learning activities are as real-world related and authentic as possible because this provides relevance and often an emotional hook into learning.
- Ensuring that the pupils learn as much from their peers as possible by providing opportunities for collective and collaborative activity.
- Encouraging learners to choose their own strategies for learning.
- Reducing the amount of written recording or text-based learning in favour of more physical–tactile, visual–spatial, musical or team-based approaches.
- Encouraging learners to spend more time showing, telling and teaching each other.
- Creating opportunities for learners to reflect on how they solved problems, handled their tasks or made sense of their learning.

Remember at the start of this case study I said that Daniel already had the features of a really good teacher. His dedication and professionalism, however, moved him to a new and exceptional level and the practice in his classroom is now truly inspirational. Children bound through the doors and seem to eat out of his hands. Everybody achieves and helps others to achieve. The last occasion I spoke to Daniel was late on a Thursday afternoon. I was just about to leave the classroom when

I glanced down at his lesson planner and inside the front cover were the following words which had become a code for his classroom practice.

Keep your thoughts positive
because thoughts become your words.

Keep your words positive
because words become your actions.

Keep your actions positive
because actions become your habits.

Keep your habits positive
because habits become your values.

Keep your values positive
because values become your future.

The journey from emotional literacy to intelligence

In 1998 Daniel Goleman wrote:

> Emotional literacy implies an extended mandate for schools by taking up the slack in terms of socialising children. This daunting task requires that teachers go beyond their traditional mission and that people in the community become more involved with schools. In this sense, emotional literacy goes hand in hand with education for character, for moral development and for citizenship. Emotional competence may be decisive in determining the extent to which any given child or teenager is undone by economic or family forces or finds a core resistance to survive them.[104]

This section will provide information about how inspirational teachers create a sense of emotional competence that provides children with a special form of intelligence – one that seems to equip people to 'do the right things'.

There are always dangers in promoting emotional literacy. You may start to think that education is merely about helping children feel good about themselves. It isn't. Academic learning is important – children need to study real things and knowledge is essential. But emotional literacy is especially important if learners are to receive an education that provides them with moral development and a sense of citizenship, as described by Daniel Goleman. This chapter will increasingly look at ways in which academic knowledge and the social and emotional aspects of learning can work together. However simply accumulating and storing facts does not lead to a successful education. Schools too readily paint a picture that academic achievement leads to access to further education, which in turn will guarantee success in life. This is a myth because, as discussed earlier, success in life is due to other factors; and though these are often modelled in schools, they are not sufficiently well taught. Robert Ingersoll wrote: 'It is a thousand times better to have common sense without education rather than education without common sense,'[105] Therefore something else is needed.

Emotional literacy is important. It gives people the self-esteem to tackle the challenges ahead of them but it certainly doesn't guarantee success. The quote from Robert Ingersoll introduces the concept of 'common sense'. It is not a phrase I like, mainly because as a child I was constantly told off for having a lack of it. However there is much we can learn from these quotations. Rather than use the term common sense I would like to think that we build a *sense of intelligence* within our learners. Intelligence equips people to do the right thing at the right time or gives them the ability to know what to do even when you don't know what to do. I bet you are thinking, well nobody can teach a child that. You are wrong. There are inspirational teachers who can because they create the right habits of mind. Let us consider the work of Monsieur Georges Lopez from the BAFTA award-winning documentary *Être et Avoir*.

Tales of Inspirational Practice

Être et Avoir and the habits of mind

My enjoyment for teaching has stayed with me. I don't think I could have done any other job. Even now, I realise on the verge of retirement that I love this work with children. It takes time and personal involvement and the wonderful thing is the children return it. They return it over and over.[106]

These are the words of Monsieur Lopez in the enchanting documentary *Être et Avoir*. The film is a charming and intimate portrait of a single class primary school in rural France and its inspirational teacher, Monsieur Lopez. The pupils aged from four to ten are personally welcomed into the classroom each day by their teacher. You see him at work in his classroom where he provides the children with academic learning. He formally teaches the youngest children such things as letter formation and the older pupils fractions and the properties of a circle. The children also learn from real life experiences such as sledging in the snow and by going on train rides to have picnics. The pupils are very much real children who have squabbles and fights and sometimes don't make the best use of their time in the classroom. But Monsieur Lopez builds their confidence. He teaches them to take responsibility and to support each other. His classroom is a place where he peacefully directs the children's learning whilst constantly engaging them in conversation about what they are learning and how well they are progressing. I would recommend anybody to watch it. He creates in his learners what is known as a 'habit of mind'.

Arthur Costa first wrote about the need to build or infuse the habits of mind in the classroom. He defines a habit of mind as being 'a disposition towards behaving intelligently when confronted with problems'.[107] (This is the concept of knowing what to do when you don't know what to do as described previously.)

Inspirational teachers constantly build the personal qualities of their children by urging them to develop positive habits of mind. These will provide them with strategies to learn independently which will equip them to become lifelong learners. Good habits of mind lead to children (and adults) who:

- Stick to task because they persist and persevere
- Think carefully before acting and manage impulsivity
- Hear what others say because they listen to gain understanding and empathy
- Consider a range of options and think flexibly
- Learn about being an effective thinker
- Ask questions of themselves

- Make connections to past learning and experiences and apply it to new situations
- Focus so they think and communicate with clarity and precision
- Absorb information from a range of sources including through the senses
- Explore ideas in order to create, imagine or innovate
- Wonder
- Take risks
- Seek out humour in situations
- Team up with others when the time is right
- Remain open to continuous learning through developing a thirst for knowledge.

Arthur Costa claimed that infusing the right habits of mind into the learning culture of a school or classroom through modelling and explicit teaching can form the basis of a great learning experience, and will also provide children with the intelligence to do the right thing at the right time.

The journey from intelligence to wisdom

Developing good habits of mind helps children to develop intelligence. However inspirational teachers do not stop at that point. They help children to develop a sense of wisdom beyond their years. Intelligence and wisdom are different. C. Archie Danielson claimed that intelligence without wisdom is a bird without wings (and we know what happened to the dodo). Like intelligence, wisdom is about knowing what to do next, but it is then about having the skill to do it and then having the courage to do it in a virtuous manner whilst taking full responsibility for your actions. It helps individuals to make the right decisions, differentiate between good decisions and bad decisions and secure a better future. George Bernard Shaw wrote: 'We are made wise not by the recollection of our past, but by the responsibility for our future.'[108] Inspirational teachers help children to become wise and some of the strategies they use will be included in this chapter. But first let us consider the work of a man of wisdom who led an inspirational life.

Tales of Inspirational Lives

Father Pasquale de Nisco

The inspirational story of Father Pasquale de Nisco has been documented in *Outliers* by Malcolm Gladwell[109] and Conn and Hal Iggulden's *The Dangerous Book for Boys*.[110] In 1882, eleven quarry workers left the small village of Roseto in Foggia, Italy to set up a new life in the land of opportunity that was the United States. They knew that it was time to move on because the marble they quarried was virtually worked out and demand had dwindled. It was a tough decision because they loved their community. They worked hard in the week and spent the evenings and weekends with their families, and every Sunday they went to Holy Mass at the local Catholic church of Our Lady of Mount Carmel.

In January 1882 they arrived with hundreds of other immigrants who had their applications for entry processed at Ellis Island, New York before heading towards Pennsylvania where they set up a new community alongside a rutted wagon path. Here they would once again quarry but this time for slate. This was in a region where business and building was booming. Two months later a further fifteen quarry workers set sail, and then more and more. Before long a 'Little Italy' community was growing in that part of Pennsylvania and they called it Roseto after their homeland and in the centre they built a small church and called it Our Lady of Mount Carmel. Every Sunday the quarry workers and their families went to worship at Holy Mass.

The life of the quarrymen was a tough one. Accidents were frequent and life expectancy was generally short. Then in 1896 a young parish priest arrived who had wisdom beyond his years. He was called Father Pasquale de Nisco. Now around this time it was not uncommon for Catholic priests to spend their time warning of the dangers of sin and how it would lead to the fires of Hell. However Father de Nisco turned his attention to other matters because he had a vision of the kind of community Roseto needed to become. He believed that success for a community lay in educated citizenry. He spoke about the need to care for each other and support each other. He set about raising the funds to build a school, a convent, a public park and even a cemetery. He urged the townsfolk to diversify and clear the land so that they could grow fresh vegetables and after Sunday Mass he gave out seeds and bulbs. He urged people to keep their own livestock and to grow grapes in their backyards. Father de Nisco recognised that working conditions were harsh and he campaigned for better rights for the workers and led a successful strike. He set up festivals that celebrated the religious calendar and spiritual societies that helped people to study how to live a better life through understanding the scriptures. Father Pasquale left a legacy of educated citizenry for his people.

Our story stops there for a while and resumes in the 1950s when a physician called Dr Stewart Wolf moved into the community. At this time in the United States and in Pennsylvania heart disease was at almost epidemic proportions. However this was not the case in Roseto where heart attacks were virtually unheard of. In addition there were virtually no suicides, few mental health issues, drug addiction or crime. Dr Wolf scratched his head as he observed, 'these people die of old age and that is it'. He decided to find out why.

Dr Wolf started from the obvious assumption that it related to a healthy diet. On investigating further he found that the citizens of Roseto tended to cook in heavy lards rather than a healthier olive oil. He also found that they ate a large proportion of thick crust pizzas, sausages and biscotti. The reality was that 41% of the calories consumed in Roseto came from fats and this actually led to a relatively high level of obesity. Dr Wolf's research also showed a high incidence of smoking. At this point he started to look to more geographical features such as the climate and soil, but that was identical to surrounding communities where heart conditions were three times more prevalent. He looked at those Rosetans who moved out of the area and found that they did not enjoy the same level of good health.

Dr Wolf now started to look at other factors and concluded that the good health of the Rosetans was a clear legacy of the wisdom of Father Pasquale de Nisco half a century earlier. Their well-being came from the educated citizenry that he had helped to create – the twenty-two civic organisations that existed within the small community, the way in which the wealthy supported the poor, the manner in which people visited each other, cooked for each other and met socially and the fact that they regularly attended Mass at Our Lady of Mount Carmel. The community also had a clear social structure where the young respected and cared for their elders. The people of Roseto had transported a culture from Italy to the United States and were enjoying happiness and well-being as a result of the wisdom of one man.

Father Pasquale de Nisco knew what needed to be done and had the skills and courage to do it in a virtuous manner. Wisdom is different to academic intelligence, so the question is: Can schools and teachers teach wisdom?

A child of five would understand this ... Send someone to fetch a child of five.[111]

This line comes from Groucho Marx. It suggests that wisdom is not the domain of the elderly. Sigmund Freud wrote: 'What a distressing contrast there is between the intelligence and wisdom of the child and the feeble mentality of the average adult.' Young children enter schools and classrooms desperate to do the right things. Factual knowledge is important but does not guarantee wisdom. Whilst wisdom is not reserved for the elderly, a significant factor in its development is the range and number of high quality experiences a person has. Inspirational teachers know that children need things to study because facts are the seeds that later produce knowledge and wisdom, but emotions and impressions of the senses are the fertile soil in which these seeds grow. In short, knowledge is an important part of having wisdom but it is not the sole factor. Wisdom also comes from the quality of experience that brought the learning about. True wisdom comes from a close relationship with the learning process and inspirational teachers recognise this. They therefore recognise the importance of engaging all the senses and making learning an emotional experience. They create a sense of awe, wonder and spirituality in pupils that leads to the development of wisdom.

The links between awe, wonder, spirituality and wisdom

Sometimes I look around me with a feeling of complete dismay. In the confusion that afflicts the world today I see disrespect for the very values of life. Beauty is all round us, but how many seem to see nothing. Each second we live is a new and unique moment of the universe that will never be again. And what do we teach our children? We teach them that 2+2=4 and that Paris is the capital of France. We should say to each of them: do you know what you are? You are a marvel. You are unique. In the entire world there is no other child exactly like you. In the millions of years that have passed there has never been another child like you. And look at your body, what a wonder it is. Your legs, your arms, and your cunning fingers. You may become a Shakespeare, a Beethoven, or a Michelangelo. And when you grow up can you then harm another who is, like you, a marvel? You must cherish one another. You must work – we must all work – to make this world worthy of its children.[112]

This quotation from Pablo Casals is interesting because it opens up the concept of awe, wonder and spirituality. Awe and wonder in the beauty of the earth and the way in which the human body works. A sense of spirituality comes from the need to consider ourselves and others within the wider world and to leave our own unique and positive mark.

The world in which we live is a complex place and there are two ways in which children make sense of it. The first is through facts – and schools are good at providing learners with factual knowledge. It would be a sad world if children didn't know that 2+2=4 and that Paris is the capital of France. In England's schools, children learn that Henry VIII had six wives, the dates of the Second World War and how a river travels from its source to its mouth. The information a child is expected to know has been clearly laid out in the differing versions of the National Curriculum between 1988 and the present day. Most teachers are highly proficient at this work. The second way in which pupils make sense of their world is through sensations, passions and emotions and the way in which we interpret them. Only inspirational teachers create a sense of mood, energy, awe, wonder, appreciation of beauty and an awareness of natural order in this way. These teachers create an emotional response between the individual and their environment. This can create a respect, sense of love or fascination for their world or an absolute desire to change it, and in this context it helps to create wisdom.

Inspirational teachers provide their learners with three kinds of aptitudes which lead to wisdom. Firstly they provide an *academic and factual intelligence*. Secondly they should provide an *experiential intelligence* through the learning opportunities and challenges they create. Thirdly they should provide a *reflective intelligence* or wisdom. This is where the previous two come together to allow the individual to develop the skills of thinking and problem solving. Reflective intelligence is the kind of intelligence most needed in an increasingly competitive and complex world. To achieve better reflective intelligence schools need to place a greater focus on improving experiential learning. The academic learning of facts alone will never allow us to predict what will happen next or transform the elements of the world which need changing.

The question becomes: How do inspirational teachers create the best learning opportunities that lead to experiential learning which will thereby improve reflective learning and create a sense of wisdom in our learners?

Samuel Johnson considered memory to be the mother of all wisdom. Primary education should be a memorable experience that lasts for at least three generations: children should remember their experiences throughout their schooldays, be able to tell their children about it when they are parents and tell their grandchildren about it later in life. On some occasions they should tell their great-grandchildren about it. And, as they speak, the memories should come flooding back and feel vivid and real regardless of how many years have passed. It should feel that they can reach out and touch that experience one more time. The only way that can be achieved is by making learning a sensory and emotional experience that creates a sense of awe, wonder and spirituality.

Awe, wonder and spirituality are words that can trip easily off the tongue, but it is worth considering the relationship between the three terms. The inspirational teacher sees them as a progression. The diagram overleaf describes how this happens.

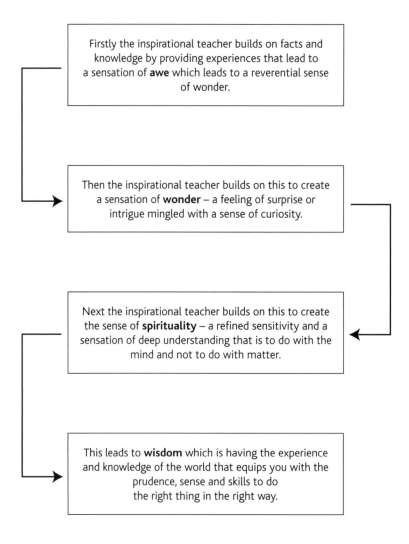

Firstly the inspirational teacher builds on facts and knowledge by providing experiences that lead to a sensation of **awe** which leads to a reverential sense of wonder.

Then the inspirational teacher builds on this to create a sensation of **wonder** – a feeling of surprise or intrigue mingled with a sense of curiosity.

Next the inspirational teacher builds on this to create the sense of **spirituality** – a refined sensitivity and a sensation of deep understanding that is to do with the mind and not to do with matter.

This leads to **wisdom** which is having the experience and knowledge of the world that equips you with the prudence, sense and skills to do the right thing in the right way.

Knowledge + awe + wonder + spirituality = wisdom

But how is this done? Well, let's start in a different sort of classroom.

Classrooms with no walls

Children in foundation stage classrooms in Britain regularly take their learning outdoors. It is a natural thing for them to do and it has been proven to work. It is as though the classroom has no walls. Too often as the children enter Key Stage 1 this ceases to be normal practice, however, and by the time children reach the end of their primary education visits out of the classroom can seem like a very occasional treat. This chapter started with a look at two of Howard Gardner's intelligences but let's take a look at another one from his list of eight – *naturalistic intelligence* – which leads to a love of the outdoors and a sensitivity to and an affinity with the natural environment. It allows learners to see patterns and relationships between the species and develop care and concern for the environment.

Whilst Gardner's naturalistic intelligence is based very much on the natural world it provides a significant message. It tells us that where learning takes place is significant, and this has been reflected in other research. Ofsted report that hands-on experiences in a range of locations contributes much to improvements in achievement, standards, motivation, personal development and behaviour.[113] They recognise that memorable experiences lead to memorable learning. Learning outside the curriculum contributes to children staying safe. Ofsted also notes that learning outside the curriculum helps to accelerate the progress of all groups of pupils especially the underachieving. Therefore the challenge is to take learning outdoors by creating more classrooms with no walls.

Tales of Inspirational Practice

Emergency landing

It was around 11 a.m. and the children in the eight Key Stage 2 classrooms were focused on their literacy lessons. They were doing word and sentence level work, writing instructions, letters of complaints and newspaper accounts. Outside it was getting noisier and noisier. Children lifted their heads to look through the windows to see the source of the sound. A helicopter was in descent and about to make a forced landing on the school field.

The teachers in school struggled to keep control of their classes. The children were desperate to watch what was going on. Most teachers succeeded. One let the children look out of the window for five minutes on the promise that they went straight back to writing their newspaper accounts based on a fictitious school football match. No problems at all existed in Class 7. This was because no one was there. The teacher was already on the way to get a better vantage point followed by thirty Year 5 children. This was because he sensed a unique learning opportunity.

Bill taught in a classroom that regularly had no walls. The children visited the local woods in every season of the year. They kicked up the leaves in autumn, felt frost on the bark in winter, built their own dens in spring which they used as hides to watch birds and saw the trees in full leaf in summer. He took the children to feel the wind on their faces and the rain on their cheeks. Every half term's topic started with a high quality educational visit and once a year it was of a residential nature. He instinctively knew how to get the best out of such experiences, and the children produced work of a stunning quality and high sensitivity.

As the helicopter became quiet he went out to speak to the pilot and co-pilot making sure the pupils kept at a safe distance. The pilot explained there had been a fault which required an emergency landing but this would soon be fixed. Then a range of negotiations took place. Before long the children were interviewing the pilot. They found out where they had recently travelled to and from. They were allowed to sit in the cockpit. They found out about radio systems and how to become a pilot. Then the children moved a safe distance from the helicopter and felt the powerful sensation when the rotors moved into action. One child announced that he had a remote control helicopter and it was agreed that he should bring it in tomorrow. Whilst all this was going on the rest of the key stage classes maintained their focus on 'wow' words, adventure stories and newspaper accounts. Strangely, by the end of the week, the children in Class 7 had used the best wow words in their adventure story about a helicopter making an emergency landing. Their newspaper accounts of the event were very good too and far in advance of the class writing reports about a fictitious football match.

The work carried on for half a term. I visited the school when the pupils were absorbed in a science experiment ... you could try it yourself. The children started with a template like the one below. They made a cut along the dotted line and folded the template to make a T shape which when dropped from a height rotates like a helicopter or sycamore seed as it falls to the ground.

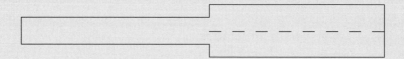

The children were engrossed in discovering whether:

- increasing or decreasing the wing span made any difference
- adding to the mass made any difference or if there was a critical mass
- the helicopter always rotated in the same direction and what controls this
- it was possible to describe the descent of the helicopter.

The children were required to report their findings back to the group in a stimulating manner.

We can't readily arrange for a helicopter to make an emergency landing on the school field, but we can take advantages of a whole range of other opportunities. The winter of 2010 was one of the most severe in the UK over recent years. *The Guardian*'s website included a story with an infamous misprint. It announced that schools were 'shit due to bad weather'. It was not the latest judgement from Ofsted but simply an article about school closures. During that winter after a particularly heavy snowfall I asked a head teacher if she had closed during the inclement weather. She replied: 'You have got to be joking – why would I want to miss a learning opportunity like that?'

Many teachers take their children out on school visits. They take them into natural environments like clifftops near the coast, or to follow the course of a river, or into landscapes of dramatic limestone scenery. They also take the children to see man-made marvels like mighty steam engines in full throttle, water wheels or windmills grinding corn, or to ride on steam locomotives, or to castles perched high in defensive positions. However not all of them have the skills and techniques to get the most out of these situations. Too many rely on collecting groups of pupils around them and using teacher talk to pass on facts and information. Others have an over-reliance on worksheets or quizzes with closed questions. They never fully create that sense of awe, wonder and spirituality that is the backbone of this chapter. Kate did though in the case study below. She was also a great believer in classrooms without walls and the need to take learning outdoors. She has a range of techniques which potentially work well in a whole variety of locations.

Tales of Inspirational Practice

You fill up my senses

Kate knew that children needed direct teaching of key skills but she was also convinced that much of the best learning should be a sensory experience. She fervently spoke of a desire to create a 'wow' classroom with no walls and regularly sought to create learning opportunities in outdoor environments. To support this she used a range of techniques which had a significant impact on children and greatly enhanced their work when they returned to the classroom. The techniques can be used in either natural or man-made environments, in locations of great beauty or even in eyesores.

During an educational visit, and shortly after arriving at a location, she encourages the children to start exploring the environment through their five senses. She asks them to carry out a sensory trail. A proforma is sometimes provided (like the one below) and in the first instance the children are asked to carry the work out individually because the exercise is about their relationship with the environment. The children absorb the location through the beauty of what they can see (or can't see), the sounds they can hear, the textures of things they can feel, the smells associated with the environment or tastes in the air such as salt from sea. The children are required to do the following exercise using strong adjectives and a richness of language.

What can I see?	
What can I hear when I close my eyes?	
What can I feel with my hands?	
What smells are around me?	
Are there any taste sensations?	

The exercise is at its best when the teacher joins in and models the process rather than merely moving around supervising pupils. After an appropriate period of time the children come back together. Sometimes they pair up and share their ideas. They feed back to each other using the 'three stars and a wish' technique. This involves the children saying three things they admire about their classmates' work whilst suggesting an area of improvement. The children also take responsibility for nominating their peers to share sections with the full class, and then time is provided for the learners to revise their own work.

Sometimes with older children, or when the technique has become well embedded, the format of the sensory trail changes. Once again using all five senses the children complete a powerful sentence beginning with each letter of the alphabet. Examples from a seaside visit to a clifftop include:

A deep mist settled on the clifftop.
Below me I can hear the crashing of the waves.
Caw caw screech seagulls from the nearby harbour.
Dampness is in the air and you can taste it on your lips.
E
F

Alternatively, if the children are being exposed to an environment that is more of an eyesore, the responses could include:

A film of oil lay on the water of the canal.
Broken and rusted machinery remain from a bygone age.
Change is urgently needed to reclaim this sombre landscape.

More recently the children have started recording their sensory trails on Flip videos so that the words and the images sit side by side. Back in the classroom the outcomes of the sensory trail can be used in a variety of ways including poetry or creating the setting for a story.

When Kate takes her learning environment outdoors she always takes high quality sketchbooks. All the children have their own and they simply sit and draw quietly. Whilst they are at work they may also note down key words and phrases which come into their mind during these close observations. They are told that their work has to reflect pride and perseverance. Her expectations are high and the children respond. As W. Somerset Maugham said, 'It's a funny thing but if you refuse to accept anything but the best, you very often get it.'

A further recent addition to Kate's work has been to get the children to look at the environment closely and note down answers to the following questions:

What should always be preserved in this environment?	
How should this environment change for the better?	
What interesting questions need to be asked?	

The purpose of the final part of this exercise is twofold. Firstly it helps to develop positive values and attitudes. More importantly it helps to cultivate a clear sense of responsibility within the learners for the environment so that hopefully when difficult decisions have to be made they will make the right ones.

Kate's work and the concept of the classroom with no walls relates closely to Gardner's concept of naturalistic intelligence.

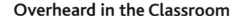

Overheard in the Classroom

Part three

Teacher: What is that you are holding?

Ryan: Sir, it's a World War Two medal. It's very special. My Grandad earned it in the war and he said I should bring it to school and see if my teachers can tell me what it is worth. Do you know how much it is worth?

Teacher: Not again Ryan. Please don't pester.

Q: Now children where does milk come from? A: Please Miss, it's Tesco!

Yes, I know this is a very old joke but within it there remains an important message about our relationship with the natural environment. Most children have a love of the outdoors and feel a sense of affinity with growing things. One of the most refreshing developments to have taken place in Britain's primary schools in the first decade of the twenty-first century has been the development of allotments. The value of children growing things is not something that has been recently recognised, but it may have become forgotten over time. In 1935 the Board of Education wrote:

> Gardening is a form of school craft that is well established, and it is generally recognised that some provision for it is as desirable in towns as well as in the countryside. It is especially desirable because it is an open air occupation and brings children into direct contact with nature. It is as valuable for girls as for boys, and there is no reason why the former should not take a full share of the work. Gardening demands skill in the use of a variety of tools and the intelligent applications of that skill to different tillage operations. In learning to raise and tend plants and to wait patiently for the results, the pupils get to know something of their needs and of their infinite variety and beauty.[114]

This extract comes from a time when we may have associated primary education with 'chalk and talk' or book and rote based learning rather than classrooms with no walls. Maybe it shows that inspirational teachers have always known what is good for children, but other forces have led us to the view that children learn best from textbooks when seated behind desks. Times have certainly changed. The passage seems to focus on the element of physical labour first and foremost. The magic of seeing things grow and the need to take responsibility comes later. We should not discount the importance of physical exercise in a time when too many children live sedentary lives.

However there is something even more important and that is the way in which gardening and allotments can stimulate children's spiritual and emotional development. Carol Williams wrote: 'Usually children spend more time in the garden than anyone else. It is where they learn about the world, because they can be in it unsupervised; yet protected. Some gardeners will remember from their earliest recollections that no one sees the garden as vividly or cares about it as passionately as the child who grows up in it.'[115] More simply Dorothy Gurney said: 'One is nearer God's heart in a garden than anywhere else on the earth.'[116] The development of school allotments allows children to take a blank canvas to try out new ideas. They cannot fully predict the outcomes but fully understand that care and responsibility will be required. This gives the allotment an element of mystery, surprise, wonder and spirituality. Not only that ... for the more hard edged amongst you it can open up a business or enterprise opportunity as well as links to other areas of the curriculum.

Tales of Inspirational Practice

Allotments

Jackie the head teacher was passionate about the allotment project. Yes, she wanted the children to experience the magic of seeing the green shoots slowly edging through the soil but she also saw it as an enterprise project that would extend into other areas of the curriculum and into the wider community.

The scheme was to involve all classes within the school. In order to promote responsibility each class had to make arrangements to appoint two allotment managers to ensure that the class fulfilled their duty within the larger project. In the first year it was agreed that the produce would be sold either to the school meals service or to the wider community. It was deemed that the project had to make a profit. However the first thing that had to be checked was whether or not this was permissible, so the children corresponded with the local council to check out the regulations. It was determined that if the children carried out the appropriate soil checks and sent the outcomes to the relevant department the plans could proceed.

The children interviewed other allotment holders and a local farmer before designing the layout of the plot and costing the purchase of seeds and other resources. The children took responsibility for preparing the land, planting seeds (the youngest children dealt with herbs and faster growing crops whilst the older children dealt with 'heavier' work). The children then took full care of the crop until harvest time arrived. Produce was supplied to the school kitchen first and then sold on a stall after school the following evening. As it had been decided that the project should make a profit further calculations needed to take place. The children firstly considered the probability of whether they would sell all the produce and from this point determined that their pricing policy would be based on selling 70% of the goods in order to break even. By the time the caretaker bought the last item (a solitary cauliflower) a healthy profit was guaranteed.

The allotment managers then met to consider how the profit should be spent and to consider plans for the future. The children said that they had enjoyed the project but wanted it to be shaped differently in the second year. They wished to use the produce themselves to prepare and cook simple dishes. The allotment managers therefore decided that the profits should be spent on purchasing cooking utensils to allow this to happen. The school also had some concerns about parenting issues and, as a consequence, they decided that the harvest at the end of the second year would be used for cook-and-eat sessions where pupils and parents came together to prepare simple meals alongside the school's parent support adviser.

Stories of allotments and extracts from the 1930s may have conjured up the sense of a wartime spirit. A message of 'dig for victory' may be coursing through your veins. Elsewhere in this book the importance of values education has been extolled, as has the importance of creating an emotional hook into learning. Our final case study of the chapter combines the two whilst maintaining the wartime ethos. The notion of the children developing an element of wisdom also comes through as they consider the values needed in their classroom to make it a better place.

Tales of Inspirational Practice

Permission to speak, Sir? An episode in inspirational learning

I recently led a training session on curriculum design at a primary school. The staff had become especially interested in creating cross-curricular thematic topics that were built around an emotional hook as described in Chapter 2. They had also taken a particular interest in visual literacy and the use of film footage in the manner described in Chapter 5. The Year 5 class were about to study the values people held during the Second World War. As I walked into Martin's classroom the children were poised ready to watch a short clip from *Dad's Army*. The children were sat with pencils ready to record certain pieces of information on a proforma like the one below.

What is made up just to make us laugh?
Which bits could actually be true?
What were the values the characters had that were necessary in the Second World War?
What questions do I need to ask?

The amount of information the children could glean from that one five-minute clip was phenomenal and they drew up many questions such as: Why were the windows taped up? What was in the cardboard boxes the men were carrying? What was the Home Guard and why were the men so old? What was an ARP warden? Why were things rationed?

However the children also saw powerful examples of the values that people required during this very difficult period. They caught evidence of team work, loyalty, bravery, creativity to solve problems, respect and caring. In the hands of their very skilful teacher a wonderful half term's work was shaped leading to a clear understanding of the war years. Moreover the children looked specifically at the values and made them into a mantra they would seek to follow during their year in Martin's class.

The journey ends here

This chapter started with the 'Fable of Fred'. I found out many years later that it had been written by Sir Alec Clegg, former influential and inspirational Chief Education Officer for the West Riding of Yorkshire for a training event. The message remains poignant. It therefore seems appropriate to finish the chapter with another thought from this same man that captures the spirit of this chapter:

> The young Michelangelo took a reference to the Pope who was to employ him on the building of the dome of Saint Peter's and on the painting of the Sistine Chapel. The reference said, 'The bearer of this is Michelangelo, the sculptor. His nature is such that he has to be drawn out by kindness and encouragement but if he be treated well and love shown to him he will accomplish things that will make the whole world wonder.'[117]

The chapter has taken you on a journey that shows how inspirational teachers systematically create their own generation of Freds through a focus on developing emotionally literate learning environments and developing a sense of awe, wonder and spirituality in children that leads not only to factual knowledge and academic learning but also a sense of intelligence and wisdom that equips them to do the right thing at the right time in the right way. I hope you enjoyed the journey and I trust you feel equipped to take your children on their own journey.

Inspirational teachers creating inspirational learners in inspirational classrooms

Finally you might like to consider how you as a teacher or your school matches up to the best practice. The following checklist explores the relationship between inspirational learners who are taught by inspirational teachers within emotionally literate classrooms that promote a sense of awe and wonder. You could score each element out of 5 and then select areas for improvement.

Inspirational Teachers	Score
In the inspirational words of George Bernard Shaw: 'What we want to see is the child in pursuit of knowledge and not knowledge in pursuit of the child.'[118]	
Teachers use praise and criticism at a ratio of at least four to one	
Teachers greet individuals by name using eye contact and find out about the children's interests	
Teachers provide opportunities to express emotions	
Teachers use displays to value children's learning	
Teachers demonstrate high expectations of themselves and others	
Teachers encourage learners to think about and talk about themselves and others positively	
Teachers make learning as real-world related as possible	
Teachers make learning a multi-sensory experience	
Teachers regularly take learning outdoors through the creation of memorable experiences	
Teachers have freedom in the curriculum to respond to changes in seasons or weather	

(continued)

Inspirational Teachers	Score
Teachers regularly create opportunities for children to respond to the natural environment and to focus on plants and animals using multi-sensory skills	
Teachers regularly create opportunities for children to respond to the man-made environment using multi-sensory skills	
Teachers plan cause and effect activities in order to provide learners with a greater understanding of their world	
Teachers develop children's sensitivity of weather, mood and atmospheres, increasing their ability to respond emotionally and spiritually	

Inspirational Learners	Score
In the inspirational words of Eric Hoffer: 'In times of change, learners inherit the earth whilst the learned find themselves beautifully equipped to deal with a world that no longer exists.'[119]	
Children feel it is OK to make mistakes. They do not fear disparagement and learn from such mistakes	
Learners regularly contribute to the learning of others through support and feedback	
Learners regularly formulate their own questions about big issues	
Learners regularly and readily connect with prior learning	
Children draw upon aspects of the natural world to aid creative expression, understanding and wisdom	
Children draw upon aspects of the man-made world to aid creative expression	

(continued)

Inspirational Learners	Score
Children demonstrate aspects of creativity in different environmental settings including the classroom, playground and local visits	
Children develop close observational skills including presenting in detail small parts of a larger object	
Children develop descriptive language alongside these observations	
Children demonstrate wonder, amazement and enthusiasm for learning	

Inspirational Classrooms	Score
In the inspirational words of Louis Rubin: 'There is a striking quality to fine classrooms. Pupils are caught up in learning; excitement abounds; and playfulness and seriousness blend easily because the purposes are clear, the goals sensible and an unmistakable feeling of wellbeing prevails.'[120]	
All learners experience success and affirmation every day	
Classrooms have an appropriate balance between written text-based activities and physical/tactile and multi-sensory approaches	
The learning within the classroom reflects all of Gardner's eight intelligences	
The class takes the opportunity to function as a team in order to make a difference	
Teaching and learning frequently take place in outside areas and away from the school site	
The classroom reflects an appreciation of the natural and human world through its provision of resources, artefacts and visual imagery	
Children are encouraged to use their creativity to develop their own local environments (classrooms, school grounds or community spaces)	

Overheard in the Classroom

Part four

Teacher: What is that you are holding?

Ryan: Sir, it's a World War Two medal. It's very special. My Grandad earned it in the war and he said I should bring it to school and see if my teachers can tell me what it is worth. Do you know how much it is worth?

Teacher: (to the rest of the class) Hey kids, gather round and look at this. It's fabulous. Let's see what we can all find out about …

Chapter 7

Not Everything That Can Be Counted Counts and Not Everything That Counts Can Be Counted

An Inspirational Approach to Assessment in the Twenty-first Century

The first step is to measure what can easily be measured.
This is OK as far as it goes.

The second step is to disregard anything that can't easily be
measured or to give it an arbitrary or quantitative value.
This is artificial and misleading.

The third step is to presume that what can't be measured easily isn't really important.
This is blindness.

The fourth step is to say what can't be easily measured
really doesn't exist.
This is suicide!

Robert McNamara[121]

Overheard in the Classroom

Visitor to class: It's the SAT tests next week – are you worried?

Pupil: No, I'm not worried. The tests are more about the teachers than the pupils, but I think they're worried.

The Prologue

Measuring what we value

Mr Plumstead was carrying out yet another school inspection. Just as the quality of head teachers and teachers ranges from 'outstanding' to 'inadequate' so does the range of inspectors. Mr Plumstead was an inadequate school inspector. His approach was not to work alongside school leaders to establish a clear mandate for the future. His approach was to focus entirely on unearthing weaknesses, and if that unnerved people along the way … then so much the better.

He had failed in his first attempt to unsettle the school. He had tried to breeze confidently in without showing his identification documents so that he could take issue with them at a later stage. However a very shrewd member of the office team had demanded to see his documentation. This was because his reputation as an inspector was already well known in the locality. However he did have more luck with his second ruse. He ordered a school dinner and waited to see if he would be charged for it. The well-intentioned secretary pointed out that the head teacher always paid for lunches taken by guests. Mr Plumstead gleefully pointed out that could be construed as bribery and placed his £1.85 on the desk in front of him.

The school he was inspecting had grown tired of government diktats, the National Curriculum and published schemes of work. It had devised a new curriculum based on the needs of the community it served. It had moved away from a content-driven, knowledge-based curriculum to one that sought to develop skills and positive attitudes in learners. The school had adopted the generic personal learning and thinking skills promoted by the QCDA.

The changes made had been very positive. Attainment and achievement had risen. Attendance and punctuality had also improved. Teachers were reporting that behaviour was better and there were more positive attitudes amongst the pupils. The teachers and the support staff were also far more enthusiastic about their work. In short, pupils and teachers were both bounding through the doors with enthusiasm.

However Mr Plumstead sensed a weakness in the school. In all the classrooms he had visited he had seen very little evidence of the pupil's short-term literacy and numeracy targets being high profile. His time as a secondary science teacher hadn't necessarily equipped him well for his life as a primary school inspector but he was determined that he would look strong and where necessary ruthless. He was now striding down the corridor with his clipboard under his arm. He had a new sense of purpose as he headed towards the room where he would be carrying out a series of pupil interviews.

The first student he met was a ten-year-old called Kevin. After a few niceties, Mr Plumstead honed in on the killer question: 'Tell me, Kevin, what are your current targets?' Kevin confidently stated that his targets were to complete his primary and secondary education, go to university (probably in Newcastle) where he would study veterinary science. Mr Plumstead said, 'Kevin, I hear what you are saying but what about your targets in the shorter term?'

Kevin responded by saying, 'Mr Plumstead, in this school we are all encouraged to have dreams and they should be targets to aim for because we can all achieve our dreams. Our school has a link with a university so we all know what qualifications we will need to gain admission. We have visited so that we know what student life will be like and about the doors that will open for us if we have the right qualifications. We are told that we must have goals in our life.'

Mr Plumstead repeated, 'Kevin, I hear what you are saying (which meant he wasn't listening) but what about your shorter-term targets?'

Kevin responded instantly: 'If I am to be successful in my aims I need to work hard in order to develop as a creative thinker and also be reflective in my learning. These are areas that are not so well developed in my profile. This is because I need to think hard about how I can make my work more original and sometimes try to transfer my learning from one area to another. I also need to reflect more fully on the work I do before I hand it in.'

Mr Plumstead now sensed his opportunity. Clearly Kevin had no idea what his short-term literacy and numeracy targets were so he moved in for the kill. Once more he said, 'Kevin, I hear what you are saying but let me put it more simply. What are your targets in English and mathematics?'

'Well, why didn't you say that?' said Kevin. 'In English I need to develop my skills of inferential comprehension so that I not only read the lines but also between the lines, and also learn to use inference better in my own writing.' Kevin went on to explain that in mathematics he was focusing on solving word problems involving two or more operations. Kevin then said, 'Mr Plumstead, I am sure you will realise that to achieve my English and mathematics targets I will need to be a creative thinker and a reflective learner.'

'Hmmph,' retorted Mr Plumstead as he stood up to leave the room. As he left Kevin looked up and said: 'Do you ever have to be a reflective learner in your job, Mr Plumstead?'

The previous chapters have looked at how inspirational teachers through their practice achieved an inspirational response from their learners. However so far within the book little reference has been made to assessment. This important dimension will now be brought to the fore. Patrick Lencioni argues that there are three signs of a miserable job and the first one he calls 'immeasurability'.[122] There can be no sense of job satisfaction if you cannot demonstrate measurable pupil progress. A wise man once said that it is easier to count the bottles than measure the quality of the wine. This chapter urges you to stop counting the bottles and suggests ways to develop a twenty-first century assessment structure.

Let me insult you – it's bound to be helpful

Consider these words of wisdom written as long ago as 1959 by the Ministry of Education with the support of Her Majesty's Inspectorate.[123] Then judge whether the message given is just as important today.

Any head teacher or assistant teacher will be wise always to consider carefully whether any formal tests they propose are really necessary, what exactly their purpose is, whether they are the best means of achieving the purpose and whether the time spent on them is justified – since it must be taken from time in which children might otherwise be learning something of value.

One word has dominated the educational world above all others in the last ten years. That word is *assessment*. Whilst much good practice has been promoted, more powerful factors have been at play which have restricted the development of high quality practice. The most negative of these has been testing. The most important measure of a school's success has been the Key Stage 2 tests that have taken place annually in mid-May. Ofsted, local authorities and parents now judge the quality of a school largely by the test outcomes. This one event in the school year is now so dominant that it distorts all that a school does and can be extremely damaging in an unwisely run school. As a consequence high quality strategies like Assessment for Learning and the National Strategies materials for Assessing Pupil Progress (APP) have not had the intended impact. This is because there has been a more powerful hidden agenda that has promoted the darker side to assessment.

Ofsted inspections are substantially driven by test outcomes. The test results are part of a limiting judgement which means that if they are not deemed to be strong enough, the school will fail. As a consequence too many schools in our most challenging areas can only dream of being judged satisfactory. The now defunct National Strategies, which were launched under the banner of *Excellence and Enjoyment* in 2003, sometimes were akin to a secret police force which operated under a new banner of 'Excellence and Enforcement'. Often the National Strategies tried to spur schools to improve their test results by giving them insulting and derogatory titles like 'hard to shift', 'notice to improve', 'coasting' or 'satisfactory but stuck'. These labels were provided regardless of the circumstances in which the school was operating and more often than not were well meant but unhelpful. The pressures placed on schools has left too many of them feeling trapped when it comes to considering assessment issues. They felt the need to constantly prepare children for – by teaching to – the tests. They have often been duped into thinking that testing is the only accurate method of assessing pupil progress. This has restricted the development of assessment strategies that could promote high quality inspirational teaching and assessment. It has also left us with assessment structures that are unfit for purpose in the twenty-first century.

Assessment that fails the test

The way in which the statutory test results have dominated primary education over the last decade will leave a damaging legacy that will be hard to remove. Inevitably it will have restricted the development of confident inspirational teachers who create inspirational pupils. The practice has also restricted the development of more inspirational and life-changing forms of assessment. This negative legacy may include views such as:

- Standardised test scores are the main and most accurate indicators of student learning and progress.

- Paper and pencil tests are the only tried and tested means of effectively assessing progress.

- Assessment is somehow separate to the rest of the curriculum or timetable because it takes place in special weeks and times or in special places using different methodologies.

- It is outside assessment agencies that provide an objective and true picture of a pupil's knowledge and learning.

- There is a clearly defined body of skills and knowledge that children need to master to demonstrate in a test situation and the other aspects of a school's curriculum are less significant.

- If something can't be tested in a uniform way then it isn't worth teaching.

- The quality of a school and its curriculum can only be as good as the test scores.

- All pupils should be tested at the same time using the same testing instruments because it is important to be able to compare and contrast one child's achievement with another's.

- Simple scoring systems are the best way to analyse a child's learning.

- The prime purpose of assessment structures is to rank pupils so that school leaders understand their level within the school.

- Assessment should be based on traditional models and scales.

- Our best teachers prepare children to achieve well in tests.

If all, or even just a few, of these views pervade the workings of a school it will restrict the development of inspirational teachers who create high quality opportunities that lead to deep learning. Change is needed and it needs to be rapid. David Lazear argues that these factors belong to the old paradigm of assessment and a new paradigm needs to develop.[124] He believes that education has been stuck with the old paradigm for far too long and it shows little sign of shifting. If the children in our schools today believe that the overall purpose of education is to do well in tests then they will also believe it when they are parents and grandparents. Therefore it will take a further three generations to shift.

Inspirational teachers have intuitively developed assessment structures that are fit for purpose in the twenty-first century. They also embrace newer methods which are developing as part of Assessment for Learning and the APP initiative. The reason for this is that the inspirational teacher is fully aware of the relationship between high quality teaching, rich and meaningful learning experiences and the use of strong and appropriate assessment structures.

Inspirational teaching, learning and assessment

The old saying states that you are only as strong as your weakest link, and the reality is that teaching, learning and assessment are all equally important links in the chain. However in too many classrooms there have been one or more weaknesses in that sequence. The significance of weak spots in the relationship between teaching, learning and assessment can be seen by carrying out the activity overleaf.

The first circle in the Venn diagram indicates that the quality of teaching has been of an inspirationally high quality. The second circle indicates that the children have then been provided with challenges which have allowed them to make an inspirational response as a result of the rich and vivid learning activities that have been planned for them in order to fulfil the intended learning outcomes. The third circle represents high quality assessment and well-established assessment opportunities that judge the progress made towards achieving the learning intentions or targets, so the child is currently functioning against agreed criteria, marking and feedback that will secure both future engagement and progress. Look at the seven numbers which have been placed at different points on the diagram. Now think what it would be like if you had just observed a lesson that was judged to fit into each of those locations on the diagram.

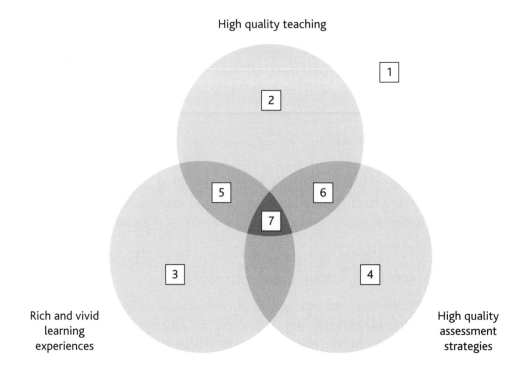

I wonder if you have come up with the same conclusions as me?

The bottom of the class lesson: The lesson at point 1 on the diagram would be an inadequate lesson with poor teaching followed by undemanding and closed tasks. Using a descriptor relating to the transfer of learning devised by Robin Fogarty the pupils would be 'sleepers' who would miss the key points of what was being studied.[125] They would not see connections to previous learning or possible ways to transfer the content of the lesson into other areas of the curriculum or life.

The fur coat and no knickers lesson: A lesson at point 2 could appear very attractive on the surface but would not have much to offer on the learning front if you looked a little closer. It would be typical of a teacher who has been strong and engaging in their delivery but then provided pupils with closed or undemanding tasks, or where there has been little attention placed on precise learning outcomes. Using Fogarty's scales the learners would be 'duplicators' who may be able to recount the lesson in exactly the way it was delivered.

The it fell on stony ground lesson: Discovery favours the well-prepared mind but the lesson at point 3 has failed because the teacher has not spent sufficient time preparing and stimulating the children's minds. As a consequence the pupils have been provided with clear and well-differentiated learning activities. However learning has been restricted because of a less than convincing delivery by the teacher, possibly because teacher talk has dominated. Using Fogarty's scales on this occasion the learners would be classed as 'replicators' who will probably be able to recall the learning but only if it is presented in an identical way.

The cart before the horse lesson: A lesson delivered at point 4 could be so focused and driven on achieving a learning intention, test outcome, target or level of attainment that insufficient attention is spent on how this will be achieved or how the learning will be retained in the longer term. In short, the pupil believes the lesson is about passing an assessment.

The missing piece of the jigsaw lesson: Imagine the sense of frustration because you have just assembled 999 pieces of a jigsaw but the final piece is missing and you are left slightly deflated. Such a lesson is depicted at point 5 of the diagram. We may have seen strong teaching followed by rich learning activities but with inadequate attention placed on the ongoing assessment of progress or providing feedback. At the end of the activity insufficient notice has been taken of national or school-based assessment criteria, or providing marking and feedback that would enhance future learning. Using Fogarty's scale the learners will be 'strategists' who will have taken a great deal from the lesson and will be able to transfer learning into other situations. However a sense of frustration in this lesson could occur because the learner may never know just how well they have performed.

The Teflon saucepan lesson: In the lesson at point 6 quite simply nothing sticks! Whilst the teaching has been strong and a range of high quality assessment strategies have been used, the learning may not be either deep or embedded because of a missing element – the memorable activity where children have been required to produce an inspirational response to the stimulus.

The pot of gold at the end of the rainbow lesson: This lesson is depicted at point 7. The teacher has taken the children on a wonderful learning journey. The activities have been stimulating. The children are clear on the progress they have made and as a result of self, peer and teacher assessment they are ready to engage positively with future learning. As a result of this they have become 'creators' of their own learning using Fogarty's scales. They will be able to use the information, skills and attitudes developed within the lesson as a springboard to future creative and original thinking. They will be able to see unusual connections and patterns that will aid the transfer of learning into a wide variety of areas.

Assessment fit for the twenty-first century

The Cambridge Review of Primary Education rightly stressed the absolute importance of children achieving the highest possible standards in all aspects of communication, language and literacy, mathematics and ICT. More radical proposals were made to combine other subjects and aspects of the curriculum. The suggestions provided teachers with far less prescription and much greater flexibility over both content and delivery. A key driver in education should be to produce responsible citizens, confident individuals and successful learners. Readers from the start will know that these are the statutory aims of the secondary curriculum. If we are serious about educational continuity, the same key principles should apply for primary education – as recommended in the Rose Review (the one that was later scrapped). These seem perfectly logical principles to me – and principles that very few people could disagree with. They are ideals which would equip children well for life in the twenty-first century. To achieve such ideals schools will need to consider their assessment systems again. Some systems will need maintaining and others extending. Schools will especially need to consider afresh how they assess progress towards developing responsible citizens, confident individuals and successful learners. Let us start with the systems they may need to maintain or extend.

Assessment: The cod liver oil element

This chapter will endorse new methodology and structures for assessment that promote inspirational teaching and inspirational learning, but it is important to consider the absolute essentials as well. Schools and pupils need them and what follows later in this chapter is dependent on them being in place. For example all schools will need clear structures for assessing and tracking pupil progress in all aspects of communication, language and literacy, mathematics and ICT. There does need to be a shift away from an over-reliance on testing or children carrying out special pieces of work during assessment weeks. One school leader bluntly told me: 'You can't fatten the pig if you spend too much time weighing it.' Our prime purpose is to teach the children and not test them. Strides are being made through the materials being provided under the APP banner which were provided by the National Strategies; it would be a shame if this impetus was lost.

I call this section the 'cod liver oil element' – you might not like it but it's good for you. It may well leave a bitter taste but, if taken regularly, it will lead to healthily growing learners.

As a minimum, through ongoing formative assessment all teachers must be able to provide accurate assessments against level descriptors for all pupils within the identified core subjects. This should equip them to take part in a professional dialogue about individual children, their class, their key stage and the subject as a whole. To do this all schools need a tracking system that is simple, visual and user friendly. It specifically needs to:

- Record the accurate assessments made by staff.
- Highlight where each child is in relation to age-related expectations.
- Show the progress each child has made over time.
- Identify children who seem stuck, slow moving or falling behind, and therefore who needs additional support.
- Map pupils to appropriate intervention programmes.
- Monitor the progress made by an individual child on a regular basis.
- Stimulate discussions about individual pupils or groups of pupils within regular pupil progress meetings.
- Be used alongside other self-evaluation strategies such as work scrutiny and lesson observations in order to ensure a school has a truly accurate picture of the progress being made.

Assessment fit for the twenty-first century curriculum

If we are serious about developing a generic set of skills and qualities young people will need then it is time to look with a fresh pair of eyes and develop a more creative approach to assessment. The methodology must demonstrate more clearly how assessment is linked to high quality teaching and learning. Many inspirational teachers have always believed the following statements to be true:

- There are no standard learners and therefore assessment, like teaching and learning, needs to be varied and sometimes individualised.
- Direct assessment at the time of learning gives a fairer and more accurate picture of progress.
- Pupil-created portfolios (which could include some formal tests) produce a more holistic view of the learning that has taken place.
- The lines between the curriculum and assessment should be blurred and assessment should be taking place continuously.
- The best assessment has a strong human touch because it involves a range of people (teachers, support staff, pupils, peers and possibly parents).
- Teaching students how to learn, how to think and how to be intelligent in as many ways as possible is the main goal of education.
- Not all learning can be assessed in a standardised manner.

- The pupil should be seen as an active creator of their own knowledge and their capacity to do this should be a key part of the assessment process.
- The main consideration in the assessment process should be to help teachers teach more effectively and to help pupils improve their life chances.
- Assessment should be used to celebrate and enhance pupils' learning, to deepen understanding and to aid the transfer of knowledge and skills from one area to another and into everyday living.
- Assessment structures should be based upon what we now understand about the development of the human brain, thinking skills and the relationship between the curriculum and real life.
- The best assessment systems should provide learners with an understanding of self.
- The best learning and assessment will transform a student as they question, expand and deepen their knowledge and understanding.

Making the shift to classroom-based systems of assessment

The inspirational teacher recognises the need to shift away from more formal testing and assessment systems and move towards multimodal approaches for assessing pupil progress. The words of Campbell, Campbell and Dickinson written in 1992 remain true today:

> Assessing in natural contexts, in familiar environments, and with familiar tools and activities enables pupils to demonstrate their knowledge more effectively than through decontextualised, standardised approaches. The boundaries between assessment and learning begin to dissolve when assessment occurs whilst students are actively engaged in their regular classroom experiences.[126]

Schools therefore need to find appropriate ways of assessing pupil progress – in all aspects of communication, language and literacy, mathematics and ICT. However a drastic shift is needed to develop new forms of evaluation which align with assessment in the real world. The phrase, 'We should measure what we value rather than value what we can measure', has become over-used but to date it has had insufficient impact. Schools will always be assessed on how well they are achieving in reading, writing, mathematics, science and ICT, and this will be against nationally agreed criteria. However our most inspirational schools and their insightful leaders have devised other success criteria that they feel measures their performance better. This has grown from an analysis of pupil needs and is one of the key features of a successful school. After a series of survey inspections relating to curriculum innovation in primary schools in 2008, Ofsted reported that the best schools have:

- A clear philosophy for learning.
- Staff that discussed issues critically.
- The curriculum but not the philosophy was constantly changing.
- A strong sense of locality and the needs of pupils.
- The ability to assess precisely what they value.[127]

But how can this be achieved?

Assessing personal learning and thinking skills

The first way in which this should be done is to return to the personal learning and thinking skills which were explored in Chapter 1 and consider how we can develop a rigorous approach to assessment that will aid the development of seamless learning across all phases. To date no effective measurement scales have been produced and this needs to be remedied. Teachers and pupils should know about progress within the six personal learning and thinking skills and what needs to be done next. When teachers are sharing the learning objectives with their class they should also clearly state which of the identified personal learning and thinking skills will be developed and used within the rich learning activities that have been planned.

The appendix near the end of this book provides a measurement tool for each of the six personal learning and thinking skills under five phases. Phase 1 relates broadly to children in the foundation stage. Phase 2 relates to Key Stage 1. Phase 3 to lower Key Stage 2. Phase 4 relates to upper Key Stage 2 and Phase 5 is aimed at pupils in Key Stage 3. The materials could help provide that elusive continuity across all phases. The statements would be most useful if used across a learning community or cluster of schools in a drive to improve continuity and progression – and provide that elusive seamless education.

Tales of Inspirational Practice

The Learning Skills Curriculum

The curriculum meets the needs of pupils extremely well. The energy that the school has put into remodelling the curriculum to make it relevant, creative and alive for pupils has been instrumental in helping teachers to raise standards. The curriculum makes a significant contribution to the promotion of equality and the eradication of intolerance.

This is just one quote from an Ofsted report from one of the schools within the Clifton Partnership Education Action Zone in Rotherham, South Yorkshire. The community of schools have focused considerable attention on developing their 'Learning Skills Curriculum' for the last few years. Like QCDA, the schools have identified six generic learning skills. Whilst these broadly align with those provided nationally, a far greater emphasis is placed on the absolute importance of communication and language. The schools have worked on Lev Vygotsky's theory that language is a primary psychological tool which transforms social experience into higher mental processes. The six skills identified are:

1. communication
2. working with others
3. critical and creative thinking
4. problem solving
5. reflective learning
6. resilience.

The schools working within the learning community all serve areas of significant social deprivation. To date they have all had successful Ofsted inspections. Further details about this powerful work can be found on their website (http://www.clifton-partnership.org.uk).

Portfolio assessment

Too many schools in the UK have placed far too much emphasis on testing their students. We know that a talented novelist would never set out to produce a great piece of work within a set period of forty-five minutes against the clock in a sterile environment starved of the resources that are normally required. They will plan, draft and redraft. They will demonstrate pride and perseverance until the task is completed. We all know this to be true but the reality of tests is that they are cheap and easy to administer, so they remain high profile even though they may not produce an accurate measure of a pupil's ability. The very nature of testing is that it primarily highlights the gaps in a child's learning and what they can't do rather than their strengths. So why not focus on the learner's best work?

The portfolio is a highly personalised approach to assessment. Pupils build up collections of their best work. It can be used to demonstrate academic progress and skill development. It allows teachers, pupils and peers to celebrate achievement by annotating the work. Emily Grady observes:

> The most obvious benefit of this type of assessment is that most of the contents of the portfolio are actual pieces of student work, not approximations supplied by a score on a standardised test. The portfolio represents a range of efforts and tangible achievements; it presents a learning history. In a well designed portfolio system, the student and staff select the pieces of work to be included. The student has the chance to revise it, perfect it, evaluate it and explain it. It is different from work completed just to fulfil an assessment or written only for the teacher's eyes; a piece created for the portfolio bears a piece of the student's identity. It represents the student in a concrete and authentic way that a test score can not do.[128]

Those of you who have been involved in monitoring the quality of teaching may well have seen, and been suspicious of, colleagues who seem to be able to deliver a high quality lesson when they are being observed when other self-evaluation strategies highlight weaknesses. For example, it is often during data trawls and pupil interviews, and especially during work scrutiny exercises, that weaknesses in teaching and learning come to the surface. The use of portfolios builds from this methodology but focuses on the positive inspirational learning that has taken place rather than the negative.

The portfolio model of assessment of learning matches real-world practice. It is obvious why an artist or photographer will present a portfolio of their best endeavours, but increasingly tradesmen carry photographs of their best work alongside references from contented customers. Is it not true that the websites of many businesses are portfolios of the very best they can do to show what they are capable of producing? In this context the portfolio is a key instrument in building confidence because it focuses on success. The same is true when they are used as an assessment tool in schools. They can be an integral part of the assessment process because learners are constantly receiving feedback. Pupils gain confidence by the acknowledgement of their strengths, get an insight into how to improve and then plan how to bring these improvements to fruition.

Inspirational teachers will always want – and persevere to get – the best out of their pupils and will therefore want to work alongside learners to produce portfolios that:

- Tell the learning journey over a period of time (it could be a year or a term/half term if it is a portfolio that reflects a thematic cross-curricular study).

- Provide regular evidence of self-reflection and self-evaluation and especially learner-annotated comments when significant strides have been made in learning or when a child feels they have excelled and produced their best piece of work in that subject/aspect to date.

- Include the teacher's assessment of the progress being made and what needs to be done next, both in the context of the key knowledge, skills and understanding with communication, language and literacy, mathematics and ICT. It also includes the teacher's assessment of progress within QCDA's generic personal learning and thinking skills identified earlier in this chapter.

- Incorporate peer observations and evaluations for the areas identified above.

- Include evidence of the learning process including first plans, early drafts or even photographs of the learning process as well as the final product.

- Incorporate parental comments and evaluations for the areas identified above.

- Reflect learning that has been carried out both independently and collaboratively.

- Provide evidence of when a target has been met.

- Include additional work that may have been voluntarily carried out away from the classroom.

For genuine success the ongoing construction of the portfolio is essential. Pupils and teachers should be working in true partnership in order to be constantly adding inspirational samples of work that reflect true endeavour. Regular meaningful dialogue between the pupil and the teacher is essential in order to promote high standards and expectations. As part of this dialogue teachers also should be regularly selecting samples of each child's best work to share with others. This could be through celebratory assemblies, class discussions, school magazines and newsletters or displays.

When the process is carried out rigorously it will promote responsibility, pride and perseverance. This is so important. As a school inspector I have viewed far too many folders of pupils' work and exercise books that are filled with unfinished tasks which will have left children with a sense of feeling unfulfilled. The use of portfolios encourages pupils to demonstrate how they have learned both independently and in collaboration with others. The portfolios will reflect creativity and originality of thought. Youngsters will be able to show examples of new learning and how learning has been transferred into new areas of life. Additionally school leadership teams should be making even wider use of the portfolios in order to ensure that high levels of inspirational teaching and learning are taking place across the school. They should be used to check the appropriateness of the following areas.

The quantity of work: Portfolios will give a clear indication of how much high quality work is being produced within a school and how often children are making significant gains in their learning. It will give information about the balance of inspirational work generated within each subject or aspect area. Within critical areas such as children's literacy work there should be evidence of regular and purposeful opportunities for children to record across a range of genres. Important information can also be extracted about the quality of teaching and the extent to which the range of assessment foci have been covered. There should also be clear evidence of how regularly children are applying their learning in mathematics in real life situations. School leaders should also be able to see clearly how frequently ICT is being used to extend and enhance learning.

The quality of presentation: School leaders should use the portfolios to establish whether there is an appropriate level of pride in the children's work. Information can also be obtained about the quality of teaching within the basic skill of handwriting. They should also establish whether children are developing the skills of presenting their work in a range of ways that are appropriate to the task.

The quality of the activities: This book is built around the basic premise that inspirational teachers create inspirational pupils through the focused rich and vivid experiences and activities they provide for pupils. Portfolios provide an analysis of how this ideal is being achieved and enables school leaders to establish:

- Whether the activities have been inspirational, appropriate, purposeful and well matched to the learning intentions.
- Whether there is enough emphasis being placed on the process of learning as well as the outcome.
- If the balance between directed, independent and collaborative work is appropriate.
- The degree to which tasks have been open ended.
- The impact of any intervention programmes that a child might have accessed.

The level of challenge: The portfolios should be cross-referenced to other assessment information such as the school's tracking system to ensure that children have received a stimulating level of challenge that has been achievable. A simple technique when looking at a child's mathematical work could be to see if there is an appropriate balance between correct and incorrect answers.

The level of differentiation: Analysing a selection of portfolios will provide school leaders with information about the quality of differentiation. Whilst some tasks will be differentiated by outcome based on the level at which the child is functioning, other information will also become apparent. This will include the level of expectation placed on the different groups of pupils, the range of resources and support materials provided, how additional adults have used support learning and how the learning of more able pupils has been extended.

Progress through the year and transfer of learning: The portfolio should provide information at a glance on the extent of improvement from the earliest to more recent examples. Portfolios should provide evidence about the extent to which there is increased challenge when an aspect of work such as a genre of writing is revisited. School leaders should be able to establish the degree to which pupils are being encouraged to transfer learning from one area to another. Portfolios should also be used to cross-reference the assessed work within them to the information entered within tracking systems in order to check for accuracy.

Marking and feedback: Monitoring portfolios will allow leadership teams to establish:

- Whether the teacher's marking has been geared to the learning intentions.
- The degree to which the strengths have been successfully celebrated.
- Whether ways forward have been identified.
- Evidence of effective self or peer evaluation taking place.
- The impact of previous feedback.
- Whether school policies are being followed.

Seamless education: When leadership teams analyse the portfolios of the best work it will give them a clear insight into the extent to which there is genuine continuity and progression and the extent to which school policies are being embedded.

Tales of Inspirational Practice

Portfolios: a different model

The pride that goes into the portfolios at Andy's school is phenomenal. The practice is well established although it has constantly been reshaped over the years. The idea first stemmed from an Ofsted inspection many years ago which criticised the way in which work scrutiny was carried out. As a consequence the school started to build up portfolios which modelled the work taking place within curriculum subjects. At this stage the portfolios represented the range of work within a subject, samples of levelled work from lower, average and higher attaining pupils, examples of planning, digital photographs taken whilst the lessons were in progress and examples of how changes were made to the teaching of the subject.

As time moved on the school shifted away from a subject-based model towards one whereby each class produced a portfolio which told a detailed story of what was happening in each class during every term. In each portfolio are samples of work from pupils in each subject. The folder represents the best the class can produce and the children strive to get their work into the portfolio. The children add their own comments on the work they have produced as well as grading it using a traffic light system. The portfolios contain work from all the ability groups. The portfolios also include information around pupil progress, how many children have reached their targets, digital photographs which depict the learning process, samples of school planning and evaluations of the work being carried out.

The portfolios are produced almost as a labour of love. They are not seen as another chore to be squeezed into the busy life of teachers. They form a celebration of the wonderful things achieved by a teacher and the talented children in his or her care. However beyond the celebratory factors the portfolios are used for a variety of other purposes. They form a key part of the discussions during performance management reviews and other members of the staff use them as a library of ideas. Many aspects of the portfolio are made available during parents' meetings – and finally they have silenced Ofsted who made the initial criticism.

Our best teachers have three great fears. The first of these is anonymity because they are individuals who thrive on the opportunity to do it their way. They will share with others and learn from others but have no desire to be clones of each other. It is therefore essential that school leaders recognise and acknowledge the strengths of their best teachers. This process is like putting money in the bank because it pays back with interest. However strong teachers will immediately recognise faint praise and therefore it has to be based on strong assessment structures. This takes us to the second great fear of inspirational teachers which is a lack of accountability and for this reason they welcome and embrace assessment whilst poor teachers despise it and seek to denigrate it. Inspirational teachers relish rigorous assessment structures because they need to know how well their learners are progressing and how they are performing professionally. The third great fear is irrelevance. Our best practitioners will only work at their best when they know they are providing an educational diet that will make a difference to the children in their care, and that is why the assessment structures must measure the right elements. Our best teachers know the absolute importance of assessment but they recognise that at present we are not getting it right.

This chapter started with a quotation from the Ministry of Education written in 1959 which raised concerns about an over-reliance on testing. The people responsible for our schools failed to listen to this advice. They could have taken us a long way down the route of transforming assessment. Let us go back to the same chapter of that dated text. This time it is promoting the use of pupil reviews:

> The review should take the form of a teacher looking back at what a child has achieved over a significant period of time – all he has written, the books he has read, the things he has made, his advance in speech, his management of himself and of social situations, his powers of concentration and persistence, and the way he uses his body and limbs. The value and completeness of such a review depends, of course, on the teacher having, in some form, a record which makes the picture clear at least to him. If others, besides the child's own teacher contribute, so much the better. Such cumulative reviews as this, though they may not be amenable to expression in precise terms, give opportunities for

human understanding, with which no formal test can compete, and they are the kind of statement most appropriate to a professional estimate of young children's progress.[129]

Those of us involved in education today believe it is fast paced and we all run at ninety miles an hour. When we read this recommendation, fifty years on, we realise that insufficient progress has been made in how we assess our pupils. Many of the principles promoted here should be a routine part of school life by now. Politicians have always been too scared to make the changes that are really needed and thereby actually slow down educational reform. As a consequence we constantly get pulled back to a very traditional view that children learn best when they are sat alone behind a desk working from textbooks and worksheets and when their progress is regularly tested. It is inspirational teachers who will bring about true change to our assessment structures. Are you up for the challenge?

Overheard in the Classroom

Michael: What level is my writing at now, Miss?

Teacher: You are a Level 2C.

Michael: Is that good?

Teacher: You are working really hard.

Michael: But is a 2C good now I am seven years old?

Teacher: You have done some lovely work.

Michael: But is a Level 2C good?

Teacher: You always do your homework.

Michael: But is a Level 2C good for the end of Key Stage 1?

Teacher: No, it means you are just below the level you should be at.

Michael: I have tried hard and now I don't think I will ever be average.

Teacher (to herself): There has to be a better way.

Chapter 8

Inspirational Teachers, Inspirational Classrooms

The mediocre teacher tells
The good teacher explains
The superior teacher demonstrates
The great teacher inspires.

William Arthur Ward[130]

Overheard in the Classroom

Mr Keating: I have a secret for you boys. We don't read and write poetry just to be cute. We read it because we are members of the human race. Poetry, romance, beauty and love are what we stay alive for ... And you may contribute a verse. What will your verse be?

From *Dead Poets Society* (dir. Peter Weir, 1989)

The Prologue

Fred (Part 2)

Do you remember the story at the start of Chapter 6? It was about a little boy called Fred whose experiences in life from keeping bees and pigeons, to going on shopping trips and visiting York and Malham led to profound learning. Then a learned educationalist who visited Fred tried to reproduce this learning through textbooks until he began to entertain a horrible suspicion that the reverse process did not work. In other words, whereas Fred grew in understanding because he started with the experience and read to feed the interest which derived from it, those children who started with the reading failed to develop understanding because the interest was not there. The learning was in a vacuum unrelated to the context of the lives that absorbed them.

But the learned educationalist pushed his suspicions aside and said: 'The facts derived from books are making no impact because they are not being effectively taught. It is ineffective teachers who cannot impart the facts who are causing the trouble. What we want is some way of ensuring more teachers impart more facts more efficiently. We will have external examiners who will set tests to find out whether the children have learned the facts. Those who have not had the facts imparted to them efficiently will fail to pass the tests and when lists are published the incompetence of the bad fact imparters will be revealed to the world and that will ensure they impart better facts in the future.'

But before the examinations had taken place, the learned educationalist died. Therefore he never learned whether or not the sound learning of facts about pigeons, bees, flowers, vegetables, York and Gordale, produced the same understanding in the mass of children that the practical experience of them had given to Fred on his island with his mother, father, aunt and uncle.

Once this machinery had been put into motion it went on turning. Hundreds of other people started to write books full of more and more facts and these were forced into millions of children and the capacity of the children to disgorge them at will was tested by thousands of examiners. And what was forgotten was that all of this started in an attempt to deliver understanding that derives from experience to those who have not had the experience.

In due course a few inspirational teachers came to the fore and they took a look at what was happening and they started to redress the balance. They recognised the importance of providing experiences and bringing excitement into the classroom. They saw the need to take the children to York and Gordale. They knew that the best learning required an emotional involvement. They knew that the future lay in providing children with fewer facts and encouraging them to find out more and more for themselves.

And the influence of those inspirational teachers began to spread – but they need more recruits. Are you ready to join? If so read on!

It's the classroom that counts

It was once stated that 'every child is a locked door'. Some teachers have the key, others search for the keys and others simply don't even look. Another famous observer once wrote that 'all children are gifted but some open their packages quicker than others'. Inspirational teachers are passionate practitioners who seek to aid this process by putting their whole heart, mind and soul into their work and bringing learning to life:

> Good teaching is not just a matter of being efficient, developing competence, mastering technique and possessing the right kind of knowledge. Good teaching also involves emotional work. It is

> infused with desire, pleasure, mission, creativity, challenge and
> joy. Good teaching is a profoundly emotional activity.[131]

Our best teachers regard teaching and learning as an emotional activity because
they are driven by a moral imperative which is deeply energising. Michael Fullan argues that if you scratch a good teacher you find a moral purpose.[132] So
will you go the extra mile for the children in your care and help the magic of
childhood be enhanced by electrifying learning opportunities? I hope so. Our
profession needs you and it needs you now, because it is classroom practice
that really makes a difference to children's chances. Compulsory primary education has now been with us for almost 150 years and sometimes it is difficult
to assess how far we have progressed over that period. At the time of writing
considerable attention is being placed on narrowing gaps wherever they exist.
These gaps include the difference between the attainment of boys and girls,
of white British pupils and those who speak English as a second language
and those pupils who are entitled to free school meals and those who are not.
However many school leaders may be focusing on the wrong gap to narrow.
Too much of the variation in pupil outcomes is due to what happens in the
classroom. The quality of what happens on a daily basis is too variable. Some
children experience inspirational teachers and some don't – and it shows.

> Recent research on the impact of schools on student learning
> leads to the conclusion that 8–19% of the variation in student
> learning outcomes lies between schools and a further amount
> of up to 55% of the variation in individual learning outcomes
> between classrooms within schools.[133]

> Studies of school effectiveness and school improvement indicate
> that the classroom effect is greater than the whole school effect
> in explaining student progress.[134]

In 2000 Jonathan Smith observed: 'Children and pupils see much more of us
and in us than we would like to imagine. They study us, as they study their
books and often with considerably more interest. They read us. They see our
body language and see through it; they spot where we scratch ourselves, they
pick up the giveaway expressions in our eyes, they work out our values and
smile at our evasions, they perceive our natures and assess our flash points.

No actor on the stage is more carefully studied.'[135] His comments are very true. Children know how to respond to each individual teacher. They know who has high expectations of their own performance and who doesn't. Andrew Hargreaves summed the situation up eloquently when he wrote: 'It is what teachers think, what teachers believe and what teachers do at the level of the classroom that ultimately shapes the kind of learning that young people get.'[136]

So it is all down to the individual teacher in his or her classroom. Experience tells me that there are two extremes in the classrooms our children encounter. There are those that I describe as hopeful and those I describe as woeful, and a whole range of others that lie between the two.

Hopeful teachers in hopeful classrooms

Enter into our best classrooms and you will find a buzz from the electricity being generated. Children will be totally absorbed in rich learning experiences that are carefully planned to fulfil a range of learning objectives, some of which could be academic and others are based on the skills and attitudes young people will need to pass successfully through life. Time will fly, nobody will look at their watches and there will be sighs of disappointment when the lesson draws to a close. Children will share their work with pride and celebrate the successes of each other. The teacher will have a strong set of values that the children are fully aware of, either because they are explicitly shared with the pupils or somehow they are naturally absorbed into the ether of the classroom. These values include a belief that:

- There are many different ways to learn and many ways to record learning.
- Effective learners take responsibility for their own learning and believe they can achieve and succeed.
- Learning takes place within a social context and the learners believe they have a duty to help each other achieve.
- Speech and dialogue are key processes within learning but the balance between teacher talk and pupil talk is appropriate and natural.
- Mistakes are an integral part of the learning process and are made in a supportive context without fear of disparagement.

- Effort is rewarded within the learning process because of the teacher's high quality skills with ongoing assessment.
- There is no tension between pupils and teachers.
- Positive exchanges predominate and children are spurred on to even greater achievements.

However there is an opposite of this situation.

Woeful classrooms in woeful schools

You will know when you are in the woeful classroom environment and you will also know you won't want to stop there for long. The first and most striking feature is that teacher talk dominates because the teacher sees it as their job to impart learning. It is as though it is the only methodology they understand or are able to work to. Much of the learning is carried out alone and often in silence. The teacher sees it as important that the child should get the learning right first time and if they don't it is the child's fault. Indeed they believe that some children are not good at learning. In the woeful classroom there can be regular moments of stress and tension between the teacher and pupils and often between pupils and pupils. Shouting can occur along with instances of mocking amongst the children. We probably all recognise this type of class-room. Fortunately they are becoming fewer in number. However if you get a critical mass of woeful classrooms within a school you potentially get a woeful school.

You will also know when you walk into the woeful school. In the entrance there will probably be one or more pupils working in silence or standing by a wall because they have been sent out of lessons. The displays will look tired or out of date and there will be no noticeboard to formally welcome you or friendly smiling and welcoming photographs of the staff. You will get no sense of the school's achievements or any awards they hold (maybe because they have none). Notices will abound stating what pupils are not allowed to do. Even when the assembly is a positive experience it will probably finish off with the children being reminded about rules they have broken. You will get a clear sense that decisions are taken based on what the staff need rather than what is in the best interests of the children.

Celebrate the pratfalls

Maybe woeful classrooms in woeful schools exist simply because teachers lack imagination. Alternatively it could be because the teacher can only teach in the way in which they were taught. Perhaps the teachers are too frightened to 'let the children go' and make their own choices or take responsibility for their own learning because they fear they will experience a 'pratfall'.

But what is a pratfall, I hear you ask? It is one of those situations where you metaphorically fall flat on your face. Inspirational teachers clearly take risks by making bold decisions in order to produce exciting activities that produce inspirational responses from their learners. Whilst they recognise that being creative with children and their learning requires very thorough planning, they also know if it can go wrong ... it will go wrong. Therefore they take the ultimate care when planning. You will have heard the phrase 'you make your own luck in life'. Anthony Robbins wrote, 'the meeting of preparation with opportunity generates the offspring we call luck'. It is not the case that some teachers are luckier than others. Our best teachers have a formula that serves them well in their work and it guarantees successful outcomes.

High Quality Preparation + Risk Taking = Success and Good Fortune

The formula is transportable to all areas of life. Follow it well and I believe you will experience success.

Many teachers fail to take risks with their lessons because they fear that they will have a pratfall. As long as they are not occurring all the time I think the occasional howler should be celebrated. Teachers in the twenty-first century live and work in a world of high accountability. All of this leads to a danger that individuals pull back within themselves and reject risk taking in their teaching. Teachers who take risks should be encouraged even if it does occasionally go wrong.

When you experience a pratfall you may feel stupid but actually they can be extremely beneficial. Firstly the analytical practitioner will examine what went wrong and learn from their practice. Secondly occasional pratfalls have actually been proven to increase your likeability especially if you take responsibility for your errors and create a sense of humility. Richard Wiseman, whose writing introduced me to the concept of the pratfall, quotes the example of the former US president J. F. Kennedy:

> In 1961, Kennedy ordered troops to invade Cuba at the Bay of Pigs. The operation was a fiasco. And historians still view the decision as a huge military blunder. However, a national survey taken after the failed invasion actually liked Kennedy more despite his disastrous decision. Two factors could account for this seemingly strange finding. Kennedy didn't make excuses or pass the buck for this botched operation, but instead immediately took full responsibility. Also, until that point, Kennedy had been seen as a superhero – a charming, handsome, powerful man who could do no wrong. The Bay of Pigs made him appear far more human and likeable.[137]

When a teacher experiences a pratfall they have two alternatives. The first is to pull back, stop taking risks and play safe for the future. Our inspirational teachers don't do this because they are strongminded and determined. They take the second alternative and learn from their mistakes and set off once more in the pursuit of excellence.

Pursuing excellence

Many of the best teachers I have spoken to talk about the influence other excellent practitioners have had on them. They have used the skills of these people as a model to pursue excellence. Try it for yourself: think of a teacher who you really admire. Firstly consider the beliefs they hold about teaching. Don't rush these thoughts and make sure you get absolute clarity. Secondly reflect on the values they espouse in the classroom through the interactions with the learners. Thirdly consider the thinking steps they go through in their planning and how ongoing assessment in lessons influences their practice. Finally think about their actual behaviour during lessons including the body language and physiology they adopt. Then simply model the excellence you have just analysed only doing it 20% better. The process is reflected in the diagram opposite.

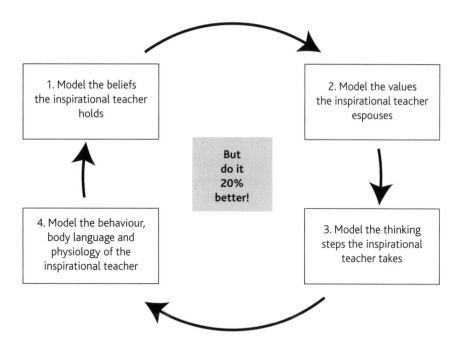

High quality teaching requires practitioners who are confident in their ability. To teach well you have to feel good about yourself. Our best teachers constantly seek to improve themselves, but don't always take the time to reflect on how they are developing their pedagogical expertise. Teachers work in a world that is often dominated by data and the need to prove their effectiveness in terms of pupil progress through National Curriculum levels. As a consequence they may seek the next short-term strategy that will have an impact on their school's results and which will help them to secure the best possible outcomes in the league tables. These high accountability stakes build up a sense of fear which could prevent a teacher from being bold and imaginative in their teaching.

Here is my tip to help build up the confidence to take risks. Imagine the time has reached 3.45 p.m. on a Friday. The classroom is finally quiet, apart from the distant sound of the school cleaners. Just pause and record one final piece of information. Although it will take just minutes, don't rush at it. I want you to invest your professionalism in the process. Use a high quality notebook and pen and note down how your practice has improved over the week, which people you have affected positively and those you might need to thank because they have contributed to your success. Finally, if you think you had a pratfall, consider how you will plan your comeback as an inspirational teacher or school leader the following week. When you have completed the task and you are about to close the classroom door behind you, look back one more time and remember the best bit of the school week. You will then go home buoyant to enjoy the weekend and return the following week feeling ready to conquer the world. Then when you are next asked to demonstrate evidence of your professional development simply slide the notebook in front of the person opposite you. The activity works just as well for head teachers as it does for classroom practitioners, and heads can also pass their notebooks to the sternest of Ofsted inspectors as a record of how the school has improved week by week. The format below may help the process.

What improvements have I made? *Make a list of five improvements from the trivial to the significant*
Which people have I affected positively? *These could be both learners or adults within the learning community*
Who do I need to thank? *Never take those people who help you for granted. Thanking them is like investing capital in the bank because it pays future dividends*
Pratfalls Have I had any pratfalls? What was I trying to achieve when I had the pratfall? Was it the right thing to achieve? How will I pick myself up, dust myself down and start all over again?

And finally.... some thoughts to see you on your way

We should never doubt the power of positive words. The use of the strategy described above can be extremely powerful and may spur us on to perform even better. Sometimes the spoken word lacks clarity and what we write is more focused and memorable. This takes me to one final influence on the inspirational teacher – and that is the power of quotations. Thomas Love Peacock wrote: 'a book that furnishes no quotations, is ... no book – it is a plaything'.[138] At one end of the spectrum quotations have the power to help us make it through the working day or inspire us to change the lives of children. The right words directed to the right person at the right time can change anything from the course of our habits or relationships to governments and wars. In school, we were taught that adding quotations to our essays adds credibility. In life, quotes can give our soul the spark it needs to revive our passions and persist in the face of immeasurable difficulties.

If we wish to succeed in life we should never underestimate the power of words, especially quotations. Carry one in your bag, write them on the classroom whiteboard or find one for every week of the year to write in your diary. They are mere words but they can offer considerable strength. When it all goes wrong, rely on your personal selection of quotes. This book has used some of my favourite quotations from educationalists, scientists, actors, philosophers, comedians, fictitious cartoon characters and religious figures. I urge all teachers and school leaders to build up their own collection because they can be deeply energising. With a set of quotations you will never be alone and anything will become possible because you have the power to make it so – and you can quote me on that.

And so I will leave you with three final thoughts to help you create inspirational teachers and inspirational learners. You might like to add them to your own collection of empowering and energising quotations:

> Teachers do what they believe in extraordinarily well, but what they are told to do merely to a mediocre standard.[139]
>
> John Abbott

Those of us who work in the field of education are neither bank clerks who have a little discretion nor assembly line workers whose actions are largely repetitive. Each child we teach is wonderfully unique and each requires us to use in our work that most exquisite of human capacities, the ability to make judgements in the absence of rules. Although good teaching uses routines, it is seldom routine. Good teaching depends on sensibility and imagination. It courts surprise. It profits from caring. In short, good teaching is an artistic affair.[140]

Elliot W. Eisner

Of some of our teachers, we remember their foibles and mannerisms, of others their kindness and encouragement, or their fierce devotion to standards of work that we probably did not share at the time. And of those who inspired us most we remember what they cared about, and that they cared about us, and the person we might become. It is the quality of caring about ideas and values, this fascination with the potential growth within people, this depth and fervour about doing things well and striving for excellence, that comes closest to what I mean in describing a 'passionate teacher'.[141]

Robert L. Fried

Overheard in the Classroom

Mr Keating: Gather ye rose buds whilst you may. In Latin we would say *carpe diem*. What does that mean?

Pitts: He's in a hurry.

Mr Keating: It means 'seize the day'. Boys you must seize the day and make your lives extraordinary … No matter what anyone tells you your words and ideas could change the world.

From Dead Poets Society (dir. Peter Weir, 1989)

May your words and ideas also change the world. Good luck.

Appendix

Assessing Pupils' Personal Learning and Thinking Skills

The grids below are referred to in Chapters 1 and 7. They seek to promote continuity and progression in the key personal learning and thinking skills children will need to develop if they are to lead a fulfilled life in the twenty-first century – as reflective learners, team workers, creative thinkers, independent enquirers, self managers and effective participators.

Phase 1 equates to the levels that would be expected in the foundation stage.
Phase 2 equates to the levels that would be expected in Key Stage 1.
Phase 3 equates to the levels that would be expected in lower Key Stage 2.
Phase 4 equates to the levels that would be expected in upper Key Stage 2.
Phase 5 equates to the levels that would be expected in Key Stage 3.

Reflective Learners

Reflective Learners (Phase 1)	Score
I can tell you what activities are on offer.	
I can choose an activity and select my resources with an adult.	
I can say what I am good at.	
I can play, listen and talk.	
I can give reasons for my ideas.	
I can say what I have done at the end of a task.	
I can say whether I worked well.	
I can recount my experiences to an adult.	
I know how to be fair.	
I know that it is important to try hard.	

Reflective Learners (Phase 2)	Score
I can decide how to do my work with friends and adults.	
With my friends I decide which resources I need and get them for myself.	
I can say which bits of work I find easy or difficult.	
I can describe some of the different ways in which we learn.	
I reflect at the end of a task.	
I can say which things I did that worked well in a task and what I might do differently next time.	
I sometimes see links to previous experiences.	
I understand that I need to be positive to perform well.	
I know it is important to make the right choices in my work and in school.	

Reflective Learners (Phase 3)	Score
I look for two different ways to carry out a task and then choose one of them.	
Independently, I decide on what resources I need and then access them from the classroom or elsewhere in school.	
I can say what you need to get better at (including my personal targets).	
I am aware of the different learning styles.	
I plan at which point to reflect on a task.	
I reflect on the task and suggest alternative approaches as necessary.	
I can use pre-existing skills and knowledge (sometimes when prompted).	
I can keep trying even when things are hard.	
I understand that using my initiative can be scary.	
I want to make a positive difference.	

Reflective Learners (Phase 4)	Score
I recognise the need to break down problems into steps.	
When planning I look for possible alternatives and eventualities.	
I can recognise the strengths and weaknesses in my plans.	

(continued)

Reflective Learners (Phase 4)	Score
I know about the different learning styles and can choose a suitable learning style for the activity I am doing.	
I plan appropriate places in my work to stop, reflect and revise if necessary.	
I can use reflections on my work to plan my future learning.	
I use my previous learning to help me complete tasks.	
I reflect on how well I have completed a task and my level of understanding.	
I am excited by new challenges and the opportunities they provide.	
When considering issues with an ethical dimension I try to make a difference.	
I understand that using my initiative can sometimes be scary.	

Reflective Learners (Phase 5)	Score
I can break down problems into manageable steps and draw up an action plan which includes a variety of techniques.	
I plan out the resources I need before commencing a task.	
I can describe the skills and qualities I possess and how I am working to address weaknesses.	
I am flexible in my use of learning styles and select which ones to use according to the task.	
I plan when to stop and reflect on my progress in a task and revise my plans when necessary.	
Within my learning I make increasingly complex or abstract links to learning elsewhere.	
I can accurately assess the quality of my own learning.	
I do not focus on negative things unnecessarily and can move on.	
I use a positive attitude to get the best out of every situation.	
I can reflect on whether my actions have an ethical dimension and make decisions as a responsible citizen.	

Team Workers

Team Workers (Phase 1)	Score
I take part in groups (verbally or non-verbally).	
I copy the verbal and non-verbal responses of others.	
With an adult present I listen for a period of time in a group.	
I encourage others to take turns (e.g. pass items within a circle).	
I enjoy working in a group for playground games or in a turn-taking game.	
I can work alone.	
I can take a role in role play.	

Team Workers (Phase 2)	Score
I contribute verbally within a group.	
I tell other people when they have done well.	
I know and can say what you need to do to be an effective listener.	
I help others participate and show or tell them what they need to do.	
I work well in group activities.	
I know that sometimes I have to work on my own and sometimes in a group.	
I can allocate and adopt roles within play/role-play situations.	
I can share.	
I know what a leader is.	
I sometimes act as the leader.	
I know that the choices I make will have an impact on others.	

Team Workers (Phase 3)	Score
I take part in a team taking account of the needs to let others contribute.	
I notice when other members of the group are working well.	
I listen well and know when others are listening well.	
I communicate well in familiar groups.	
I work well with groups that do not include my usual friends.	

(continued)

Team Workers (Phase 3)	Score
I know when I have made a positive contribution to a team.	
I sometimes take the lead within a team.	
I choose when it will be best to work in a group and when it would be better to work alone.	
I understand that teams work best when jobs are allocated.	

Team Workers (Phase 4)	Score
I show respect when I work in collaboration with others.	
I can describe the skills of others and try to put them into practice.	
I am usually an effective listener and respond well to the person who is speaking.	
I have an understanding of how other people in a group feel.	
I can persuade people that I have a good idea	
I make decisions having listened to others.	
I can commit to ideas that are not my own.	
I can confidently lead a familiar group.	
I can work alone or with small groups to contribute to a piece of work.	
I will happily take on a role within a group.	

Team Workers (Phase 5)	Score
I can be engaged, self-motivated and committed to making group work successful.	
I am willing to refine and develop my skills through observing others.	
I am an effective listener who filters information and responds appropriately whilst taking full account of the needs of others.	
I understand democracy and my responsibility to a group.	
I know when it is appropriate to work with others to seek a solution.	
I can combine the independent and collaborative elements within a task.	
I can take up roles and assign roles within a group and revise them along the way.	

(continued)

Team Workers (Phase 5)	Score
I can reflect upon the strengths of a good leader.	
I can confidently lead an unfamiliar group.	
I take part in correctly evaluating how my team has worked.	

Creative Thinkers

Creative Thinkers (Phase 1)	Score
I happily share my ideas with an adult.	
I can sort things observing similarities and differences by using colour, shape, size, etc. and sometimes use a less obvious classification.	
I am willing to try new activities.	
I am happy to have a go and not worry about being wrong.	
I use my imagination when playing (e.g. making up stories or events).	
I like to solve problems.	
I like making things.	
I like to play and experiment with resources and materials.	
I sometimes ask 'why' questions.	
I sometimes say how I would do my work differently next time.	

Creative Thinkers (Phase 2)	Score
I like to give ideas to my teacher or group.	
I make connections through play and experimentation.	
I explore and experiment with resources and materials.	
I ask questions about how and why things work or seek to dismantle them to learn more.	
I make links between previous learning and experiences with adult support.	
I understand that trying new things is taking a risk.	
I sometimes think of more than one way to do my task.	

(continued)

Creative Thinkers (Phase 2)	Score
I like to make things from my own ideas.	
I will remain patient when the solution is not readily to hand.	
I sometimes think in unusual or amusing ways.	
I investigate objects and materials using my senses.	
I suggest changes to my work using adult support.	

Creative Thinkers (Phase 3)	Score
I am excited by problems and the challenges they provide and will persevere to reach a conclusion.	
I generate creative ideas drawing upon personal experiences and knowledge.	
I respond well to imaginative ideas.	
I remain patient if solutions are not readily to hand.	
I have the confidence to take calculated risks.	
I get excited by challenges and the opportunities they provide.	
I am prepared to put forward my ideas or answers to a larger group.	
I make connections through play and experimentation.	

Creative Thinkers (Phase 4)	Score
I rise to the challenge when the solution is not clear.	
I can remain focused in activities over a longer period of time to seek solutions.	
I can suggest creative ideas using information from things I have learned in the past.	
I put forward ideas even if they are not the same as others.	
I evaluate my designs and ideas and use my learning to improve them.	
I have the confidence to decide when a risk should be accepted or reduced.	
I like to put original and unique ideas into my work.	
I try alternative and different approaches.	

(continued)

Creative Thinkers (Phase 4)	Score
I sometimes seek to respond to tasks and problems in amusing ways.	
I discover and make connections through play and experimentation.	
I ask 'why', 'how', 'what if' and unusual questions.	

Creative Thinkers (Phase 5)	Score
I use failure as a way of learning what to do differently next time.	
I relish the opportunity to take on new challenges.	
I create plans that anticipate changing circumstances.	
I use my previous learning to create new solutions by 'thinking outside the box'.	
I generate imaginative and unusual approaches to my work that are often very successful and fulfil the desired learning outcome.	
When working in a group I respond well and build upon the imaginative ideas of others to solve real problems in a collaborative manner.	
I regularly try to think differently from others in order to reach a higher level of understanding in my learning.	
I ask complex 'why', 'how', 'what if' and unusual questions which relate to living in the modern world (e.g. How does your personal philosophy compare with people of the past? How can studying a period of history help us with a contemporary issue? What is my personal agenda for achieving cross-cultural understanding?).	

Independent Enquirers

Independent Enquirers (Phase 1)	Score
I am willing to try new activities.	
I like making things and playing/experimenting with new resources.	
I listen carefully so I know what I have got to do.	
In activities I can express my ideas to friends and adults.	
I can use trial and error methods to overcome problems in play situations.	

(continued)

Independent Enquirers (Phase 1)	Score
I test out ideas practically (e.g. press, push, pull a new toy).	
I can tell a known adult what I did.	
I observe and notice similarities and differences through sorting and matching.	
I can say what I have done and how I did it.	
I can say what I have done and how I could do it differently next time.	
During an activity I can tell a known adult what has happened or what I saw.	

Independent Enquirers (Phase 2)	Score
When working with my group I offer ideas.	
I formulate and ask questions with my friends and adults.	
I explore, devise and test ideas using resources and play.	
With help I make links to my previous experiences.	
I recognise when a plan is helpful and can follow it.	
With help I collect information using surveys.	
I keep focused on an activity until I have completed it.	
After carrying out a survey I can offer a conclusion using cause and effect strategies.	
I answer relevant questions about how and why things work.	
I can sort, organise and classify familiar and less familiar objects by comparing and contrasting.	

Independent Enquirers (Phase 3)	Score
I test out ideas practically using a range of methods with adult support.	
I can choose a good way to solve a problem.	
I can generalise from one situation to another.	
I can draw conclusions and explain them.	
I can follow a brief to complete a task.	

(continued)

Independent Enquirers (Phase 3)	Score
I find different ways to show my findings.	
I ask questions about why things happen and how things work and think about how I can find out.	
I use materials and resources to carry out tasks that are set for me to explore cause and effect.	
I use data collecting techniques effectively (e.g. surveys, questionnaires).	
With my teacher I carry out tasks which help me compare and contrast (e.g. life in the 1960s and now, two contrasting locations, two different religions).	

Independent Enquirers (Phase 4)	Score
I listen, filter information and respond appropriately.	
I use thinking pattern maps such as lists, writing frames, webs or Venn diagrams to organise my work.	
I describe a range of methods to test out ideas and select the most appropriate.	
I make reasoned judgements which I can justify.	
I can clarify information systematically.	
I draw conclusions, explain and evaluate in depth.	
I evaluate and learn from my previous experiences.	
In my work I look for cause and effect.	
I compare and contrast in an effective manner.	
I ask relevant questions about why things happen and how things work and discover ways to find out.	
I choose different techniques to collect and organise information (e.g. listing, grouping, ordering).	
I choose from a range of data collecting techniques.	
I predict the answer to a problem before seeking to solve it.	

Independent Enquirers (Phase 5)	Score
I construct hypotheses based upon a wide range of sources and ideas.	
I generate and evaluate a range of options to test hypotheses.	
I make reasoned judgements, deductions and decisions.	
I design and evaluate classification systems and systems for collecting data.	
I predict and justify the answer to a problem before solving it.	
I draw conclusions, make inferences and formulate ideas based upon my findings.	
Where appropriate I transfer the steps of solving a problem into symbolic formulae.	
Through discussion and independently I draw conclusions, make recommendations and am willing to make revisions if necessary.	
I create plans that anticipate changing circumstances.	
I carry out investigations to understand cause and effect (e.g. key historical events, how environmental factors influence human geography).	
I carry out investigations to compare and contrast (e.g. the key features of different cultures, various artists' techniques).	

Self Managers

Self Managers (Phase 1)	Score
I have fun doing tasks.	
I know that I have to behave differently in different settings and at different times.	
I know that I have to do some things for myself.	
I can tell an adult what I have been doing.	
I can describe what I have been doing.	
I can become engaged in tasks which are not of my choice for short periods of time.	
I like to receive praise from adults and know when I have done well.	
When helped by an adult I manage distractions well.	

Self Managers (Phase 2)	Score
I can say what I enjoyed about a task.	
I work very well on the tasks I enjoy.	
I recognise some elements of what I need to do in order to be ready to learn.	
I make links to my previous experiences.	
I can identify what distracted me and can think of ways I could have avoided it.	
I know I have targets and know what some of them are.	
I know that sometimes learning is difficult for all of us.	
I carry out the tasks that I have been set.	
I like to please my teacher and receive rewards.	
I use the resources I have been given to help me to complete tasks.	
With the help of adults I organise the things I need to take home from school and also bring to school.	

Self Managers (Phase 3)	Score
I know which elements of a task I will enjoy.	
I know the behaviours I need in order to be ready to learn.	
I often use things I have learned in the past to help me to complete a task.	
I take actions to avoid distractions and make good use of the time available.	
I know my targets and can say how the task I am carrying out will help me to achieve it.	
I stick at tasks which I do not always enjoy and complete them well.	
I take care in the way in which I present my work.	
I will ask others for support when I need to.	
I will think about the resources I need within the classroom to complete the task and often access them for myself.	
I am motivated by the rewards for completing a task well.	

Self Managers (Phase 4)	Score
I engage well with all learning activities.	
I take all the appropriate actions so that I am ready to learn including taking responsibility for collecting my own resources.	
I regularly reflect on my prior learning and pre-existing skills.	
I recognise potential distractions and take action quickly to limit them.	
I know my targets and what I have to do to achieve them.	
My work reflects pride in terms of presentation and style.	
I persevere and don't focus on negative things and I often keep going for the pleasure it provides rather than external rewards.	
I seek to complete tasks in a way that represents my unique character and personality.	
I complete tasks well and I am proud of my achievements.	
I complete tasks which have a financial element effectively.	

Self Managers (Phase 5)	Score
I enjoy learning because I see it as a strategy for self-improvement.	
I relish the opportunity to take on a challenge and develop new skills.	
I recognise the need to maintain a positive attitude within my learning.	
I take positive actions to address issues which prevent me from learning including avoiding distractions.	
I complete tasks well within the appropriate time scales.	
I collect the resources I need for a task from a widening range of options (e.g. libraries, internet, CD-ROMs).	
I organise my time carefully and always complete longer pieces of work to the appropriate time scale.	
I make increasingly abstract links to prior learning and wider concepts.	
I can describe my long-term goals and know the short-term targets that I need to achieve along the way.	
I take responsibility for setting some of my own targets.	
I know when to seek the support of others and do not see it as failure.	

(continued)

Self Managers (Phase 5)	Score
I know what motivates me and provide my own rewards for sticking at a task.	
When appropriate my work reflects my own unique character (e.g. through the opinions and arguments expressed, the use of empathy or an artistic interpretation).	
I effectively plan and carry out activities which involve financial planning and the need to stick to a budget.	
I am fully aware of the consequences of profit and loss.	

Effective Participators

Effective Participators (Phase 1)	Score
With adults present I listen well for a period of time within a group.	
I respond to what has been said.	
I ask questions of known adults.	
I contribute in small group discussions.	
I can say how something makes me feel.	
I use pictures and writing to communicate.	
I take part in expressive art forms (e.g. being creative, exploring media and materials, creating music and dance, developing imagination).	
I know when I am being fair.	

Effective Participators (Phase 2)	Score
I know the skill that I need to be an effective listener.	
I respond well when speaking and listening with others.	
I formulate and ask questions with peers and adults.	
I speak well within small discussion groups.	
I express my ideas and opinions and can give some reasons for holding them.	
I express some of my ideas in a written or visual form.	

(continued)

Effective Participators (Phase 2)	Score
When working with my teacher I experiment with how ideas can be conveyed through the arts.	
I give encouragement to others.	
I am aware that other people have feelings and I try not to upset them.	
I know when I am being fair and try to make the right choices between right and wrong.	

Effective Participators (Phase 3)	Score
I know what you have to do to be an effective listener and listen for increasing periods of time.	
I enjoy and respond well when interacting with others.	
I make positive contributions during discussions.	
I work with others to reach an agreement.	
I encourage others through the support and feedback that I give them.	
I formulate questions to ask with peers and adults.	
I speak audibly within a discussion group.	
With support I make choices about the most effective method to record information and ideas.	
I recognise similarities and differences between myself and other people.	
I can recognise and label the thoughts, behaviours and feelings of others and try to make people feel good.	
I recognise the causes of other people's emotions and actions.	
I try to make good choices that will help me become a responsible citizen.	

Effective Participators (Phase 4)	Score
I show fairness and consideration to others.	
I am willing to commit to an idea that is not my own.	
If I believe my idea is best I try to persuade others to support my ideas.	
I take responsibility and have self-confidence when completing a task.	
I give constructive support and feedback to others in a helpful way.	

(continued)

Effective Participators (Phase 4)	Score
I recognise similarities and differences between myself and others and know that this is a good thing.	
I take an interest in, watch, listen and learn from other people.	
I can recognise and describe the feelings of others.	
I seek to understand the views of others.	
I can anticipate how others will respond when I do something.	
I know about significant issues that exist and how a responsible citizen should behave.	
I take opportunities to make a difference and to make things better.	
I understand that solving ethical issues often has a financial element.	

Effective Participators (Phase 5)	Score
I am an effective listener who respects the ideas of the person speaking.	
I will sensitively ask challenging supplementary questions to seek greater understanding.	
I enter into extended dialogue with larger groups, sometimes with people other than peers and those I know well.	
I negotiate with others to ensure a good outcome.	
I can broker win-win agreements.	
I can speak to different audiences maintaining their interest.	
I select and use a variety of appropriate methods of communication (e.g. written word, ICT, the arts).	
I anticipate how others will feel and always behave responsibly.	
At appropriate times I help others by giving suitable support and feedback in a sensitive way.	
I make decisions as a responsible person and seek to make a difference for the better.	
I recognise the similarities and differences between myself and others and can use this information responsibly.	

Notes

1. Willy Russell, *Blood Brothers*. London: Methuen, 1983.

2. Catherine Hurley, *Could Do Better: School Reports of the Great and Good*. London: Simon & Schuster, 1997.

3. Sir Peter Lampl writing for The Sutton Trust in 2008. Available at http://www.suttontrust.org.uk

4. Unicef, *Child Poverty in Perspective: An Overview of Child Well-Being in Rich Countries*. Florence: Unicef Innocenti Research Centre, 2007.

5. Ken Boston quoted in 'Exam Strain on Schools'. *The Observer*, 26 March 2006.

6. 'Shift Happens'. Available at http://www.youtube.com/watch?v=ljbI-363A2Q

7. Lord Sandy Leitch, *The Leitch Review of Skills*. London: HMSO, 2006.

8. Ken Robinson, *The Element*. London: Penguin, 2009.

9. Will Ryan, *Leadership with a Moral Purpose*. Carmarthen: Crown House, 2008.

10. *Times Educational Supplement*, 17 July 2009.

11. Guy Claxton, *What's the Point of School?* Oxford: One World Publications, 2008.

12. R. F. Dearden, *The Philosophy of Primary Education*. London: Routledge and Kegan Paul, 1968.

13. Mike Hughes, *And the Main Thing is … Learning: Keeping the Focus on Learning – for Pupils and Teachers (Jigsaw Pieces)*. Cheltenham: Education Training and Support, 2007.

14. Ofsted, *Improving City Schools* (Ref. 222). London: Ofsted, 2000.

15. Antonio R. Damasio, *Descartes' Error: Emotion, Reason, and the Human Brain*. New York: G. P. Putnam's Sons, 1994.

16. J. Z. Young, *Philosophy and the Brain*. Oxford: Oxford University Press, 1997.

17. From evidence submitted to the National Commission on Teaching and America's Future in 1999.

18. Howard Gardner, *The Unschooled Mind*. New York: Basic Books, 1993.

19. 'More Long-Term Migrants to UK'. Available at http://news.bbc.co.uk/1/hi/uk/7574382.stm

20. Robert Putnam, *Bowling Alone, The Collapse and Revival of American Community*. New York: Simon & Schuster, 2000.

21. Daniel Goleman, *Emotional Intelligence: Why It Can Matter More Than IQ*. London: Bloomsbury, 1996.

22. Available at http://www.qcda.org.uk

23. Competition entry entitled 'My Ideal School' in Tim Brighouse and David Woods, *Inspirations*. Stafford: Network Continuum, 2006.

24. *Times Educational Supplement*, 5 March 2010.

25. *Times Educational Supplement*, 12 March 2010.

26. Robin Alexander (ed.), *Children, their World, their Education: Final Report and Recommendations of the Cambridge Primary Review*. London: Routledge, 2010.

27. For further information visit http://www.values-education.com

28. See Julie Duckworth, *The Little Book of Values*. Carmarthen: Crown House, 2008.

29. Ofsted, *Curriculum Innovation in Schools* (Ref. 070097). London: Ofsted, 2009.

30. Ofsted *Learning Outside the Classroom* (Ref. 070219). London: Ofsted, 2009.

31. Daniel Goleman, *Emotional Intelligence: Why It Can Matter More Than IQ*. London: Bloomsbury, 1996.

32. Robert Coles, *The Moral Intelligence of Children*. New York: Random House, 1997.

33. Robin Alexander, *Culture and Pedagogy: International Comparisons in Primary Education*. Oxford and Boston, MA: Blackwell, 2001.

34. Robin Alexander (ed.), *Children, their World, their Education: Final Report and Recommendations of the Cambridge Primary Review*. London: Routledge, 2010.

35. Jonah Lehrer, *The Decisive Moment*. Edinburgh: Canongate, 2009.

36. Richard Gerver, *Creating Tomorrow's Schools Today*. London: Continuum, 2010.

37. Dr W. H. Cockcroft, *Mathematics Counts (The Cockroft Report)*. London: HMSO, 1982. Available at http://www.educationengland.org.uk/documents/cockcroft

38. *Times Educational Supplement*, 5 March 2010.

39. Quoted in Alexander, *Cambridge Primary Review*.

40. Sir Ron Dearing, National Curriculum and Assessment, 1993

41. David Blunkett quoted in Brighouse and Woods, *Inspirations*. Stafford: Network Continuum, 2006.

42. Ministry for Education and Research (Norway): Ministry for Education and Research, 1991.

43. The Singapore Curriculum and Framework 1998.

44. Michael Gove in an interview with *The Times*, 6 March 2010.

45. Unicef, *Child Poverty in Perspective: An Overview of Child Well-Being in Rich Countries*. Florence: Unicef Innocenti Research Centre, 2007.

46. Editorial in *The Independent*, 7 January 2000.

47. Robin Alexander, *Culture and Pedagogy: International Comparisons in Primary Education*. Oxford and Boston, MA: Blackwell, 2001.

48. Ben Page, Chairman, Ipsos MORI Social Research Institute, 'Understanding Learners'. Lecture delivered at Harnessing Technology: Building on Success Conference, Birmingham, 6 November 2007.

49. Quote accredited to E. M. Forster.

50. Susan Cowley, *Getting the Buggers to Think*. London: Continuum Press, 2004.

51. Howard Gardner quoted in Brighouse and Woods, *Inspirations*. Stafford: Network Continuum, 2006

52. See http://www.interculturalstudies.org/faq.html

53. Edward de Bono, *Six Thinking Hats*. Boston, MA: Little, Brown and Company, 1999.

54. Edward de Bono, *Six Action Shoes*. Boston: Harper Collins, 1992.

55. Neil Postman, *The End of Education: Redefining the Value of School*. New York: Knopf, 1996.

56. Edward de Bono's message of the week, 26 February 2007. Available at http://www.edwarddebono.com

57. QCA and the Department for Education and Employment, The National Curriculum, Handbook for Primary Teachers, 2000.

58. Ian Gilbert, *The Little Book of Thunks*. Carmarthen: Crown House, 2007.

59. Lilian G. Katz, *The Dispositions of Educational Goals*. Urbana, IL: ERIC Clearinghouse on Elementary and Early Childhood Education, 1993.

60. Carol McGuiness, *From Thinking Skills to Thinking Schools*. London: DCSF, 1999.

61. Oliver Caviglioli and Ian Harris, *Reaching Out To All Thinkers*. Stafford: Network Educational Press, 2009.

62. David Hodgson, *The Little Book of Inspirational Teaching Activities*. Carmarthen: Crown House, 2009.

63. Thomas L. Friedman, *The World is Flat*. London: Penguin, 2006.

64. James Caan quoted in an interview in *The Independent*, 25 February 2010.

65. Board of Education, *Handbook for Teachers*. London: HMSO, 1935.

66. Guy Claxton, *What's the Point of School?* Oxford: One World Publications, 2008.

67. Gilbert Highet, *The Art of Teaching*. New York: Random House, 2000 (orig. pub. 1950).

68. A. J. Oswald, Happiness and Economic Performance. *Economic Journal* (1997): 1815–1831.

69. Malcolm Gladwell, *Outliers*. Harmondsworth: Penguin, 2008.

70. Sutton Trust, *Annual Report 2008*. Available at http://www.suttontrust.com/about-us/annual-reports/annual-report-2008

71. Anthony Robbins, *Unlimited Power*. New York: Simon & Schuster, 1986.

72. Jim Collins, *Good to Great*. New York: Harper Collins, 2001.

73. Sir Jim Rose, *Independent Review of the Primary Curriculum: Final Report*. London: DCSF, 2009. Available at http://publications.education.gov.uk/default.aspx?PageFunction=productdetails&PageMode=publications&ProductId=DCSF-00499-2009

74. 'We Are The People We Have Been Waiting For'. Available at http://www.youtube.com/watch?v=RUODHGy60no

75. Catherine Brentnall, *Enterprise through the Curriculum*. Rotherham: Rotherham Ready, 2009.

76. QCA and the Department for Education and Employment, The National Curriculum, Handbook for Primary Teachers, 2000

77. DCSF Sir Jim Rose, *Independent Review of the Primary Curriculum: Final Report*. London: DCSF, 2009. Available at http://publications.education.gov.uk/default. aspx?PageFunction=productdetails&PageMode=publications&ProductId= DCSF-00499-2009

78. Lenny Henry quoted in National Advisory Committee for Creative and Cultural Education, *All Our Futures: Creativity, Culture and Education*. London: DfEE, 1999.

79. National Advisory Committee for Creative and Cultural Education, *All Our Futures: Creativity, Culture and Education*. London: DfEE, 1999.

80. Rebecca Clarkson and Marian Sainsbury, *Attitudes to Reading at Ages Nine and Eleven: Full Report*. Slough: NFER, 2008. Available at http://www.nfer.ac.uk/nfer/ publications/RAQ01/RAQ01_home.cfm?publicationID=77&title=Attitudes%20 to%20reading%20at%20ages%20nine%20and%20eleven:%20full%20report

81. Guy Claxton, *What's the Point of School?* Oxford: One World Publications, 2008.

82. PIRLS, see http//timss.bc.edu/pirls2006

83. Guy Claxton, *What's the Point of School?* Oxford: One World Publications, 2008.

84. Maria Tatar, *Enchanted Hunters: The Power of Stories in Childhood*. New York: W.W. Norton, 2009.

85. Department of Education and Science, *A Language for Life (The Bullock Report)*. London: HMSO, 1975.

86. Inspire Rotherham, *Where We Stood (Celebrating the Best from Five Anthologies of Creative Writing by the Young People of Rotherham, 1995–2008)*. Rotherham: Rotherham School Effectiveness Service, 2009.

87. M. Sainsbury and I. Schagen, Attitudes to Reading at Ages Nine and Eleven. *Journal of Research in Reading* 27(4) (2004): 373–386.

88. Olivia O'Sullivan and Sue McGonigle, *The Power of Reading, Project Research Summary 2005–09*. London: Centre for Literacy in Primary Education, 2010. Available at http://www.clpe.co.uk/pdf/por_research_briefing_jul09.pdf

89. M. O. Martin, I. V. S. Mullis, E. J. Gonzales and A. M. Kennedy, *Trends in Children's Reading Literacy Achievement 1991–2001: EA's Repeat in Nine Countries of the 1991 Reading Literacy Study*. Chestnut Hill, MA: Boston College, 2003.

90. Prince of Wales Arts and Kids Foundation, 'Half of Britain's Kids Don't Read Books' (press release, 2004). Available at http://www.artsandkids.org.uk

91. Quoted in Inspire Rotherham, *Where We Stood* (*Celebrating the Best from Five Anthologies of Creative Writing by the Young People of Rotherham, 1995–2008*). Rotherham: Rotherham School Effectiveness Service, 2009.

92. Department for Education, The Importance of Teaching, www.education.gov.uk/schools/teachingandlearning/schoolswhitepaper/60068570/the-importance-of-teaching/

93. Anthony Seldon, *The Observer*, 14 February 2010.

94. United Kingdom Literacy Association, *Raising Boys' Achievement in Writing*. London: UKLA, 2004.

95. United Kingdom Literacy Association, *Raising Boys' Achievement in Writing*. London: UKLA, 2004.

96. Florence Beetlestone, *Creative Children, Imaginative Teaching*. Philadelphia, PA: Open University Press, 1998.

97. See http://www.takeonepicture.org

98. Tim Brighouse quoted in National Advisory Committee for Creative and Cultural Education, *All Our Futures: Creativity, Culture and Education*. London: DfEE, 1999.

99. Gervase Phinn, *Teaching Poetry in the Primary Classroom*. Carmarthen: Crown House, 2009.

100. Maria Tatar, *Enchanted Hunters: The Power of Stories in Childhood*. New York: W.W. Norton, 2009.

101. See http://www.jeremystrong.co.uk for information about Jeremy Strong.

102. I later discovered 'The Fable of Fred' was written by Sir Alec Clegg (former Chief Education Officer for the West Riding of Yorkshire) for a training event.

103. Andrew Curran, *The Little Book of Big Stuff about the Brain*. Carmarthen: Crown House, 2009.

104. Daniel Goleman, *Emotional Intelligence: Why It Can Matter More Than IQ*. London: Bloomsbury, 1996.

105. Robert Ingersoll, *The Works of Robert Ingersoll* (12 vols). New York: Dresden Publishing Company, 1902.

106. *Être et Avoir*, dir. Nicholas Phillibert, 2002.

107. Arthur L. Costa and Ben Kallick, *Habits of Mind: A Developmental Series*. Alexandria, VA: ASDC, 2000.

108. George Bernard Shaw quoted on http://www.brainyquote.com

109. Malcolm Gladwell, *Outliers*. Harmondsworth: Penguin, 2008.

110. Conn and Hal Iggulden, *The Dangerous Book for Boys*. New York: HarperCollins, 2007.

111. Groucho Marx quote from *Duck Soup*, dir. Leo McCarey, 1933.

112. Pablo Casals, *Joys and Sorrows*. London: MacDonald and Co., 1970.

113. Ofsted, *Learning Outside the Classroom* (Ref. 070219). London: Ofsted, 2009.

114. Board of Education, *Handbook for Teachers*. London: HMSO, 1935.

115. Carol Williams, *Bringing a Garden to Life*. New York: Bantam Books, 1998.

116. Dorothy Gurney quoted in Florence Beetlestone, *Creative Children, Imaginative Teaching*. Philadelphia, PA: Open University Press, 1998.

117. Sir Alec Clegg, *About Our Schools*. Oxford: Blackwell, 1980.

118. Tim Brighouse and David Woods, *Inspirations*. Stafford: Network Continuum, 2006.

119. Eric Hoffer, *Vanguard Management*. New York: Berkley Publishing Group, 1998.

120. Louis Rubin, *Artistry in Teaching*. New York: Random House, 1985.

121. Robert McNamara quoted in Charles Handy, *The Empty Raincoat: Making Sense of the Future*. London: Hutchinson, 1994.

122. Patrick Lencioni, *The Three Signs of a Miserable Job: A Fable for Managers (And Their Employees) (J-B Lencioni Series)*. San Francisco, CA: Jossey-Bass, 2007.

123. Board of Education, *Primary Education: Suggestions for the Consideration of Teachers and Others Connected with the Work of Primary Schools*. London: HMSO, 1959. Available at http://www.educationengland.org.uk/documents/primary

124. David Lazear, *Multiple Intelligence Approaches to Assessment*. Carmarthen: Crown House, 2004.

125. Robin Fogarty quoted in David Lazear, *Multiple Intelligence Approaches to Assessment*. Carmarthen: Crown House, 2004.

126. L. Campbell, B. Campbell and D. Dickinson, *Teaching and Learning through Multiple Intelligences*. Stanwood, WA: New Horizons for Learning, 1992.

127. Ofsted, *Curriculum Innovation in Schools* (Ref. 070097). London: Ofsted, 2009.

128. Emily Grady, *The Portfolio Approach to Assessment* (Fastback Series 341). Bloomington, IN: Phi Delta Kappa Educational Foundation, 1992.

129. Board of Education, *Primary Education: Suggestions for the Consideration of Teachers and Others Connected with the Work of Primary Schools*. London: HMSO, 1959. Available at http://www.educationengland.org.uk/documents/primary

130. William Arthur Ward quoted in Duncan Grey, *Grey's Essential Miscellany for Teachers*. London: Continuum, 2005.

131. Tim Brighouse and David Woods, *Inspirations*. Stafford: Network Continuum, 2006.

132. Michael Fullan, *The Moral Imperative of School Leadership*. Thousand Oaks, CA: Corwin Press, 2005.

133. Paul Cuttance, 'Quality Assurance Reviews as a Catalyst for School Improvement in Australia'. In A. Hargreaves, A. Lieberman, M. Fullan and D. Hopkins (eds.), *International Handbook of Educational Change*. London: Kluwer Academic, 1998.

134. L. Stoll and K. Riley, School Effectiveness and Improvement: Recent Research. *Management in Education* 3(2) (1999): 16–22.

135. Jonathan Smith, *The Learning Game: A Teacher's Inspirational Story*. London: Abacus, 2002.

136. Andrew Hargreaves, *Changing Teachers, Changing Times: Teachers' Work and Culture in the Postmodern Age* (Professional Development and Practice Series). New York: Teachers' College Press, 1994.

137. Richard Wiseman, *59 Seconds: Think a Little, Change a Lot*. New York: Borzoi Books.

138. Thomas Love Peacock, *Crotchet Castle*. Harmondsworth: Penguin, 1969.

139. John Abbott, *Learning Makes Sense – Recreating Education for a Changing Future*. Letchworth: Education 2000, 1994.

140. Elliott Eisner, *The Educational Imagination*. New York: Macmillan, 1979.

141. Robert L Fried, *The Passionate Teacher*. Boston: Beacon Press, 1995.

Acknowledgements

During 37 years of working in schools I have had the privilege of experiencing many truly inspirational teachers who have achieved inspirational responses from their children. I would particularly thank the following people whose considerable talents, successes or stories are represented in this book:

Catherine Brentnall, Richard Chapman, Carol Connell, Lynda Hilbert, Chris Houghton, Andy Jessop, Kay Jessop, Peter Mountstephen, Amy Parry, Del Rew, Liz Ruston, Jackie Ryan, David Saunders, Helen Simpson, Claire Sneath, Kate Taylor, Joanne Walker, Sue Warner and Barry Gow and his team at the Clifton Partnership of Schools.

Index

Praise for
Inspirational Teachers, Inspirational Learners

Inspirational Teachers is a carefully created and rewarding adventure through the world of inspiring education. Every teacher should take a chapter to school with them and aim to deploy as many ideas as possible. The book actively promotes the development of sound pedagogy with a passion for learning and mixes in a combination of excellent delivery skills for good measure. *Inspirational Teachers* is suitable for all, whether you are comfortably outstanding, challenging mediocrity or just aiming a little higher. The book shoots from the hip and provides a delightful range of pithy quotes and snippets of conversations about learning. As Will Ryan says, we should never forget the potential of powerful and well-chosen words to guide us as they have done for so many people in so many different situations.

Marcus Cherrill, ICanTeach.co.uk

This publication provides school leaders with an innovative framework to evaluate, enhance and develop a relevant primary curriculum for the twenty-first century. Recent experience of using these stimulating materials has enabled all of our staff to be engaged in the process of developing a rich and inspiring creative curriculum.

A 'must read' for senior leadership teams in this post-National Curriculum era.

John Henderson, Executive Head Teacher of
Canklow Woods and Whiston Worrygoose primary schools

The materials in this book were the basis of a fabulous training day with Will Ryan. The whole collaborative was buzzing. The excellent mix of ideas provided stimulating thinking and challenge, a context for curriculum development and for our visioning work. The content provided excellent and real ideas that reflect real school life. The message from the executive governors and staff was that this was the 'best training day ever'. The materials in this book will remind you of why you came into the profession. It was a great way to start our journey of collaboration with two schools.

Mark Wheeler, Executive Head Teacher of
Trinity Croft and Thrybergh Fullerton schools

Will Ryan is one of those unique educators who 'walked the walk' before he started to 'talk the talk'. I have been privileged enough to be in an audience of teachers during one of his inspirational sessions and his book manages to take that inspirational magic and reproduce it in ink, on paper. Will's book is full of humour, common sense and passion, much like a great lesson.

Over the years too many people have created a mythology around teaching and learning that has over-complicated what is, at its heart, a very simple set of principles; translate tough concepts into the tangible, make it matter, be inspirational and provide contexts and experiences. In this book, Will nails it! We are entering very challenging times for education; teachers are feeling increasingly stressed, their jobs and the way they practise are under threat and they are desperate for someone or something to provide inspiration and guidance. Will's book may well be a significant beacon.

If you are looking for inspiration, wanting to be reminded of just why you have devoted your professional life to working with kids; if you want to feel that education and our young really do have a positive future then read this book, be inspired and continue to build a system worthy of our children!

Richard Gerver, educational commentator, author and broadcaster

From the beginning I wanted to read more. Will explained how the book would be useful and the effect it would have on pupils. Throughout the book there are interesting quotes and anecdotes which make it very readable. Readers are given the opportunity to reflect on their own practice regularly. There are scenarios of good practice that Will has observed and teachers could use these to develop their own inspirational ideas. A valuable read for any primary school teacher.

Angela Tuff, education consultant

Will gives a very convincing argument for doing the right thing for our children. His brilliant stories make you laugh and seethe in equal measure. I laughed at the fantastic wisdom of children and seethed at the way some of our brilliant teachers are made to feel inadequate because they are not following the latest teaching fashions.

Will's enthusiasm for teaching is contagious. He speaks from the heart whilst drawing on a wealth of research from some of the most inspiring educationalists in the world. Yet it is his practical approach, with so many examples of great ideas, that makes this book such a useful tool for teachers.

Two things really stand out in reading the book:

Firstly, it challenges the reader to think about what is really important for our youngsters if they are going to succeed in a rapidly changing world. Secondly, Will's call to action when he asks us, 'Will you go the extra mile for the children in your care and help the magic of childhood be enhanced by electrifying learning opportunities? I hope so.' And so will everyone else that cares about children's success!

Chris Quigley, Director Chris Quigley Education Ltd

Will Ryan's book, *Inspirational Teachers, Inspirational Learners,* does not just tell you how education and educationalists have to change their thinking. It explores real and concrete areas for change, that need to be seriously looked at for twenty-first century teaching and learning.

Following significant and very welcome changes to the Scottish education system from 5-14 to Curriculum for Excellence, this book is a real gold mine of ideas and examples for those educators who have found it challenging to change their ways of thinking and teaching. For those following the English system, currently in the process of change, this book gives a real heads-up, with tangible examples of exemplary practice that coax real ideas, some tried and considered, to move primary school education firmly forwards. Furthermore, the checklists planted carefully throughout the book will help to guide any teacher, department or school towards inspirational learning.

Read this book to gain a real sense of can-do, of wanting, perhaps *needing* to become an inspirational teacher, to encourage inspirational learners to be the very best they can be.

Dawn Lobban, primary school teacher and mentor to NQTs

Ranging from *The Beano*'s Bash Street Kids to Lorenz's butterfly effect, and with words such as 'joy', 'passion', 'awe and wonder' featuring throughout, this book is certainly an inspirational read. Although aimed more towards primary teachers, the ideas it contains are equally applicable to the secondary sector.

Will Ryan captures some of the really pertinent agendas of today's educational world, arguing strongly for schools to place inspiring children and young people at the heart of curriculum development and school improvement. Contained within the book are amusing but thought-provoking anecdotes which encapsulate the thinking behind the practice.

Whilst each chapter can be read individually, the sum is far more than its parts and the book offers strong messages to school leaders and classroom teachers who may be feeling disempowered by government edicts and who would prefer to put joy and a passion for *real* learning back in the classroom but perhaps lack the courage. This is a book of hope for twenty-first century education and those who work within it.

Jan Sargeant, Senior Adviser (Secondary), North Yorkshire Local Authority

Wow – what a great book!

The book arrived at lunchtime and I took a sneaky peek as I ate my lunch – it looked interesting. However, I had to wait until later that evening to properly sit down and have a read. I then couldn't put it down. It even took precedence over the next few episodes of 24 I was currently watching on DVD. If you are a 24 fan you will know just what a great commendation that is! Four hours later I had finished the book – now I need to read it more slowly, with more thought towards application.

But what of the content? Well, that is summed up in a quotation Will himself uses on page 163: Alan Bennett talks about the best moments in reading being when you read something that you yourself have already been thinking. This is just what this book is like – a summary of my thoughts on thinking from the past year or so. I run a consultancy and training company which runs workshops for teachers and school management across India. Our latest developments have been courses on 'Thinking Skills' for Primary and Secondary teachers. So far these have proved very popular with schools, as teachers realize the need for children to be thinking. We cannot continue to teach the same things now and into the future as we have been for the last 50 or even 20 years. Students now need skills more than content – a change which is going to take India (a very exam and content based education system) a long time to adapt to. It was eye opening for me to see the tables on pages 73 and

74 showing the survey results which I assume were from England. It seems India is not so different after all.

Although the book is very UK based, it is concept based enough that it is applicable to other countries around the world. It also refers to many popular books/videos out there – The Outliers/We are the people we have been waiting for/Shift Happens – all offerings I have discovered and enjoyed over the past few months.

I shall be incorporating some of Will's thoughts and concepts as I re-evaluate my training sessions on 'The Role of a Teacher' for schools' orientation weeks. As we fashion inspirational teachers so we will create inspired learners.

Joy Townsend, Destiny Education Mumbai Pvt Ltd

Someone urgently needs to give Michael Gove a copy of this book or, better still, just make Will Ryan the new Education Minister. He presents a clear vision for education in the twenty first century that is creative, enterprising and, yes, inspirational.

Despite including some rather depressing examples of everything that is wrong with this country's education system, this is overwhelmingly a hopeful book, with a finely drawn vision of everything that teaching and learning should be. In this age of increasing accountability, over-prescription and emphasis on testing, it is easy to see how creativity, originality and critical thinking have been stifled in our schools. Will Ryan strikes a careful balance between exploring what went wrong with education and putting forth his agenda for change. This agenda includes broad sweeping philosophical ideas that will inspire a cognitive shift in mindset, along with concrete examples of creativity and inspiration in action. I defy anyone to read this book and not feel energised by its contents. Most of the ideas and examples come from primary schools, but the message is equally relevant for secondary teachers.

Provocative quotes are used throughout the book to inspire argument and debate. One that Will uses to close the book sums it up perfectly: *Teachers do what they believe in extraordinarily well, but what they are told to do merely to a mediocre standard* (John Abbott). Will Ryan's inspirational book will remind teachers to do what they believe in and believe in what they do.

Selena Gallagher, PhD

This important and urgent book opens with one of the saddest education stories I have ever heard. As a head, the author had talked to an eight-year-old pupil in his school who was bemoaning the boredom inherent in a project on rivers that involved her cutting out parts of diagrams from a pre-published worksheet and sticking them on to another piece of paper to illustrate the water cycle.

The child argued that this was "a load of rubbish" and proceeded to describe with great enthusiasm aspects of the real life of a river that lay at the end of the lane from the school. Some years later he chanced, as a local authority adviser, on the same girl, now a teacher herself. She told him that one of her latest lessons related to the journey of a river, making use of a lesson downloaded from the internet that involved a diagram and the children sequencing sections of text to piece together the story of the water cycle.

When reminded of her response to this same task as a pupil and asked why she hadn't been able to act on her own advice, the answer was sadly predictable. The drive to ensure a 5 per cent improvement in standards in English and maths meant no "extras" like out-of-school visits, with their attendant health and safety risks, no story settings until the following term, and no deviation because all she had to do was use the Qualifications and Curriculum Development Agency schemes to ensure the topic was covered.

This prologue encapsulates most of the charges that Mr Ryan levels with unerring accuracy at the state of education in England: a results drive to the point of madness, inflexible management (one could hardly call it leadership), a lack of imagination in interpreting the national curriculum, the stifling of intellectual curiosity in the young and the inhibition of creative teaching. The triumph of Dickens' Mr Gradgrind, one might think, is almost complete.

Is it any wonder that a 2007 Unicef report on the wellbeing and happiness of children ranked the UK as the worst of the 21 wealthy nations surveyed? Should we not despair when a colleague of Mr Ryan's tells him that her son went through 35 mock Sats papers before the tests?

Despair, fortunately, is something this book has no truck with. Its subject is inspiration and it is the author's unwavering belief that inspiration is the birthright of every child, and creative teaching the key to providing it.

Inspirational Teachers Inspirational Learners sets out to show how, even in the present circumstances, this can be achieved. Literacy and the arts are key; awe, wonder and emotional and spiritual intelligence need to be nurtured; learning outside the classroom is essential; there needs to be passion, courage and faith.

Ofsted does not come out of his anecdotal evidence well. That is, perhaps, predictable. But his biggest challenge is to school leaders: "The prime duty of any school leader is to take a dynamic and inspirational lead on the curriculum … it should course through every vein to create a passionate community where everyone wants to learn …".

The tick-box mentality of many school managers, with their insistence on paperwork and uniformity, gets short shrift: "I have become firmly convinced that the size and degree of elaboration within planning documents is inversely related to the quality of action and learning."

But any head wanting to take up the challenge of creating an inspirational curriculum will find plenty of practical help here with encouraging enterprise, "awakening joy in creative expression" and pursuing alternative means of assessment. This is a book that aims to effect improvement and realise an ambition, not simply moan about the current climate and the sterility of many of our classrooms.

Particularly important are his claims for a return to what might be called "real literacy", with story at its heart. A study by the National Foundation for Educational Research suggests that while standards of literacy achieved by pupils have risen, a love of reading in boys and girls – Harry Potter notwithstanding – has declined.

It is not unrealistic to attribute this at least in part to one of the most damaging trends of the past few years: the rise and rise of the use of extracts, rather than the enjoyment of shared whole books. Stories inspire; children need to be exposed to full texts; daily story time needs to return to every primary classroom.

Mr Ryan brings a wealth of practical experience as well as idealism to this book. The questions he asks schools to ask of themselves are enlightening and his suggestions for moving towards a more creative and inspirational curriculum are well grounded. The anecdotal sections of the text make their points with humility and humanity, and although in some cases they provoke anger and frustration they also point the way to remedies. In short, *Inspirational Teachers Inspirational Learners* is itself an inspirational text that should be on the reading list of all educational administrators and on the bedside table of all school leaders and classroom teachers.

The verdict: 10/10.

Martin Spice, TES Magazine, 6 May, 2011

Leadership with a Moral Purpose
Turning Your School Inside Out
Will Ryan

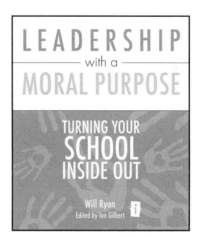

ISBN 978-184590084-7

Leadership with a Moral Purpose gives all primary heads aspiring, newly appointed or those who think 'There must be something more than this!' – the ideas, techniques, tools and direction to turn their schools Inside-Out and inspire them to lead with the heart and with the soul.

What's more it will give Heads the confidence to do those things they know are right because they are right for the children, right for the staff and right for the community.

Contents include developing an 'Inside Out Vision' for:

- the school
- the classroom
- inclusion
- social and emotional aspects of learning
- positive attitudes
- a professional learning community
- leadership
- parents

Twenty-First Century School Assembly and Classroom Activities

Will Ryan photography by Jane Hewitt

If you took the time to do the calculations you would discover that during their primary school years, a child will spend roughly 70 days in assembly, and possibly a further 52 days during their secondary years. This can be either time that is simply lost and forgotten or hours that can be used to make a difference – to create confident individuals and responsible, deep-thinking citizens for the future. Will Ryan has created a resource that will allow busy school leaders and teachers to deliver outstanding assemblies that make a beneficial impression on the lives of the young people listening.

ISBN 978-178135007-2

Part I, Our World in the Twenty-First Century, aims to help children to become responsible global citizens who will help to change the world for the better. While Part II, Creating Responsible Citizens in Our Schools and Communities, aims to promote a sense of aspiration and ambition within learners and also provide ideas for how they can make a positive difference to the school and the locality.

Each assembly idea is presented in three ways:

- Three Star Assemblies: 'Help, I've hardly any time to plan an assembly!' For these assemblies, you can simply pick up the book and read the story or account and follow the activities planned.

- Four Star Assemblies: These are for the occasions when you've got a bit longer to prepare, gather resources or get the children involved.

- Five Star Assemblies: Perhaps it is because Ofsted are about to arrive, but you want this assembly to be the best assembly ever!

The book is aimed at Key Stages 2 and 3 (ages 7–14) and contains beautiful and thought-provoking colour photographs throughout, which are included on a free accompanying CD, making it even easier to jump straight into outstanding assemblies.